Le Corbusier
Public
Buildings

GREAT ARCHITECTS REDRAWN

images
Publishing

Le Corbusier
Public
Buildings

GREAT ARCHITECTS REDRAWN

CONTENTS

Foreword / 005

Preface / 009

Part 1

Spatial Composition Analysis of Public Buildings from a Macro Perspective / 013

Plan Composition / 014
Façade Composition / 065
Section Composition / 082
Form Composition / 098

Part 2

Spatial Composition Analysis of Public Buildings from a Micro Perspective / 103

Columns / 104
Windows / 114
Staircases / 128
Ramps / 136
Sunshading / 143
Drainage Structures / 149

Part 3

Case Studies / 153

Administration Building / 154
Museum / 220
Exhibition Hall / 264
Religious Building / 318
School / 350
Sports Facility / 374
Public Building (Water Conservancy) / 388
Complex / 396
Commercial Building / 430
Monument / 448
Hospital / 460

References / 464

Image Credits / 465

Epilogue / 466

Explanation of the classifications in the book:
The research cases included in this book are works featured in *Le Corbusier Complete Works*, with the exception of small houses, apartments, and planning projects, and center on common public building types, such as museums, administration buildings, and religious venues. Hence, the book is titled *Le Corbusier Public Buildings*.

It should also be noted that, according to the definition of "public building" as determined by China's current design code, school dormitories such as Pavillon Suisse, Cité Internationale Universitaire and Maison du Brésil, Cité International Universitaire should be classified as "residence," however, as these buildings also have public activity spaces set up for students, they have been included in the book.

The author also refers to the classifications of Le Corbusier's works on foreign websites and includes them in the category of "School" within the book. In addition, municipal public facilities, Château d'Eau and Bâtiments de l'Écluse, are included in the "Public Building (Water Conservancy)" category; Unité d'Habitation, as a representative of other similar works, is included in the "Complex" category because of its complex function.

FOREWORD

Drawing is a crucial tool for architects to record and describe space. During the whole process, from the initial conception of a building to the final completion of its construction, drawing plays a dual role by conveying the designer's intention and guiding the engineering construction of the project.

If the drawing is an important medium for the architects to project the space concept into the object (architecture) in the real world, the reductive analysis and interpretation on the existing buildings—existing as the result of the projection of the space concept of the architects—likewise requires the mapping and drawing of the buildings in order to complete the interpretation of the space concept of the designers.

The architectural works designed by Le Corbusier, the most famous modernist architect and artist of the twentieth century, have been significant objects for research and analysis. In 2001, for example, Tadao Ando, the famous Japanese architect, organized students of the University of Tokyo to sort out the drawings of 106 residential works by Le Corbusier, as well as make their models, and in the same year, also held an exhibition titled Le Corbusier Residence in Tokyo, to exhibit the drawings and models of Le Corbusier's residential works.

Yu Fei's book, *Le Corbusier Public Buildings*, references the public buildings designed by Le Corbusier as the object of observation and makes a detailed analysis of the eighty public buildings designed by Le Corbusier through drawing, modeling, and omni-directional interpretation. It should be said that this is a comprehensive reorganization, analysis, and summary of the public buildings designed by Le Corbusier.

The analytical process through the annotation of the architectural works presented in this book demonstrates a method of research in practice, which starts with the most basic interpretation and drawing in architecture. When drawing the object's plan, elevation, section, and when conducting the 3D modeling, the draftsperson, existing as an analyst, can understand the thinking and feeling of the original designer in the process of "projecting" his work.

Wang Yun
BUCEA Graduate School of Architecture Design and Art

Table A Biography of Le Corbusier (Charles-Edouard Jeanneret-Gris)

1887	Born in Switzerland.
1900	Attends the École des Arts Décoratifs at La Chaux-de-Fonds, where he studies the art of enameling and engraving watch faces. There, he meets artist Charles L'Eplattenier, his first teacher, and begins to take an interest in painting and architecture.
1905	With the help of L'Eplattenier, he is commissioned by Louis Fallet, a member of the Board of the Art School, to design a villa. It is his first design commission.
1907	First long trip to visit the Charterhouse of Ema at Galluzzo in Tuscany, Italy. Works at Josef Hoffmann's studio in Vienna for several months. Influenced by Adolf Loos's design ideas.
1908	Travels to Paris and visits Frantz Jourdain, Charles Plumet, Henri Sauvage, and Eugène Grasset. Meets Tony Garnier. Works as a draftsman at Auguste Perret's Studio.
1910	Visits Germany for investigation and observation. Establishes ties with the Deutscher Werkbund. Works for Peter Behrens's architectural practice in Berlin for five months. Meets Walter Gropius, Mies Van der Rohe, and Heinrich Tessenow.
1911	Starts the journey east, via Prague, Vienna, Budapest, Istanbul, Athens, various cities of Italy, and once again, the Charterhouse of Ema at Galluzzo.
1912	Travels to Zurich and Paris to complete the construction of two villas: Villa Jeanneret-Perret and Villa Favre-Jacot.
1914	First puts forward the concept of mass-produced Maison Dom-Ino.
1916	Builds Villa Schwob and the Cinéma "La Scala," his last projects at La Chaux-de-Fonds.
1917	Lives at 20 rue Jacobs, Paris. Sets up his first architecture studio at Astor. Works as the consultant to reinforced-concrete utility companies.
1918	Meets the painter Amédée Ozenfant and co-writes *Après le Cubisme* with him. Paints his first purist painting of La cheminée. Holds "Purist" exhibition at the Galerie Thomas in Paris with Ozenfant.
1919	Launches *L'Esprit Nouveau* magazine with Amédée Ozenfant and poet Paul Dermée, publishing twenty-eight issues between 1920 and 1925.
1920	Prints the first issue of *L'Esprit Nouveau* magazine. Adopts the pseudonym Le Corbusier for his architectural persona. Meets Fernand Léger.
1922	Begins an architectural partnership with his cousin Pierre Jeanneret. Establishes his architectural office at 35 rue de Sèvres, Paris. Exhibits the plan of a contemporary city for three million people at the Salon.
1923	Publishes *Vers une Architecture*.
1925	Builds Pavillon de l'Esprit Nouveau, Paris. Publishes *L'Art Décoratif d'Aujourd'hui*, *L'Urbanisme* and *La Peinture Moderne*.
1926	Death of Georges Edouard Jeanneret, father of Le Corbusier. Publishes *Almanach d'architecture*.
1927	Enters the competition for the League of Nations building in Geneva. Wins first prize, but not the commission of construction, and so lodges a protest with the jury committee. Sees the buildings of Antonio Gaudí.
1928	Is the founder member of CIAM (Congrès Internationaux d'architecture moderne); first annual conference held at La Sarraz Castle, Switzerland. Visits South America on a lecture tour to Rio de Janeiro, Buenos Aires, and Montevideo. Travels to Moscow. Publishes *Une Maison – un Palais*.
1929	Exhibits an apartment interior in the Salon d'Automne Paris, in collaboration with Pierre Jeanneret and Charlotte Perriand. Second CIAM conference held at Frankfurt am Main. Embarks on his first trip to Algiers.
1930	Marries Yvonne Gallis. Publishes *Précisions sur un état présent de l'architecture et de l'urbanisme*. Third CIAM conference held in Brussels. Visits Moscow, where he meets Ysevolod Meyerhold, Aleksander Tairov, and Serguëi Eisenstein.
1931	Takes part in the design competition for the Palace of Soviets, Moscow. Contributes to the magazine *Plans*. Travels across Spain with Pierre Jeanneret, and to Morocco, Algeria, and Marseilles.
1932	Takes part in the planning competition for the exposition Internationale des Arts et Techniques in Paris. Publishes *The Crusades: Twilight of Academism*.

Table A Continued

1933	Is a member of the review committee of the new magazine *Préludes*. Moves into a penthouse apartment at 24 rue Nungesser-et-Coli, Boulogne-sur-Seine. Participates in the fourth CIAM conference. Contributes to the Athens Charter.
1934	Frequently visits Algiers. Lectures in Rome, Milan, Algiers, and Barcelona.
1935	First trip to USA. Puts on "Primitive" art exhibition in his penthouse apartment. Publishes *Aircraft and La Ville Radieuse*.
1936	Second trip to South America. Gives advice to Lúcio Costa, Oscar Niemeyer, Alfonso Reidy, and others for the Ministry of National Education and Health building in Rio.
1937	Publishes *Quand les Cathédrales étaient Blanches*. Fifth CIAM conference held in Paris. Builds the Pavillon des Temps Nouveaux.
1938	Publishes *Des canons, des munitions? Merci! Des logis S.V.P. (Guns and Ammunition? No Thanks! Give Us Housing Please)*.
1940	Pairs is attacked and occupied by Germany. Le Corbusier closes his office at 35 rue de Sèvres and leaves for Ozon in the Pyrenees.
1941	Publishes *Destin de Paris* and *Sur les Quatre Routes*. Extends stay in Vichy.
1942	Begins study on "Modulor." Publishes *Constructions "Murondins"* and *La maison des hommes*. Official trip to Algiers, as well as instructional planning for Algiers.
1943	Publishes the *Charte d'Athènes* and *Entretiens avec les étudiants des Écoles d'architecture*.
1945	Publishes *Trois Établissements Humains*, *Manière de penser l'urbanisme* and *Propos d'urbanisme* Commissioned to build Unité d'Habitation, Marseilles. Investigation trip to USA with Eugène Claudius.
1946	Assumes role as consultant to the committee responsible for the United Nations Headquarters building in New York. Second trip to USA. Meets Albert Einstein at Princeton.
1947	Visits Bogotá. Sixth CIAM conference held at Bridgwater, England. The foundation of Unite d'Habitation, Marseilles is laid.
1948	The study on "Modular" notes achievements. Holds several exhibitions in USA. Begins collaboration with Pierre Baudouin on the design of tapestries.
1950	Publishes *Modulor I* and *Poèsie sur Alger*. Starts working on the La Chapelle de Ronchamp. Receives inspection delegation from Punjab of India.
1951	Official consultant to the administration of Punjab for the planning of the new capital city of Chandigarh. Commissioned for planning of Ahmedabad. Refuses invitation to planning competition for the UNESCO Headquarters in Paris.
1952	Begins the projects for Chandigarh. Construction of the Chapel at Ronchamp. Discusses the construction planning of Couvent with Father Couturier. Builds Le Cabanon at Roquebrune, Cap-Martin, France.
1954	Designs nine mural tapestries for the High Court in Chandigarh. Publishes *Une Petite Maison*.
1955	Construction of Unité d'Habitation, Marseilles. Publishes *Poème de l'Angle Droit* and *Modulor II*.
1956	Refuses a teaching post at the Ecole des Beaux-Arts. Visits Chandigarh for the inauguration of the High Court building by Jawaharlal Nehru. Publishes *Les plans de Paris 1922–1956*.
1957	Holds a large retrospective exhibition curated by W. Boesiger at Municipal Gallery of Zurich. His wife, Yvonne Le Corbusier, passes away.
1958	Visits USA for the investigation on Carpenter Visual Arts Center of Harvard University. Builds Philips Pavilion at the World's Fair in Brussels. Designs the visual composition *Poème Electronique*, music by Edgar Varèse.
1960	Construction of Couvent Sainte-Marie de la Tourette begins. Publishes *L'Atelier de la Recherche Patiente* and *Secret*. His mother, Marie Charlotte Amélie Jeanneret-Perret, passes away at the age of 100.
1961	Builds Carpenter Visual Arts Center of Harvard University. Makes frequent trips to Firminy to build Maison de la Culture and housing units.

Table A Continued

1962	Visits Brazil for the project of the Embassy of France in Brasilia. Construction of the Assembly Building in Chandigarh begins. Study on *The House of Men* (Pavillon d'exposition ZHLC in Zurich).
1964	Receives a commission to design a project for the Venice Hospital. Palais des Congrès, Strasbourg, the Embassy of France in Brasilia, and Olivetti, Centre de Calculs Électroniques are in the research stage.
1965	Submits the new design project for Venice Hospital to the authorities of Venice. Publishes *Le Voyage d'Orient*. On August 27, Le Corbusier passes away from a heart attack while swimming at Cap-Martin.

PREFACE

This book originated from my master's dissertation titled *An Analysis on the Spatial Composition of Public Buildings Designed by Le Corbusier from 1910 to 1965*, written during my study at Wang Yun Laboratory, Research Centre of Architecture, Peking University. In the summer of 2014, I made the first building model of Le Corbusier's Palais des Filateurs, Ahmedabad, to complete the space research project. I had felt the charm of the space in his works, but had also found that the drawings of plans, elevations, and sections, and the only two or three photos of local spaces from his portfolio were not equipped to reflect the basic spatial composition of his works. That's when I got the idea to create models for his works.

In 2001, *Le Corbusier HOUSES*, edited by Ando Tadao Laboratory, Department of Architecture, Graduate School of Engineering, the University of Tokyo, was published, introducing all the residential works of the architectural giant of the twentieth century. However, his architectural practices were not limited to residences, but also included a large number of art galleries, museums, churches, and other public buildings. This led me to determine the research object of my dissertation—all the public buildings of Le Corbusier.

The role and influence of Le Corbusier in the promotion of the Modern Architecture movement needs no further elaboration. There are countless studies and literature about Le Corbusier all over the world, but there remains a lack of systematic review and research of the public building works in his career. In this twenty-first century, after undergoing the tide of postmodernism, the creation of architecture currently presents a more diversified trend. Especially in China—where various construction undertakings have been carried out vigorously under the influence of BIM (Building Information Modeling), parametric design, and other technologies, as well as various trends of architectural design at home and abroad—the creation of architecture has, inevitably, fallen into a state of chaos, which seems to be the reason for the massive emergence of miscellaneous "odd buildings." In such a circumstance and context, I deeply feel that it is necessary to take a retrospective and systematic study into the classical texts and cases of modern architectures in the twentieth century.

From early homeschooling (before 1916) to late brutalism, represented by Unité d'Habitation, Marseille, Le Corbusier worked on nearly eighty public building works (the eighty works), including uncompleted projects not included in the volumes of *Le Corbusier Complete Works* (*Le Corbusier Complete Works / Complete Works*). This book introduces these works in accordance with their function types, as shown in Table B: seventeen administration buildings, eleven museums, fourteen exhibition halls, eight religious buildings, six schools, five sports facilities, two water conservancy public buildings, six complexes, five commercial buildings, five monuments, and one hospital. After collecting either first-hand or second-hand drawing information (Figure A) from *Le Corbusier Complete Works* and the website of Fondation Le Corbusier, I used CAD software to complete either reference drawings of plans, elevations, and sections of the buildings (Figure B), and

Figure A Drawing information of Podensac Château d'eau (plan, elevation, and section)

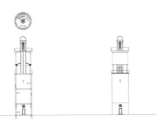

Figure B CAD drawings drawn according to the information

Figure C Three-dimensional model drawn from plan, elevation, and section introduced into SketchUp

Table B Statistics and classification of the 80 works

Administration building (17)	Museum (11)	Exhibition hall (14)	Religious building (8)	School (6)
1927–29 Palais de la Société des Nations	1929 Mundaneum, Musée Mondial (museum)	1928 Pavillon Nestlé	1929 Église, Le Tremblay	1910 Ateliers d
1928 Centrosoyuz	1931 Musée d'Art Contemporain	1930 Pavillon d'Aviation S.T.A.R.	1948 Basilique, La Sainte-Baume	1930–32 Pavillon Cité Inte nc Univ
1929 Mundaneum, Musée Mondial (administration building)	1931 Musée des Artistes Vivants	1935 Centre d'Esthetique Contemporaine	1950–54 Chapelle Notre Dame du Haut	1940 École
1931 Palais des Soviets	1935 Musée de la Ville et de l'État	1936 Pavillon des Temps Nouveaux	1951 Chapelle Funeraire Delgado-Chalbaud	1958 Ma Brésil, Cité Interm Univ
1933 Immeuble Rentenanstalt	1939 Musée à Croissance Illimitée	1936 TN-Wagon Maison Pavillon	1957–60 Couvent Sainte-Marie de la Tourette	1961–64 Ca Center for Visual Arts, H U
1936 Ministère de l'Education Nationale et de la Santé	1946 Musée et Lotissement Delaunay	1937 Pavillon Bat'a	1960–69 Église Saint Pierre	1964–69 Éco et d'A ch
1939 Station Biologique	1952 Musée de la Connaissancea	1939 Pavillon de la France à l'Exposition de l'Eau	1962 Église, Bologna	
1946 Palais des Nations Unies	1954–57 Musée, Ahmedabad	1939 Ideal Home, Arundell Clarke	1964–65 Église, Venice	
1946–51 Usine Claude et Duval	1957–59 Musée National d'Art Occidental	1950 Musée Tent		
1951–57 Palais de l'Assemblée	1964–68 Musée, Chandigarh	1950 Porte Maillot		
1952–56 Secrétariat, Chandigarh	1965 Musée du XXe Siècle	1958 Pavillon Philips, Exposition Internationale de 1958		
1952–56 Haute Cour		1962 Pavillon d'Exposition, Stockholm		
1954–57 Palais des Filateurs		1963 Centre d'Art International		
1960–65 Extensions of Haute Cour		1963–67 Pavillon d'Exposition ZHLC, Zurich		
1963–64 Olivetti, Centre de Calculs Électroniques				
1964 Palais des Congrès, Strasbourg				
1964–65 Ambassade de France, Brasilia				

then introduced the drawings into SketchUp to build three-dimensional models, where plan determines the column grid and function segmentation, and section determines the story height. After building the models layer by layer, I arranged them vertically according to the section, determined the surface according to the elevation drawing, supplemented the façade details and the interior space, and obtained the three-dimensional model (Figure C). Through this, I obtained the axonometric drawings of the eighty public building works listed in Table B.

In order to reflect the forms of Le Corbusier's works more intuitively and truthfully, Part 2 of this book includes plans, elevations, sections, and axonometric drawings of three-dimensional models of all his public buildings

Sports facility (5)	Public building (water conservancy) (2)	Complex (6)	Commercial building (5)	Monument (5)	Hospital (1)
5 Plan d'une Piscine à Vagues, Domaine de Badjarah	1917 Château d'Eau	1922 Gratte-Ciel Cartésien	1916 Cinéma "La Scala"	1937–38 Monument Paul Vaillant-Couturier	1964–65 Hôpital, Venice
6–37 Stade de 100.000 Places	1959–62 Bâtiments de l'Écluse	1934–38 Réorganisation Agraire, Ferme et Village Radieux	1931 Cinéma à Montparnasse	1951–57 Main Ouverte, Chandigarh	
9 Aménagement ation de Sport d'Hiver et d'Été		1935 Lotissement Durand, Oued Ouchaia	1936 Boutique Bat'a	1951–57 Monument des Martyrs, Chandigarh	
0–65 Maison de la Culture		1938–42 Gratte-Ciel, Quartier de la Marine, Cité des Affaires	1958–69 City Center, Chandigarh	1952 Tour d'Ombres	
5–69 Stade, Firminy		1945 Unité d'Habitation	1963–65 The Club House	1955 Tombe de Le Corbusier	
		1961 Gare d'Orsay			

for readers to explore. In the analysis of the spatial composition in the first two parts—from the abstract processing of the drawing surface to the data statistics, and then to the extraction of the conclusion—I try to express each process through intuitive means, such as diagrams for the reader to refer to. In this book, in addition to the "Five Points of Architecture," "Domino" structure system, "House is a Machine for Living" concept, and other concepts, through the display of axonometric drawings of three-dimensional models, unfolded drawings of layered space, as well as plans, elevations, sections, and other detailed drawings, the reader can glimpse the architectural language of the great modern architect Le Corbusier, and understand the thinking behind it.

Part 1

Spatial Composition Analysis of Public Buildings from a Macro Perspective

This part analyzes and compares the plan, façade, section, and form composition of Le Corbusier's eighty public buildings through different viewpoints and a macroscopic perspective. It also summarizes the commonality of the works in each section and arranges them into function types at the end of each section in order to reveal Le Corbusier's common techniques across different types of architecture.

1 Plan Composition

The plan is one of Le Corbusier's three memos for architects, and has always played an important role in determining the layout and control order of buildings. It is also called a "generator."[1]

Viewpoint Based on Shape Outlines

This section simplifies the plan of each work and refines its shape. In order to facilitate comparative analysis, only one representative plan is selected from each work—the one that can reveal the basic elements of the project, such as shape outline, column grid, and functional division (usually one or two layers of the plan). Figure 1 shows the process to simplify the abstract of the plan outline of project 03. In order to see the overall shape and pattern of the work, the subsidiary sections, such as the porch, staircase, and ramp have been removed from the image.

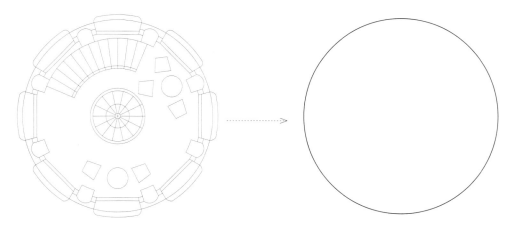

Figure 1 Abstracting the plan of project 03

This same simplified treatment is applied to each work plan and shown in Table 1.

---

1 Le Corbusier, *Towards A New Architecture* (New York: Dover Publications, 1986), 45.

015

Table 1 Plan simplification of the 80 works

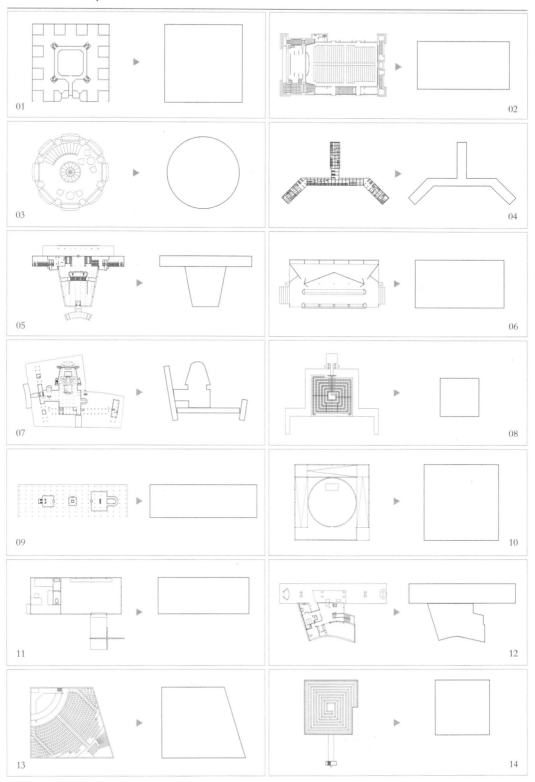

Table 1 Continued

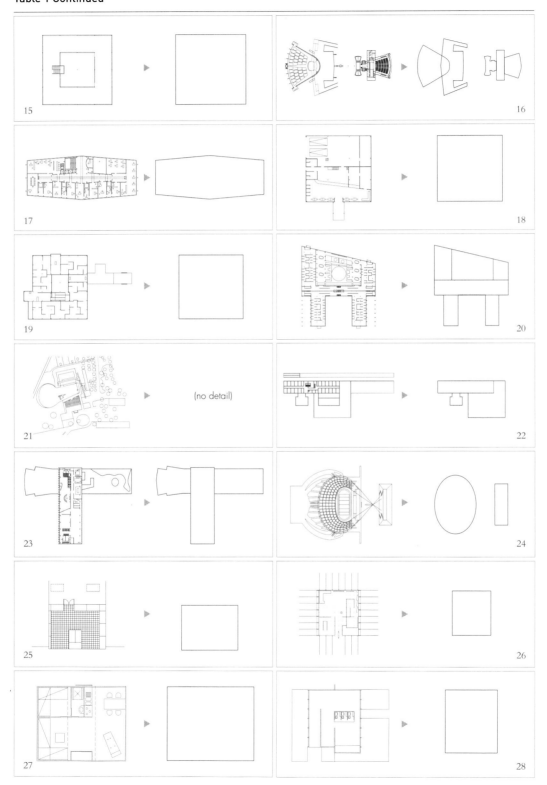

Table 1 Continued

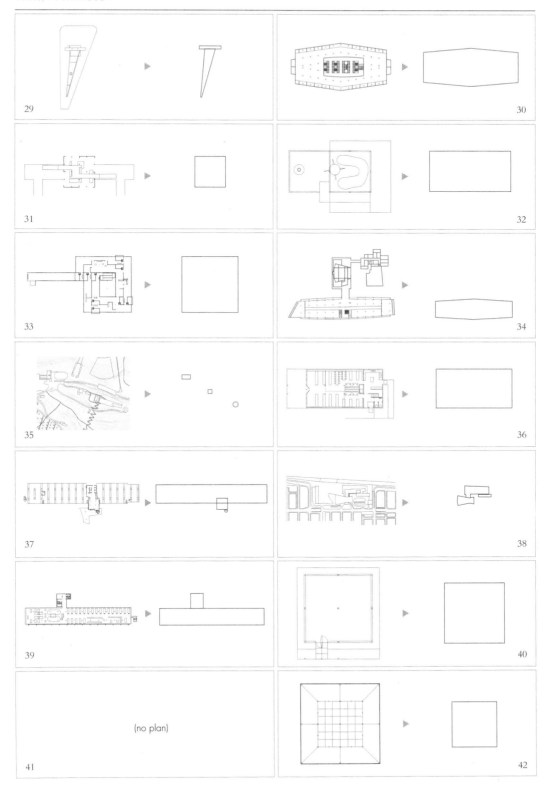

Table 1 Continued

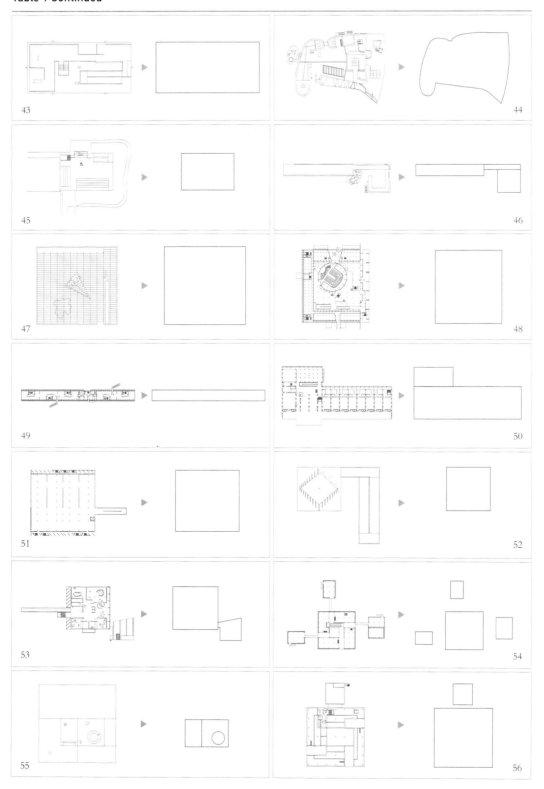

Table 1 Continued

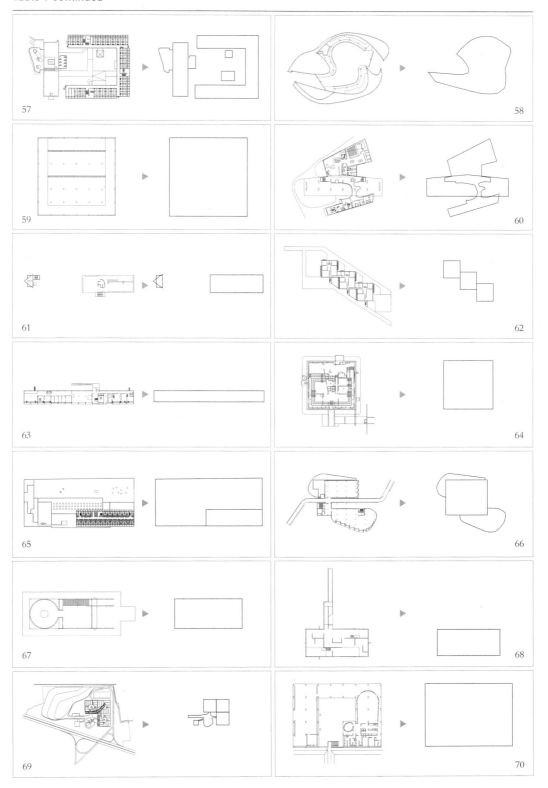

Table 1 Continued

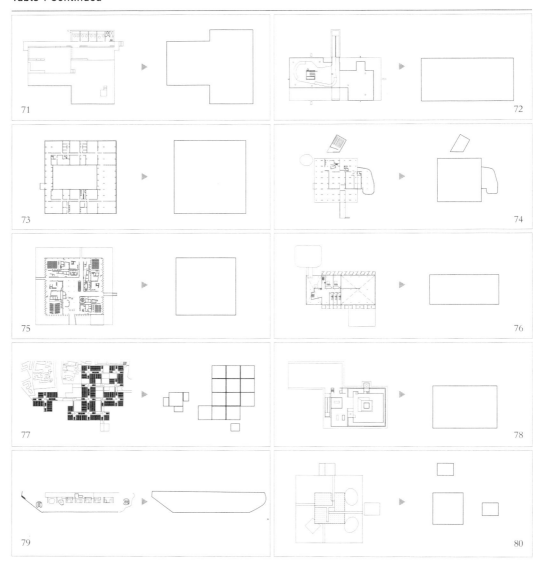

Through the comparison of the eighty plan outlines, it can be seen that most of the works show some common features, which can be divided into the following categories:

Type A: Square or square combination

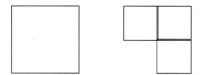

Buildings of this division, that is, with a plan that presents the characteristics of a square or a square combination are projects 01, 08, 10, 14, 15, 18, 19, 25, 26, 27, 28, 31, 33, 35, 40, 42, 45, 46, 47, 48, 51, 52, 53, 54, 55, 56, 59, 62, 64, 66, 69, 70, 73, 74, 75, 77, and 80, making a total of thirty-seven works. Project 35 (Aménagement Station de Sport d'Hiver et d'Été) is an architectural complex containing an individual square building. Project 46 (Monument des Martyrs) can be refined into a combination of multiple shapes, including squares. Project 66 (Carpenter Center for Visual Arts, Harvard University) is not a pure square, but as two curvilinear masses attached around it.

Type B: Rectangle

In this category, the outline of the plan is rectangular, and the length–width ratio of the rectangle is similar to that of two squares connected. They are projects 02, 06, 11, 32, 36, 43, 61, 67, 68, 72, 76, and 78 (a total of twelve works).

Type C: Horizontal shape or its combination

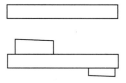

Plan outlines of this category show a long horizontal shape or a combination of a horizontal shape with subsidiary masses. They are projects 05, 07, 09, 12, 20, 22, 23, 37, 38, 39, 49, 50, 57, 63, and 65, making a total of fifteen works. Among them, the plan of project 57 (Couvent Sainte-Marie de la Tourette) presents as a combination of a horizontal shaped church and a U-shaped monk's dormitory.

Type D: Shuttle shape or its combination

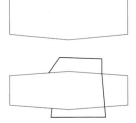

Of the eighty plans, four show features with special shuttle patterns, which are wide in the middle and narrow at both ends. They are projects 17, 30, 34, and 60. It should be pointed out that in project 60 (Maison du Brésil), one side of the slab-type apartment is a straight line—without the bulge outward—and thus, it is not a standard shuttle.

022

The four categories mentioned above are representative of a majority of works. In addition to them, there are several individual works with special plan outlines. They are unique or unusual cases (projects 03, 04, 13, 16, 21, 24, 29, 41, 44, 58, 71, and 79), which are classified as "Others."

From the data, it can be seen that Le Corbusier was most interested in the use of the square or its combination, followed by the horizontal shape, and the rectangle and its combination, with less use of unique shuttle patterns.

Table 2 The works categorized by function

Administration building	Work	05	07	09	16	17	23	34	38	39	48	49	50	53	62	69	75	76
	Type Code	C	C	C		D	C	D	C	C	A	C	C	A	A	A	A	B
Museum	Work	08	14	15	20	33	40	51	54	56	74	80						
	Type Code	A	A	A	C	A	A	A	A	A	A	A						
Exhibition hall	Work	06	11	19	26	27	28	31	32	42	43	58	68	71	72			
	Type Code	B	B	A	A	A	A	A	B	A	B		B		B			
Religious building	Work	10	41	44	47	57	64	67	78									
	Type Code	A			A	C	A	B	B									
School	Work	01	12	36	60	66	73											
	Type Code	A	C	B	D	A	A											
Sports facility	Work	21	24	35	63	79												
	Type Code			A	C													
Public building (water conservancy)	Work	03	61															
	Type Code		B															
Complex	Work	04	18	22	30	37	65											
	Type Code		A	C	D	C	C											
Commercial building	Work	02	13	25	59	70												
	Type Code	B		A	A	A												
Monument	Work	29	45	46	52	55												
	Type Code		A	A	A	A												
Hospital	Work	77																
	Type Code	A																

A ☐   B ☐   C ☐   D ⬡

The blank represents "Others"

The five categories of plan outlines are combined with the information in Table 1 (page 15) to form Table 2 (page 22); the number denotes the project number and the alphabet denotes the category of plan outline. From the table, we can see that administration buildings are of Types A and C; museum works are of Type A—the outline of the square—with only one work of Type C; exhibition halls are mainly of Types A and B; religious classifications mainly fall within Types A and B, with only one project of Type C; schools are mainly of Type A, with only one work within each of the other three main categories; sports facilities and water conservancy buildings have no obvious common methods; complexes are of Type C, with one work each of Type A and Type D; commercial buildings are of Type A, with one work that falls within Type B; monuments are of Type A, except project 29; and hospitals are of Type A.

From the perspective of method, Type A is the most widely used plan type, especially in museum buildings; the Type B plan is used more in exhibition halls; Type C—the outline of a "horizontal-stroke" shape—is mainly embodied in administration buildings and complexes; the Type D plan is used in administration buildings and is also seen in a complex and a school.

Viewpoints Based on Internal Segmentation

This section is an analysis derived from the perspective of segmentation within a plan, in two steps. The first step, is to refine all floor plans of the eighty public buildings listed in Table 3, to summarize the organization mode of their internal spaces, and to find the patterns they follow. Because the number of floors of each work is different, when abstracting and refining the plan, instead of summarizing the organization mode for each floor of each work, the most characteristic floor, or the most representative plan segmentation is used for the analysis. The second step, is to compare the abstract plans and their represented organization mode in order to determine the commonality of the method and its internal evolution with time. In project 01, for example, there is a hollow "core," which is a large classroom surrounded by compartments. The final pattern seen in Figure 2 is obtained through abstraction.

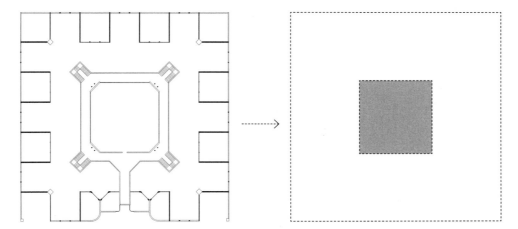

Figure 2 Abstraction process of the plan of project 01

Table 3 Individual floor plans of the 80 public buildings

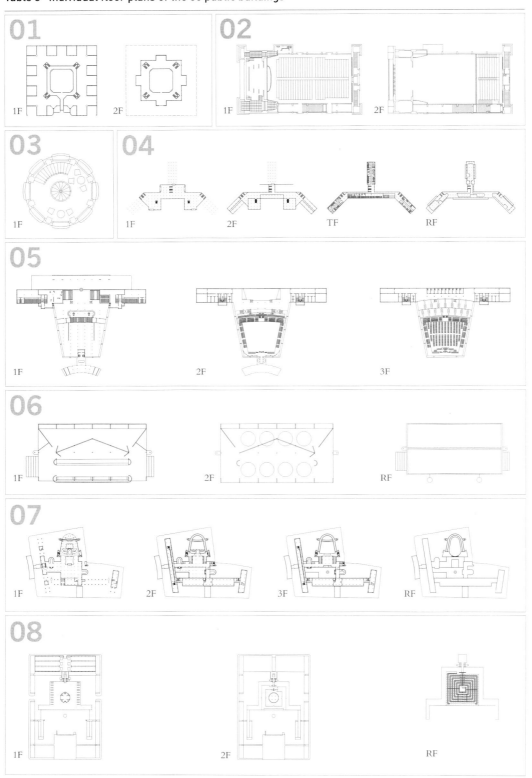

Note: -1F refers to the first floor underground (basement), 1F refers to the first floor; 2F refers to second floor, and so on. TF refers to typical floor, RF refers to roof plan, and MF refers to mezzanine floor.

Table 3 Continued

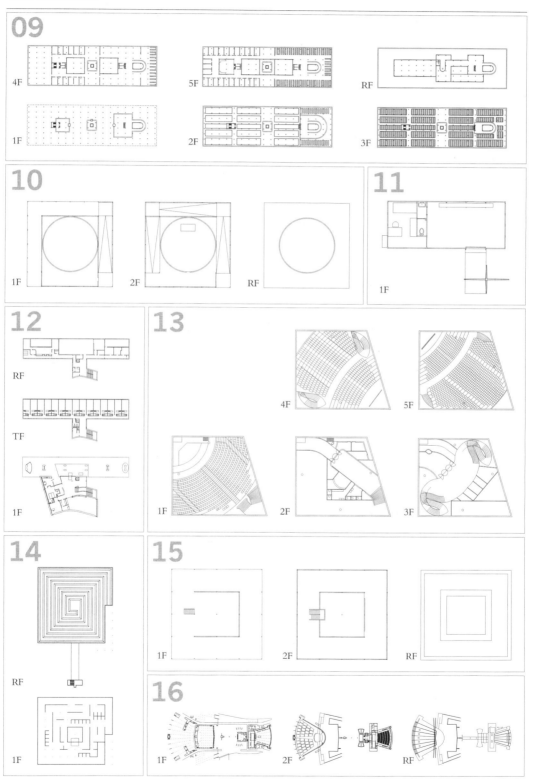

Table 3 Continued

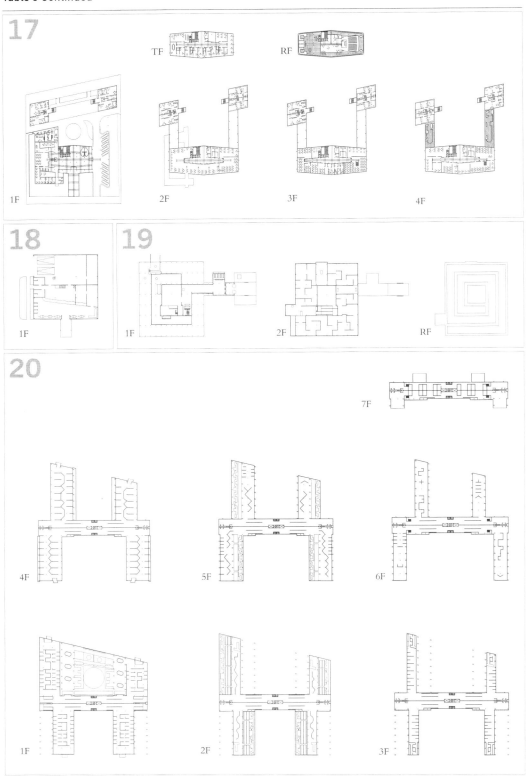

Table 3 Continued

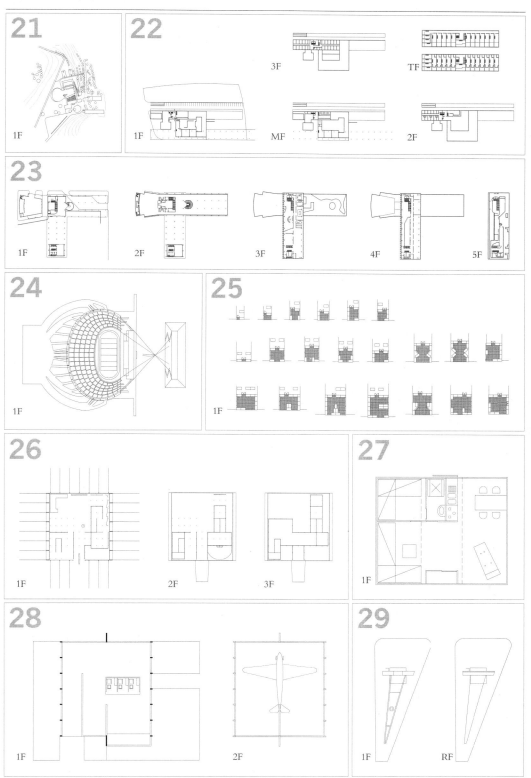

Table 3 Continued

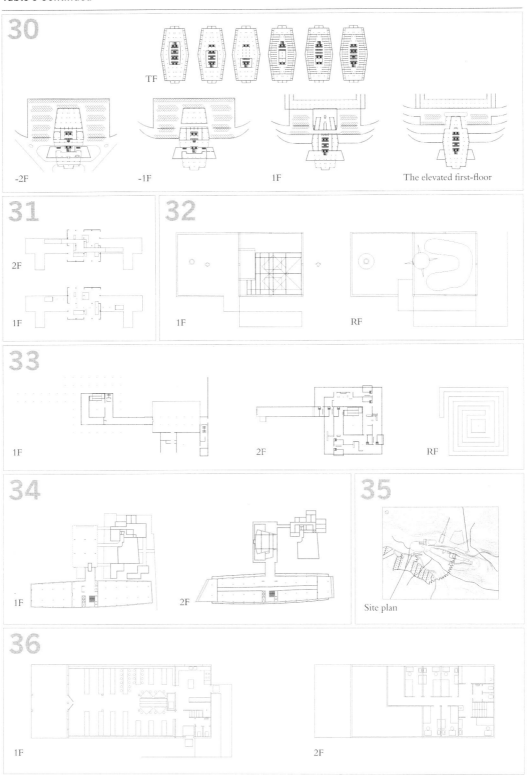

Table 3 Continued

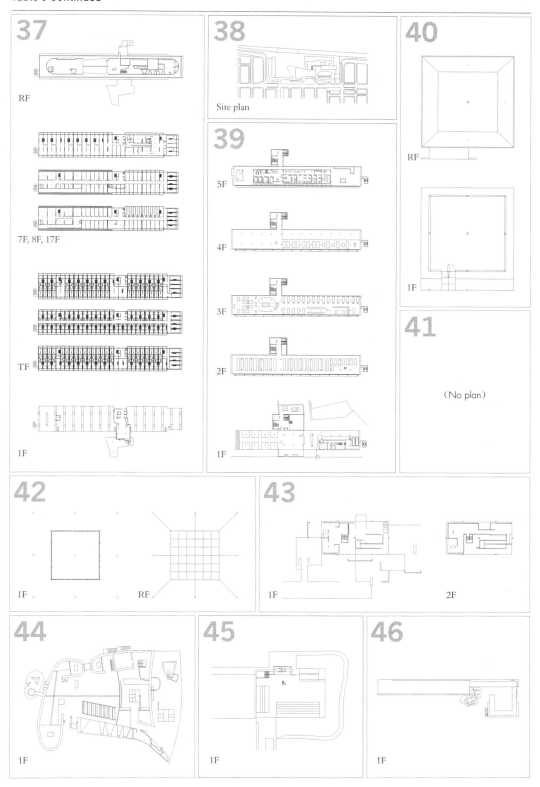

Table 3 Continued

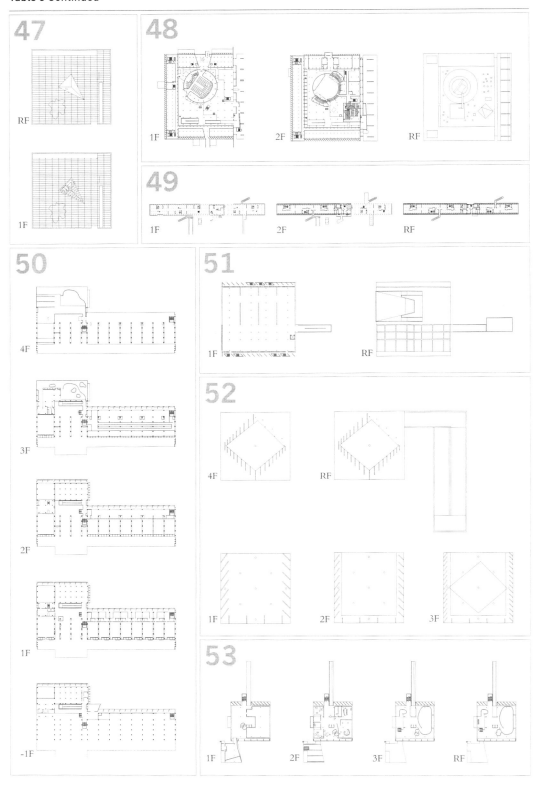

Plan Composition 031

Table 3 Continued

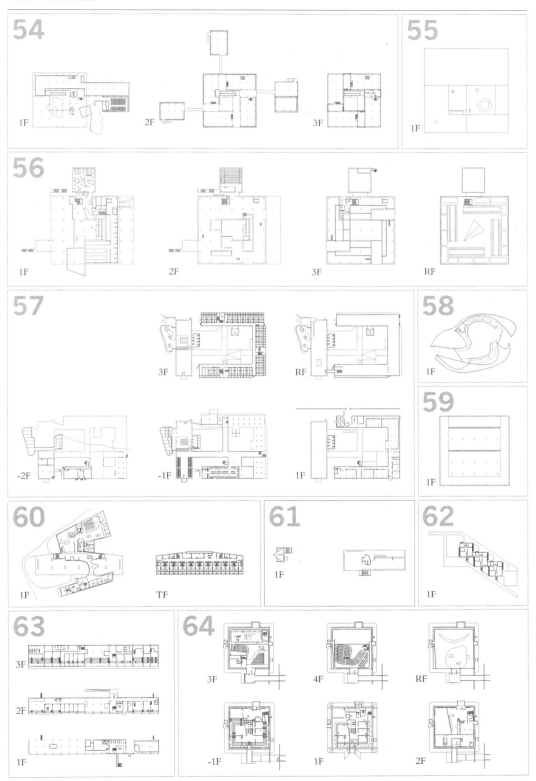

032

Table 3 Continued

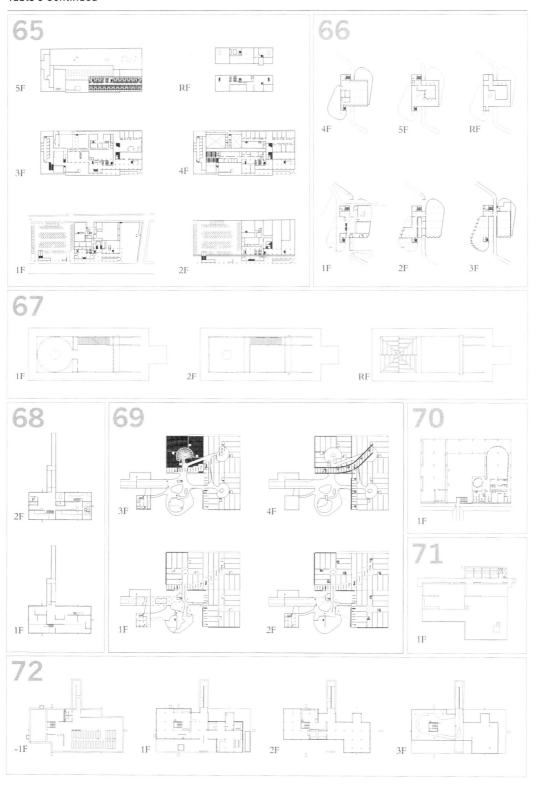

Table 3 Continued

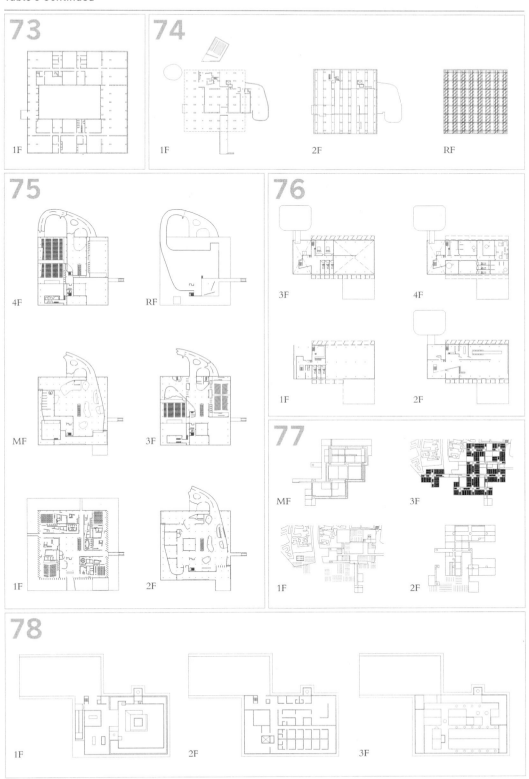

Table 3 Continued

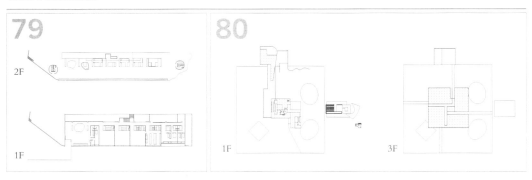

The in-plan organization modes of the eighty works are abstracted and the refined modes are summarized in Table 4.

Table 4 Abstracted plan organization modes

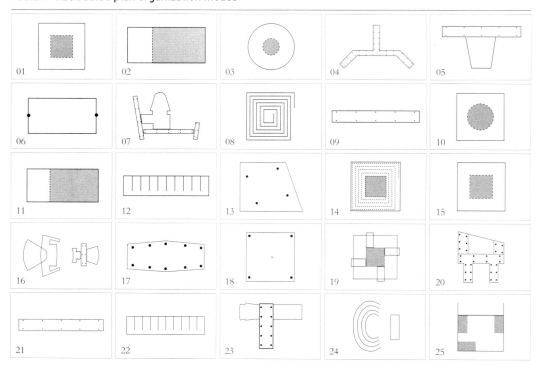

Table 4 Continued

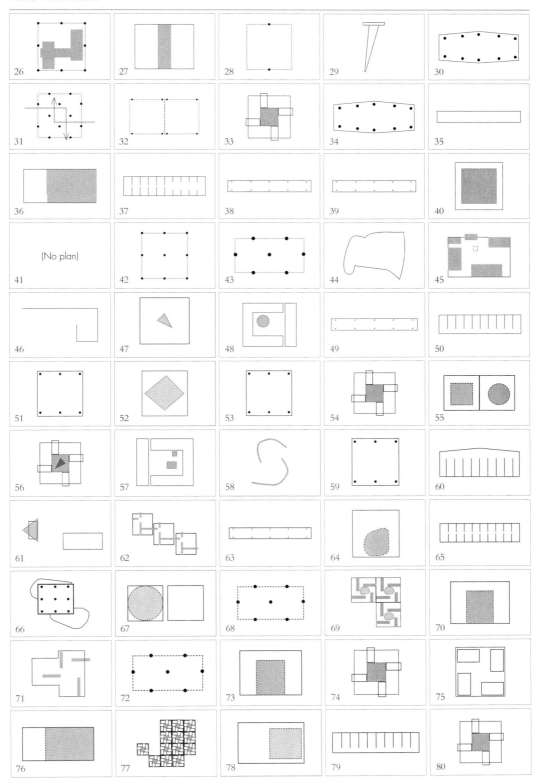

Through comparison, it can be seen that some works have a common composition in the internal space, which is found in the peculiarity of each work; the commonality should be found in the peculiarity, but not in the commonness. There are several types of this commonality.

<u>Type A:</u>

These works have a "core" in the center, which is not the "hub" of an elevator, but the "core" of a spatial organization, and they present the patterns superimposed by the basic geometries. They are projects 01, 03, 10, 15, 40, 47, 48, 52, 57, 64, 67, 70, 73, and 78, making a total of fourteen works (Table 5).

<u>Type B:</u>

These works present a " 卍 " shape, or a spiral layout around the center, forming an overlapping head-to-tail pattern. They are projects 08, 14, 19, 33, 45, 54, 56, 69, 71, 74, 75, 77, and 80, making a total of thirteen works (Table 6). It should be noted that some works of this type are composed of a single unit, while some are composed of multiple units, such as projects 69 and 77. Also, in projects 45 and 71, the " 卍 " feature is not as obvious as it is in other works, but there are traces of this tendency.

Table 5 Summary of Type A works

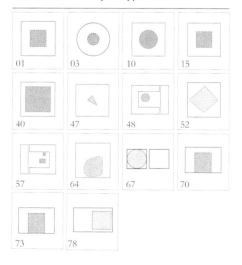

Table 6 Summary of Type B works

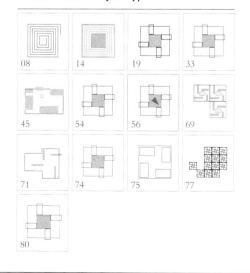

Type C:

These works have different external outlines, but the division of their internal space is based on the domino structure framework, that is, they have free division under the column grid of a standard beam-column structure. Some works combine this with a large spatial layout (projects 05 and 16). The Type C works are projects 04, 05, 07, 09, 13, 16, 17, 18, 20, 21, 23, 30, 34, 38, 39, 49, 51, 53, 59, 63, and 66, making a total of twenty-one works (Table 7).

Table 7 Summary of Type C works

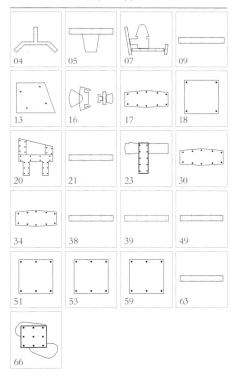

Type D:

These works are characterized by having structural elements arranged on the periphery of the plan outline, enclosing the large internal spaces of nearly two or four squares; the functional space is arranged in the large space. They are projects 06, 26, 28, 31, 42, 43, 68, and 72, making a total of eight works (Table 8).

Table 8 Summary of Type D works

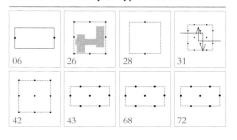

Type E:

These works show the internal separation of the determinant compartments set along a walkway. They are projects 12, 22, 37, 50, 60, 65, and 79, making a total of seven works (Table 9).

Table 9 Summary of Type E works

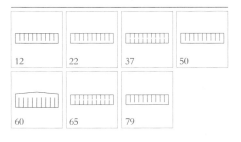

Type F:

These works have similar plan outlines and their interiors are divided into two parts, with a ratio of 2:1 in the space. They are projects 02, 11, 36, and 76, making a total of four works (Table 10).

Table 10 Summary of Type F works

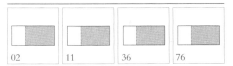

The following section describes each type of commonality by using representative works.

Type A

In 1910, Le Corbusier learned the technique of reinforced-concrete from Auguste Perret and visited the prototype of his ideal residence, Charterhouse of Ema at Galluzzo. Motivated by technique and ideal, he designed Ateliers d'Artistes (project 01) for his alma mater in his hometown, which integrated teaching and practice. Its plan is a 7-by-7 open square, with a centralized layout of workshops surrounding the large classroom and the stairs at the four corners leading straight to the second floor; Le Corbusier also strengthened the entrance and this distinction also highlights the one axis of the building (Figure 3). As the first public building proposal, Ateliers d'Artistes initiated a series of Le Corbusier's works that used this layout, with a fully centralized space.

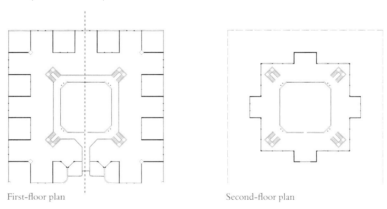

First-floor plan   Second-floor plan

Figure 3 Plans of project 01 representing each floor

In Château d'Eau (project 03) in 1917, Le Corbusier adopted a regular octagonal layout wrapped in a cylinder, as shown in Figure 4, to reinforce this layout. Supported by eight perfectly symmetrical irregular columns, the tower is partially exposed in the form of a pilaster embedded in the rounded outer wall (Figure 5), through a spiral staircase clinging to the exterior wall from the ground floor to the observation platform on the intermediate floor, and then from a spiral staircase in the center to the rooftop platform. In this part, Le Corbusier adopted the partition between the interior and the exterior to achieve the transformation of the use of space. The hollow space from the floor to the roof was transformed into a staircase leading to the observation platform (Figure 6), thus making room for viewing, which resolved the tension between the movement of traffic and those using the space. The centripetal symmetrical layout of the eight observation plans expresses a unity of non-directionality. The tower may have been the template for the design of the spiral staircases commonly seen in Le Corbusier's small houses after the 1920s.

If the plans of the first two projects retain the legacy of classicism, then in comparison, works after the late 1920s with this layout are simpler and more abstract, such as project 10, Église, Le Tremblay. In this plan, the structural columns are simplified (Figure 7); the geometry tends to be more a basic square and circle, and there are no classical pilasters, Islamic steeples, or other elements. As shown in the plan, a round open rampway along the periphery aids transportation. In a first rough sketch (Figure 8), it can be seen that Le Corbusier originally used a large cube to express the church's towering space, but later found that the cylinder embodied this sanctity better. In Musée d'Art Contemporain, Paris (project 15) from 1931, this layout is embodied in the centralized plan with two square layers inside and outside (Figure 9); there is only a double-flight staircase on the central axis, without any other partition. The focus of the space is a high-ceiling atrium space, serving as a spatial core, which is similar to the role of the spiral staircase in Château d'Eau (project 03).

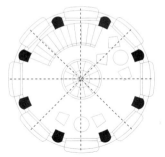

Figure 4 Plan of project 03

Figure 5 Image of tower of project 03

Figure 6 Interior sketch of project 03

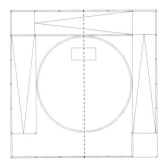

Figure 7 Plan of project 10 (the dotted line is the central axis)

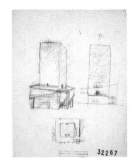

Figure 8 Rough sketch of project 10

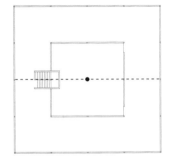

Figure 9 Plan of project 15 (the dotted line is the central axis)

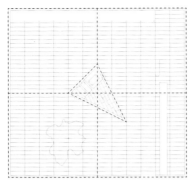
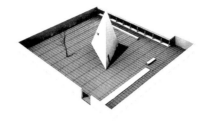

Figure 10 Plan of project 47   Figure 11 Perspective drawing of project 47

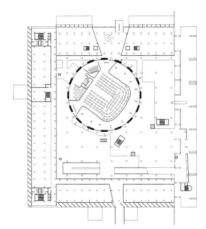

Figure 12 First-floor plan of project 48

Project 47 is a funeral chapel (Figure 10). The whole building is an enclosed courtyard, using a total of 480 floor tiles laid out in 12 columns and 40 rows. Each tile has a length of 2,450 millimeters (96.5 inches) and a width of 700 millimeters (27.5 inches), with a length–width ratio of 3.5:1. The courtyard is basically a square outline and the center of the pyramid-like chapel (Figure 11) is located at the midpoint of the whole courtyard, which is shown as a void in the diagram. Projects 52, 67, and 78 from Le Corbusier's late-career period all show Type A characteristics.

The "core" in the center of each plan of projects 01, 03, 10, 15, and 47 present a complete centrality; in some other Type A works, however, the "cores" deviate from the central position. If we partition and abstract the complex plan of Palais de l'Assemblée based on function, the core still reflects a Type A plan composition. Its circular conference hall (Figure 12), with its role as the absolute center of the picture, deviates toward one corner, unlike the square core in the center of Ateliers d'Artistes' (project 01, see Figure 3 on page 38) plan in 1910. At that time, Le Corbusier was inclined to the presentation with the deviation toward one corner.

Unlike the separate columns and cubes of Église, Le Tremblay (project 10, Figure 13), in Église Saint Pierre (project 64) from 1960 to 1969 (Figure 14), Le Corbusier fused the two into one, but the basic modes were the same. The bottom is a service function room and the upper frustum is a sacred church space. As can be seen from the plan, the frustum does not appear to be in the center of the composition, but more toward the west side, and the whole shape also appears to be distorted and contracted to the west side. The composition of the plan had become richer and more difficult to define than that of earlier works, and the form had also evolved from being simple and readable in the earlier period to being mysterious, complex, and difficult to understand in the later period. The continuation of Le Corbusier's method from the 1920s to the 1960s can be seen by comparing Figure 15 and Figure 16.

In the plan layout of Type A works, the evolution of the idea of the "core" at the center of the composition reveals that Le Corbusier's early works show the classical tendency of conservatism, embodied in elements such as the steeple and classical wall pillar; later works were abstracted and simplified, with most of the works showing the common characteristic of only one axis. There are few cases of works with their "core" at the corner, which were mainly in the later years of his practice (Table 11, page 42).

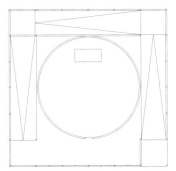

Figure 13 Second-floor plan of project 10

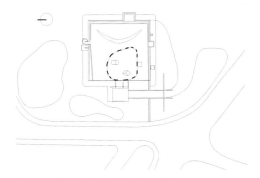

Figure 14 Site plan of project 64

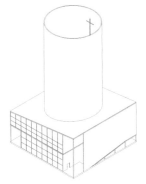

Figure 15 Axonometric drawing of project 10

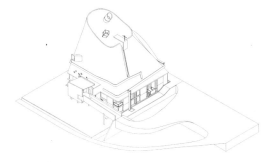

Figure 16 Axonometric drawing of project 64

Table 11 Summary of planes of Type A works

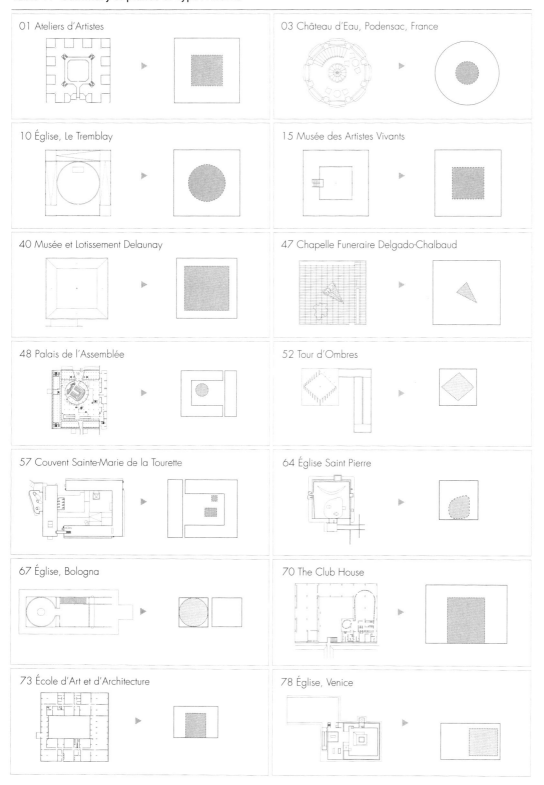

Type B

There are thirteen works that showcase the Type B plan layout, with a " 卍 " shape or spiral layout around the center. Le Corbusier's first mention of the word "spiral" was with regard to Mundaneum, Musée Mondial in 1929 (project 08):

"In order to ensure the symphony of the three passages in the trilogy of museums, in order to express the uninterrupted continuity of the expanding links in the chain, a unique basic architectural concept will bring about one organic form—spiral. The three passages will unfold along the same spiral line."
——*Le Corbusier Complete Works, Volume 1*[2]

From then on, this ideal organic form of nature appeared throughout his works, until the last sketch before the end of his life. The spiral features embodied in his works are either space-based or hidden-path-based, and no two are the same.

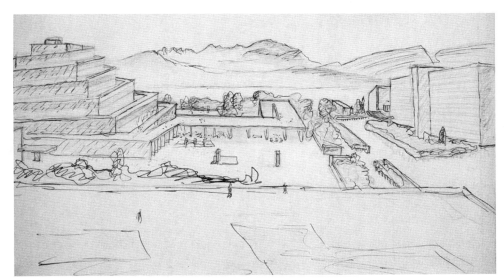

Figure 17   Sketch of project 08

The Mundaneum, Musée Mondial, built in 1929, was part of Le Corbusier's proposal to build a worldwide international center, which also included the international library, Institution of the League of Nations, and other functional institutions. *Le Corbusier Complete Works, Volume 1* shows the general idea of the museum, which visualizes the three elements of time, space, and place through architecture. For this purpose, Le Corbusier set up three ramps, so that people could first access the top by elevator and then slowly walk down along the ramps. From the above sketch, it can be seen that the infinite-spiral Utopia ideal is reminiscent of the Tower of Babel.

---

2 W. Boesiger, *Le Corbusier Complete Works*, Volume 1 (China: China Architecture Publishing, 2005), 182.

The plan in Figure 18 shows that the entire building extends outward from the center, with equal intervals between the ramps; the top floor is the platform to which the elevator and ramps have direct access. In this work, Le Corbusier presented the classical tendency of middle axial symmetry. In his concept sketch (Figure 19), a section of the museum partially summarizes the relationship of three passages, in which "a" represents the meaning of object and work, "b" represents the place, "c" represents the time, and "d" represents the transportation, loading and unloading; the bottoms of "a," "b," and "c" are continuous warehouses; also see Figure 20. He designed two routes, one each along the inside and outside of the building, through which people could walk directly from the roof ramp outside the pavilion to the ground floor without entering the building, or directly into the interior pavilion, along the ramp in Figure 20; the outdoor stairways and walkways (Figure 21) can access different floors of the interior pavilion. The floor slabs and ramps of the entire building are sloping and the ramp is both a traffic route and a usable space, presenting a trend of continuous expansion in both horizontal and vertical directions; it can be said to be a three-dimensional parking garage. The standout interior ramps on each floor and the outdoor roof ramps are staggered, forming a natural lightwell, and the ingenious design of the sections allows people to admire Le Corbusier's excellent ability in space organization. This design embodies the spiral in space and is the first attempt by Le Corbusier to practice a series of organic forms of spiral.

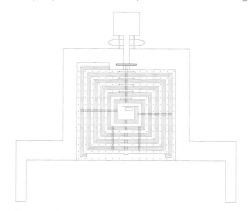

Figure 18　Roof plan of project 08

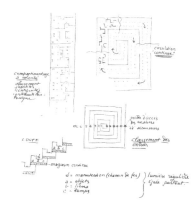

Figure 19　Concept sketch of project 08

Figure 20　Section perspective drawing of project 08

Figure 21　Perspective drawing of project 08

If the architectural technique of Mundaneum, Musée Mondial is an infinite spiral in both horizontal and vertical dimensions, then project 14 from 1931 is the beginning of the turn toward an infinite expansion of single horizontality. The building comprises one floor underground and one floor aboveground, where people enter from point A on the plan (Figure 22), walk down the stairs through an underground corridor to point B at the exhibition hall on the lower ground floor, and then walk up the stairs to the ground floor for viewing. The first-floor interior segmentation (Figure 23) is seemingly random, with the free plan under the standard frame. The part where the exterior wall stops and the section is finished with seven pillars marks the track of infinite expansion. In addition, the unique structural roof, designed to provide high-side window lighting, extends spirally outward from the center. This project seems to be a preliminary experiment in not closing the connection between the roof and the main space on the first floor; they are two separate systems that are attached.

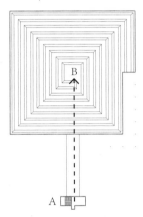 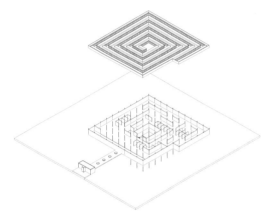

Figure 22 Roof plan of project 14   Figure 23 Layered axonometric drawing of project 14

In the Contemporary Aesthetic Centre of Pavillon Bat'a, Paris, in 1937 (Centre d'Esthetique Contemporaine, project 19), Le Corbusier gradually pushed the division of interior space under the spiral theme. Instead of using the four indistinguishable external façades, he formed the partition through the raised part on the façade (Figure 24 and Figure 25).

 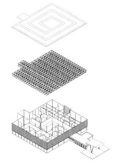

Figure 24 Second-floor plan of project 19   Figure 25 Layered axonometric drawing of project 19

The roof frame has a triangle truss with a secret passageway to allow staff to access the roof and for light regulation, rather than fixed high-side window lighting. In addition, the central hall uses the ramp to replace the stairs. This basic model was established in Musée à Croissance Illimitée in 1939 (project 33): the architecture has three partial floors and the ramp begins in the central hall; the four square exhibition halls on the second floor present a " 卍 " layout around the atrium (Figure 26), while the prominent façade is connected to the corridors in four directions and the roof is re-constructed with high-side windows. As can be seen from the model photograph (Figure 27), Le Corbusier presents this spiral theme on the floor, exterior wall, interior exhibition hall, and roof; this project can, therefore, be regarded as demonstrative of Le Corbusier's exploration into using a spatial spiral theme.

It was not until creating Musée, Ahmedabad (project 54), from 1954 to 1957 that Le Corbusier realized this concept proper. The building is composed of one main exhibition space and three subsidiary masses, and the plan of the main space presents the characteristics of the exhibition hall layout in the form of a " 卍 " around the atrium (Figure 28). In this project, instead of a typical spiral form, the roof is adapted to the local climate by adopting a flat roof that is ventilated and covered with soil and plants. Another original aspect of the project is the use of an open space in the central hall for rainwater collection, ventilation, and so on. (Figure 29). Without taking into consideration these small strategies to allow for regional climate, the core organizational form of the plan remains a space-based spiral theme (Figure 30).

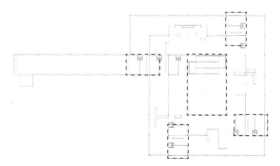

Figure 26 Second-floor plan of project 33

Figure 27 Model of project 33

Figure 28 Second-floor plan of project 54

Figure 29 Atrium of project 54

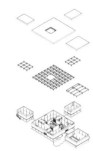

Figure 30 Axonometric drawing of project 54

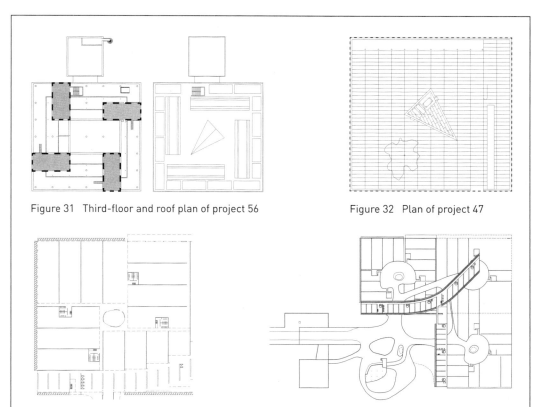

Figure 31 Third-floor and roof plan of project 56

Figure 32 Plan of project 47

Figure 33 Plan of workshop units, project 69

Figure 34 Office-floor plan of project 69

During the same period, Le Corbusier was commissioned to design a museum, Musée National d'Art Occidental in Tokyo (project 56). Its plan (Figure 31) and the basic pattern of space remains the same as that of his previous works, which are characterized by the structure of roof and hall. In the third-floor plan, the atrium is a high-ceiling hall and the exhibition hall has four floors arranged around the atrium in the form of a "卍." In the roof plan, Le Corbusier arranged four rectangular, high-window protrusions to surround the central pyramid-like roof light, forming a "卍" shape (Figure 31). This arrangement stemmed from the design of Chapelle Funeraire Delgado-Chalbaud (project 47, Figure 32) and also demonstrates the continuity and flexibility of the architect in the use of his design methods.

The arrangement is also partially applied in projects 69, 75, and 77. Olivetti, Centre de Calculs Électroniques (project 69) is a huge architectural complex that can accommodate up to 4,000 computing staff. It includes many functions, such as office, restaurant, workshop, and library. The workshop is on the first floor and consists of three units. The interior division of each unit strictly follows the features of the windmill-shaped arrangement (Figure 33). The center of the unit is a high-ceiling hall with an irregular circular dome. The four small boxes revolving around the center are stairs leading to the changing room and the three units join together to form the ground-floor podium of the entire workshop floor (Figure 34).

Looking back at Le Corbusier's method in Mundaneum, Musée Mondial, it can be seen that his approach evolved from figurative coils of a spiral spreading outward (with distinct features of the line) to the form of " 卍 " that starts at the center and hovers around the center (Figure 35 – with distinct features of the surface). The difference between the two is that the former is so limited that it can be used only in a linear spatial organization; also, the pavilion space required by the Mundaneum, Musée Mondial fits perfectly with its spiral linear ramps, while the spiral-shaped roof is separated from the bottom space. Aware of the stiff logical relationship, he hence decided to adopt the " 卍 " form in the roof of Musée National d'Art Occidental. This form is consistent with the layout of the exhibition hall on the ground floor and the spiral partition layout of the space as embodied in the roof lighting structure. As a result, the windmill-like spiral is more flexible, allowing for the head-to-tail design of four spaces under a square frame, which satisfies almost all other types of space organizations, such as the workshop of Olivetti, Centre de Calculs Électroniques; the conference hall of Palais des Congrès, Strasbourg (project 75, Figure 36), and the ward floor of Hôpital, Venice (project 77, Figure 37). These works prove once more that Le Corbusier's idea of non-functionalist design is concerned with space itself and the organizational logic of method.

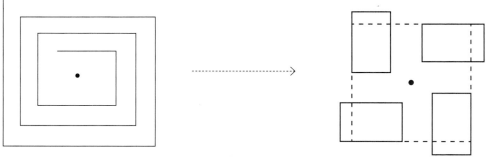

Figure 35 The evolution of a spiral line into a "卍" form

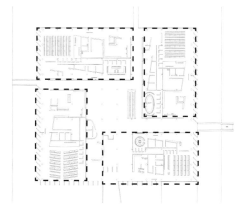

Figure 36 First-floor plan of project 75

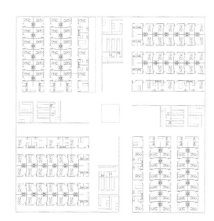

Figure 37 Third-floor ward unit plan of project 77

In the thirteen works that fall under the Type B layout, the basic plane segmentation method reflects the common spiral organization mode (Table 12, page 50). The original spiral line was inspired by the continuing upward-spiral exhibition space of the Tower of Babel. The inherent expansibility and linearity of the spiral meets the core requirements of Mundaneum, Musée Mondial. In the later development process, this type of line—expanding horizontally and vertically—began to shift to a single-dimensional, horizontal extension; at this time, the spiral line was only embodied in the roof lighting structure, separated from the spatial structure of the ground layer and the two were not included in the same organizational logic. The "line" was gradually replaced by the "plane" in the shape of "卍." The applicability of "plane" is more extensive and it can achieve unity in the logical relationship between roof and space organization. If the Mundaneum, Musée Mondial and Musée à Croissance Illimitée were based on the infinite expansion of the exhibition space, and, therefore, adopted this organic mode, then why was it still adopted in later workshops, wards and conference rooms? The core idea of almost all of these houses lies in expansion. The organic nature of the spiral is embodied in the constant extension from the center, and the standardization and extensibility that Le Corbusier began to focus on in 1910 were used more widely under the theme of the spiral. It was also a step forward to show that Le Corbusier was a rationalist who adhered to an original idea, while constantly revising it to achieve a more logical unity.

Table 12 Summary of planes of Type B Works

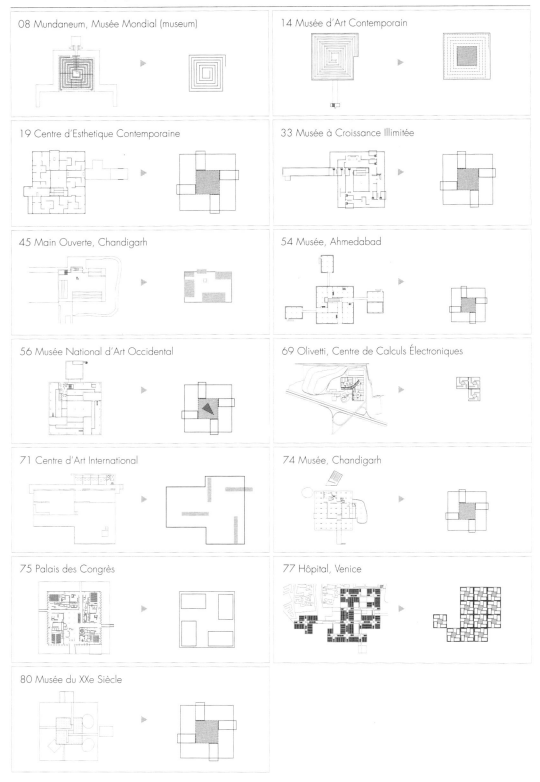

Plan Composition 051

> Type C
>
> Of the eighty public buildings, twenty-one show no features in the plane. Although they have different external contours, they are free in the division of interior space. This is an extension of the domino structure system proposed by Le Corbusier in 1914—that is, the free division of space within the standard beam-column frame of a regular geometry rather than a specific spatial organization pattern like Type A or Type B. Because of the large number of works within this category, only some of the works are discussed in this book, as listed in Table 13.

Table 13 Selected Type C works

09 Mundaneum, Musée Mondial (administration building)

This plan was designed for the international library project for Mundaneum, Musée Mondial, Geneva. The plane is the shape of a rectangle, with the reception and information office in the middle, and elevator, ramp, and other traffic core at the two ends, and a concrete frame structure; the plane can be divided freely.

18 Réorganisation Agraire, Ferme et Village Radieux

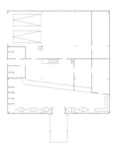

The plan is part of Village Radieux, a modern village conceived by Le Corbusier in response to a call from French peasant friends. It is a post office, where the archetype of the arch structure in the "Monol" system is used, while the interior is still composed of columns and the space is divided freely.

51 Musée de la Connaissancea

The plane of the plan is the shape of a square. The whole structure is a frame structure; the solid wall on one side of the plane is used as the load-bearing function instead of the column, the ramp is set outside the square outline, and the inner space is characterized by free division.

53 Palais des Filateurs

The prominent feature of this scheme is the long ramp leading into the second floor. It has the same frame structure of reinforced-concrete; the main façade and its back are equipped with sunshades, the interior space is divided freely, and the functional space is several independent small blocks.

59 City Center, Chandigarh

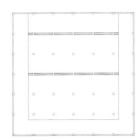

The plane of this plan is the shape of a square, with an overall frame structure. This is a standard study of the commercial center designed by Le Corbusier for the new urban planning scheme of Chandigarh, which is technically a frame with no division of the plane.

66 Carpenter Center for Visual Arts, Harvard University

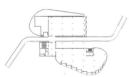

The plane of the scheme presents a variable square, with two kidney-shaped bodies over a square outline and an S-shaped ramp through the whole building, but despite these special treatments, the core organization of the scheme is still a free division under the frame structure.

Table 14 Summary of planes of Type C works

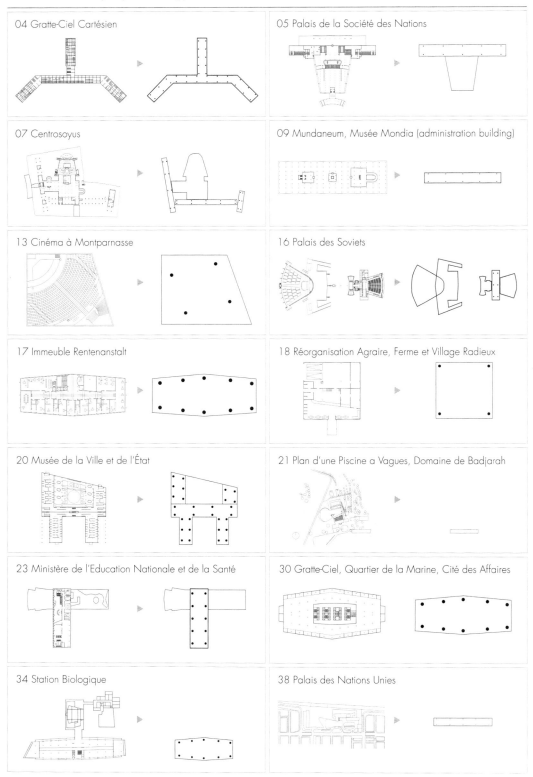

Table 14 Continued

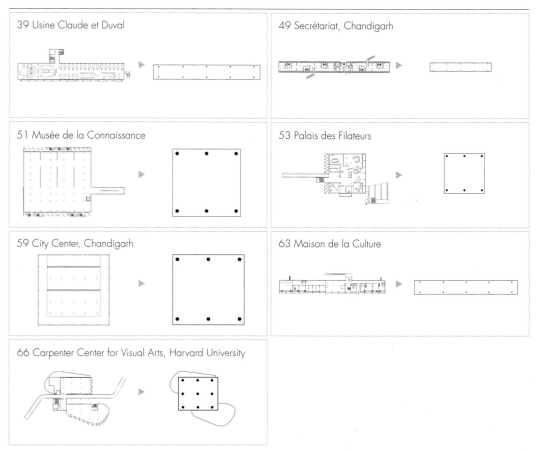

Type D

Eight projects fall within the Type D category, all of which are characterized by having structural elements arranged on the periphery of the plane contour that surrounds the interior space of nearly two or four squares.

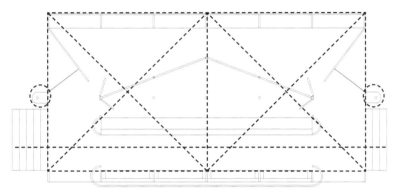

Figure 38 Plan of project 06

In the early stage of the machine age, Le Corbusier designed commercial buildings for some of Paris's middle class to accommodate and display goods, as well as to propagandize the new era's "display" buildings. Project 06, Pavillon Nestlé (Figure 38), which he designed for the Nestlé Corporation, was a detachable pavilion built for exhibition and sales, composed of metal skeletons and steel plates. In a 6-by-2 open space, it traces a linear path on the street-facing side and houses a sample exhibition room at the back, with a small cabinet enclosed in the middle of the plane. The building structure is composed of 7-purlin array trusses (Figure 39). The roof is overlaid with an inverted slope and two light boxes are arranged at one end. A base foot stall protrudes from the ends of the plane and flagpoles are placed on them. Le Corbusier used a simple steel structure in this temporary pavilion, with the plane presenting a rectangular frame made up of two squares. In this project, the foot stall and the light boxes on the roof do not fit into the main structure of the building, but stand out on the exterior outline of the building, and together, they frame a complete space for the exhibition.

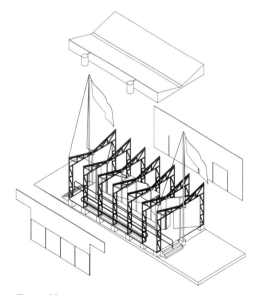

Figure 39 Axonometric drawing of project 06

Plan Composition 055

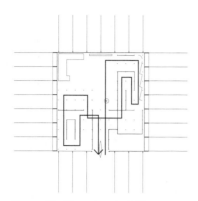

Figure 40 Plan of project 26

Figure 41 Interior image of project 26

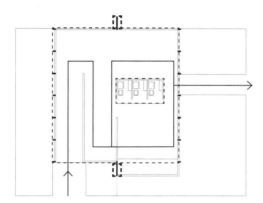

Figure 42 Plan of project 28

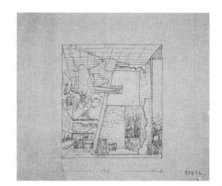

Figure 43 Interior sketch of project 28

Pavillon des Temps Nouveaux (project 26, Figure 40) is the only one of the four proposals that Le Corbusier presented for the Paris Exposition Universelle in 1937 that was built; here, Le Corbusier followed the ramps that had been revealed in the 1920s, and the plane's composition reflects the separation of structure from space. The four sides of the square outline have eight steel truss columns, jointly supporting the roof; the interior is a complete space, and the inclusion of the structure (steel frame with canvas roof) and its contents (clapboard exhibition areas with a ramp) presages the core design philosophy of Unité d'Habitation in Le Corbusier's later career—that is, free-filling under the standard framework (Figure 41).

Project 28 (Pavillon Bat'a) also presents a Type D plane composition (Figure 42). The Paris Exposition Universelle was a pilgrimage site for "commodity fetishism," and the pavilion, as a carrier for commodity, had gradually been endowed with a lofty, large-scale space, almost like a church. The plan is a showcase designed by Le Corbusier for a shoe shop in Paris. The building consists of steel columns around a square box, with three little cubicles as pedicure rooms in the middle of the square plane (Figure 43).

Pavillon de la France à l'exposition de l'Eau (Project 31) embodies the characteristics of a Type D plan, with a similar structural form of steel frames and floating roofs (Figure 44). Twelve vertical steel columns, on the periphery of the plane outline, support four undulating roofs (Figure 45). The exhibition begins with a ramp at both ends of the plane, reaches the center of the second-floor square plane, and then follows the perpendicular ramp down to the ground floor, where the two paths overlap each other. In addition, the four walls on the ground floor are attached end-to-end, around the square plane; the four plates, connected to each other, also frequently connect at the head and tail (Figure 46).

In Musée Tent (project 42, Figure 47), the plane shows that the anchor point of the outer eight ropes presents a hidden square pattern. The middle seventeen stand columns also support a square space, with eight anchors facing the middle column, and the whole plane is divided into eight equal parts in the outer outline of the square—that is, the four non-directional axes. The planning is a rough pavilion made by Le Corbusier with local trunks and simple ropes (Figure 48).

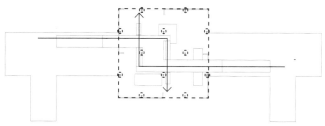

Figure 44 Second-floor plan of project 31

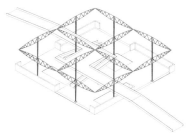

Figure 45 Axonometric drawing of project 31

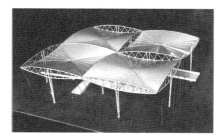

Figure 46 Model of project 31

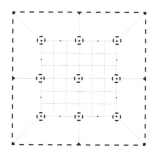

Figure 47 Plan of project 42

Figure 48 Interior image of project 42

The other three projects that fall within Type D are small exhibition halls designed by Le Corbusier from the 1950s to the 1960s (Table 15), which reflect the exposed structure columns framing the space used on the plane composition, with ramps and staircases. The plane of project 43 (Porte Maillot) is a combination of two squares, and the six steel columns supporting the roof appear independently on the four sides of the plane. Compared to the pier stud protrusion without structural function of Pavillon Nestlé (project 06), the four-sided protrusions of this plane strengthen the independence of the two squares; there is a heterogeneous H-shaped steel structure in the center of the plane. The plan composes a two-floor structure with ramps and stairs arranged within a square frame. In planning project 68 (Pavillon d'Exposition, Stockholm) in 1962, Le Corbusier throws the ramp out of the square outline and replaces double-flight staircases with two single-flight staircases. It is unique in that the roof is not detached from the main space, but the relationship between the four-sided structural columns and the roof is similar to that of projects 43 and 72, with the ramp inclined to one side. In project 72 (Pavillon d'Exposition ZHLC, Zurich), the ramp is located in the center of the plane and causes the two squares to break apart completely; a cross-column net is added between the two squares and the double-flight staircase is used again.

Table 15   Projects 43, 68, and 72

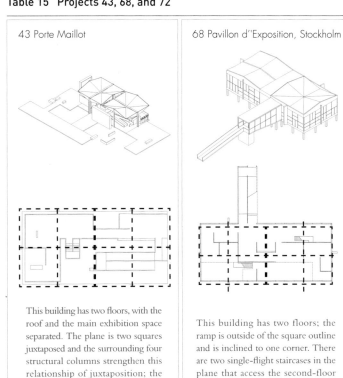
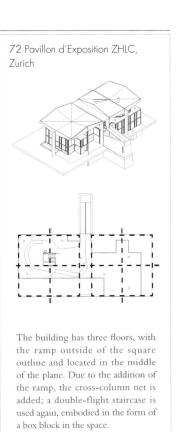

43 Porte Maillot	68 Pavillon d''Exposition, Stockholm	72 Pavillon d'Exposition ZHLC, Zurich
This building has two floors, with the roof and the main exhibition space separated. The plane is two squares juxtaposed and the surrounding four structural columns strengthen this relationship of juxtaposition; the double-flight staircase and the ramp organization are placed within the square outline.	This building has two floors; the ramp is outside of the square outline and is inclined to one corner. There are two single-flight staircases in the plane that access the second-floor exhibition room, and the umbrella-shaped roof and the main space are not completely detached.	The building has three floors, with the ramp outside of the square outline and located in the middle of the plane. Due to the addition of the ramp, the cross-column net is added; a double-flight staircase is used again, embodied in the form of a box block in the space.

Table 16 Summary of planes of Type D works

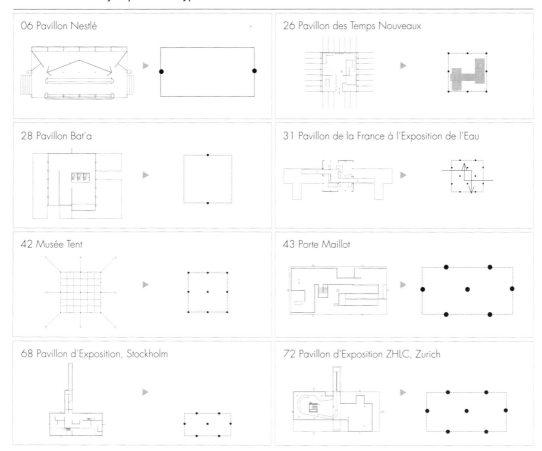

Type E

Of the eighty works, seven display characteristics that categorize them under Type E—that is, the internal separation of the main compartments are set along a walkway.

Unité d'Habitation (project 37, Figure 49) is a representative work of the Type E category. It is the prototype of the urban residential unit as conceived by Le Corbusier. The whole building is shaped like a cruise ship. Shown in the typical floor plan, the interior is divided into residential units, with twenty-nine apartments along the long side of the building and five on the short south side of the building. The plane outline of the building, which Frank Lloyd Wright satirized as "the carnage of the seaside," presents a " — " shape. At the end is an outdoor double-flight staircase that leads directly to the fourth floor. The plane presents a uniform modulus of 16 meters (52.5 feet) and a right-angle orthogonal system, and the overall building is elevated. It's worth mentioning that the top floor of Unité d'Habitation is a mix of multifunctional rooms, which once again reinforces Le Corbusier's architectural philosophy: the free plane under a fixed frame.

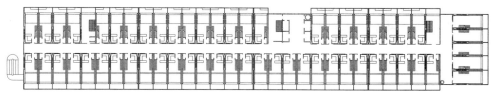

Figure 49 Typical-floor plan of project 37

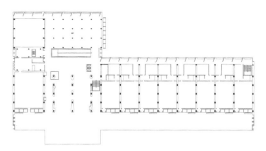

Figure 50 First-floor plan of project 50

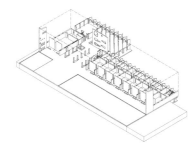

Figure 51 Axonometric drawing of the model of project 50

Project 50, Haute Cour, (Figure 50) was a major building in the square complex of the Chandigarh Government, the new capitol of Punjab Pradesh, India. Le Corbusier adopted a horizontal rectangular plane layout; the project can be divided into three parts in the plane layout, with a hall formed by the full-height slab structure in the middle, the array unit organization of many small courts on the one side (Figure 51), and an independent grand court on the other side.

Gare d'Orsay (project 65, Figure 52), which was not completed, is a city complex located on the river bank of central Paris, with three sides facing the streets and a car park and entrance at the bottom. A rectangular building offers the hotel rooms, with a concave balcony on one side of the standard floor plan and sunshade facilities on the other side; a number of circular lightwells can be seen on the roof. The ground floor has a wide area, considerable depth, and more rooms, therefore not all rooms receive light from standard windows; some receive light through the skylight.

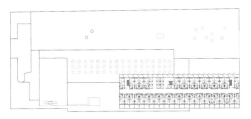

Figure 52 Fifth-floor plan of project 65

The common feature of Type E works is that the plane is divided into arrays of small rooms and these rooms show a standard, uniform nature, which are mostly used in hotels, apartments, and similar types of buildings.

Table 17 Summary of planes of Type E works

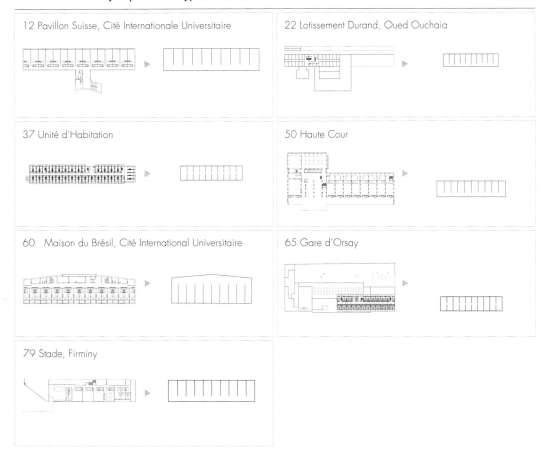

Type F

Four projects embody Type F characteristics, where the space is divided into two parts under the plane outline of a rectangle and their size ratio is close to 2:1. They include projects 02, 11, 36, and 76.

Project 02 (Cinéma "La Scala," Figure 53) is a cinema building designed by Le Corbusier and his friends in his hometown. The building has a sloping roof and retains the features of classicism. The plane outline is presented as a long strip with a length-to-width ratio of nearly 3:1. The interior is divided into two parts, one of which is a small space for the stage, and the other of which is a large space for the auditorium, with the size ratio of nearly 2:1. The building has two floors, with an attic at the auditorium end of the plan, which can be reached directly from the outer stairway, or from the interior of the first floor.

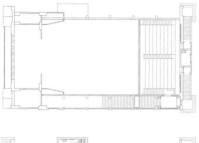

Project 11, Pavillon d'Aviation S.T.A.R., is an incomplete small exhibition hall with a rectangular plane. Its interior is divided into two parts—a large space and a small space—and their size ratio is close to 2:1, as shown in Figure 54.

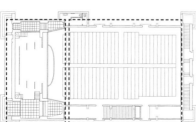

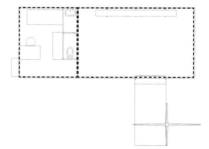

Figure 53 Plans of project 02 at each floor

Figure 54 First-floor plan of project 11

École volante (project 36) was designed in 1940. In the face of reconstruction and fund shortages, Le Corbusier explored a series of low-cost construction methods, while also pondering how to create buildings in a simpler, faster, and more efficient way. As a result, the projects of this period bear intrinsically close resemblances the temporary features of project 11. Project 36 was Le Corbusier's first gift to refugees during the war and he made sure to clarify the philosophy of this exploration:

"Modern warfare means the migration of population, and temporary barracks should also be built while firearms are being built. They can be used as a complement to guns, as residences, schools, assembly halls, etc., and thus the real builders should build standard temporary barracks as carefully as the makers of guns, which will meet a wide variety of functions with high efficiency."[3]

---

3 W. Boesiger, *Le Corbusier Complete Works*, Volume 4 (China: China Architecture Publishing, 2005), 94.

The proposal, with its strong slogan, reflects two principles that Le Corbusier always adhered to: the standardization brought about by industrial technology and the demands of the times, and the flexibility of a space to accommodate a variety of functions. The planning includes school buildings such as classrooms, craft workshops, youth clubs and canteens, all of which use the same spatial and structural patterns. Figure 55 shows the first floor of a canteen for 160 children, which consists of three parts, and which includes a porch, kitchen, toilet, and other ancillary functions at both ends, as well as a main dining area in the middle. Part of the building has two floors—at 2.2 meters (7.2 feet) and 4.5 meters (14.8 feet)—and a lower attic as a changing room and accommodation for service personnel. The building's first floor is divided into two parts: dining room and kitchen, embodying the characteristics of works in Type F category.

Project 76 (Ambassade de France, Brasilia) is the planning of the French Embassy in Brasilia, in which the building plane of the office part is also divided into two parts—one of which is the open hall of the large space, and the other is the subsidiary function of the small cubicle, as shown in Figure 56.

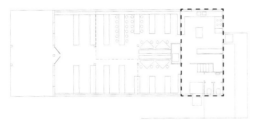
Figure 55 First-floor plan of project 36

Figure 56 First-floor plan of project 76

Table 18 Summary of planes of Type F works

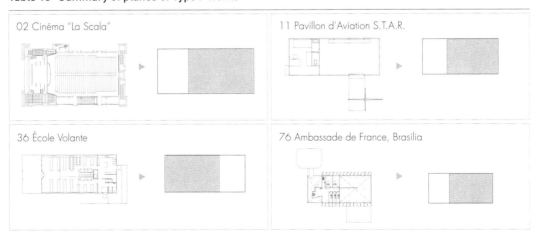

Fourteen of the eighty works do not belong to any of the six categories discussed, nor do they have anything in common with each other. By examining these eighty works, we can observe the plane partition patterns used by the different building types and the specific method used in a particular type of building, as shown in Table 19.

Plan Composition 063

Table 19 The works categorized by function

Administration building	Work	05	07	09	16	17	23	34	38	39	48	49	50	53	62	69	75	76
	Type Code	C	C	C	C	C	C	C	C	C	A	C	E	C		B	B	F
Museum	Work	08	14	15	20	33	40	51	54	56	74	80						
	Type Code	B	B	A	C	B	A	C	B	B	B	B						
Exhibition hall	Work	06	11	19	26	27	28	31	32	42	43	58	68	71	72			
	Type Code	D	F	B	D		D	D		D	D		D	B	D			
Religious building	Work	10	41	44	47	57	64	67	78									
	Type Code	A			A	A	A	A	A									
School	Work	01	12	36	60	66	73											
	Type Code	A	E	F	E	C	A											
Sports facility	Work	21	24	35	63	79												
	Type Code	C			C	E												
Public building (water conservancy)	Work	03	61															
	Type Code	A																
Complex	Work	04	18	22	30	37	65											
	Type Code	C	C	E	C	E	E											
Commercial building	Work	02	13	25	59	70												
	Type Code	F	C		C	A												
Monument	Work	29	45	46	52	55												
	Type Code		B		A													
Hospital	Work	77																
	Type Code	B																

A ▪ B ▦ C ▭ D ⸬ E ▥ F ▫

According to the statistics in Table 19, from the perspective of function:

· Administration buildings are mainly of Type C (65 percent), while fewer are of Types A, B, E, and F.
· Museums are mainly of Type B (64 percent), while Types A and C highlight two works each.
· Exhibition halls are of Type D (57 percent), while few are of Types B and F.
· Religious buildings only fall within Type A (75 percent).
· Schools are mainly of Types A and E (33 percent each), while a few are of Types C and F.
· Sports facilities are mainly of Type C (40 percent), with a few of Type E.
· Public buildings are of Type A (50 percent).
· Complexes are of Types C and E (50 percent each).
· Commercial buildings are mainly of Type C (40 percent).
· Monuments are mainly of Types A and B (20 percent each).
· Hospitals are of Type B.

Going by category, we see that Type A is more used in religious buildings; Type B is used more in museums; Type C is used more in administration buildings; Type D is used more in exhibition halls; and Type E is used more in complexes and schools; In the commercial building, school, exhibition hall, and administration building categories each, there is one work of Type F.

Although these six types are based on the core idea of building plane segmentation, there is still a commonality of some special methods among some specific cases.

In 1931, Le Corbusier and his friends designed a building in his hometown: project 13, Cinéma à Montparnasse. The basic outline of its plane is a trapezoid. Due to functional constraints, the division of its internal space basically follows the requirements of the theater. For the first-floor entrance, lounge, and other floors serving ancillary functions, the plane frame is divided by using ramps to connect the external and internal spaces in a diagonal direction. This is similar to his later work, Carpenter Center for Visual Arts, Harvard University (project 66), which uses the ramp to divide the plane (Figure 57). The S-shaped plane-dividing line of project 13 also has a high difference in the vertical (Figure 58), in the form of a ramp that extends from the entrance to the theater space at the bottom; this resembles the ramp of project 66 that is used as a divider. In project 13, Le Corbusier used this S-shaped ramp to solve the problem of connecting and dividing spaces within a limited framework. From this point of view, the method of project 13 is better than that of project 66; the latter only used this form to address the question of the boundary between the city and the building, but there is still a connection between the two.

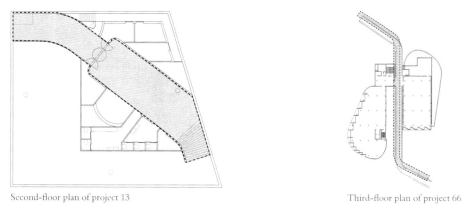

Second-floor plan of project 13　　　　　　　　　　　　Third-floor plan of project 66

Figure 57　Comparison between the plans of project 13 and project 66

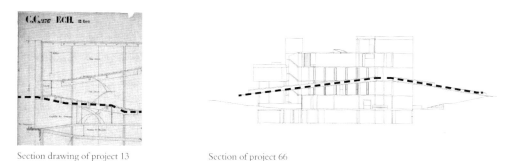

Section drawing of project 13　　　Section of project 66

Figure 58　Comparison between the sections of project 13 and project 66

2 Façade Composition

The façade, the second of Le Corbusier's three memorandums to the architect, is an element that encloses the form, which endows the work with characteristics. This section examines which characteristics the eighty works embody in the composition of their façade (Table 20).

Table 20 Elevations of the 80 public buildings

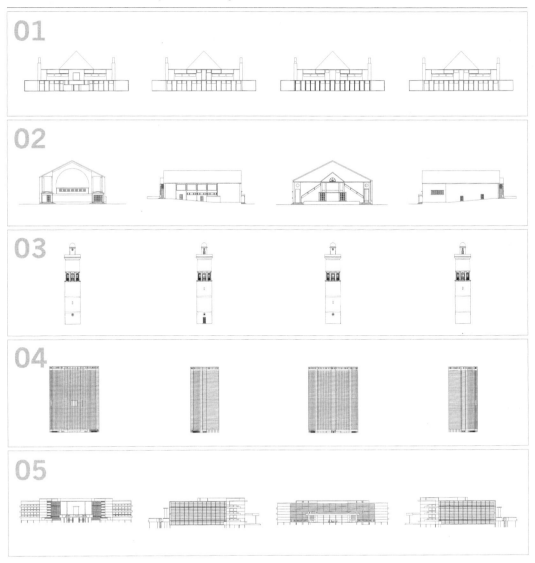

Table 20 Continued

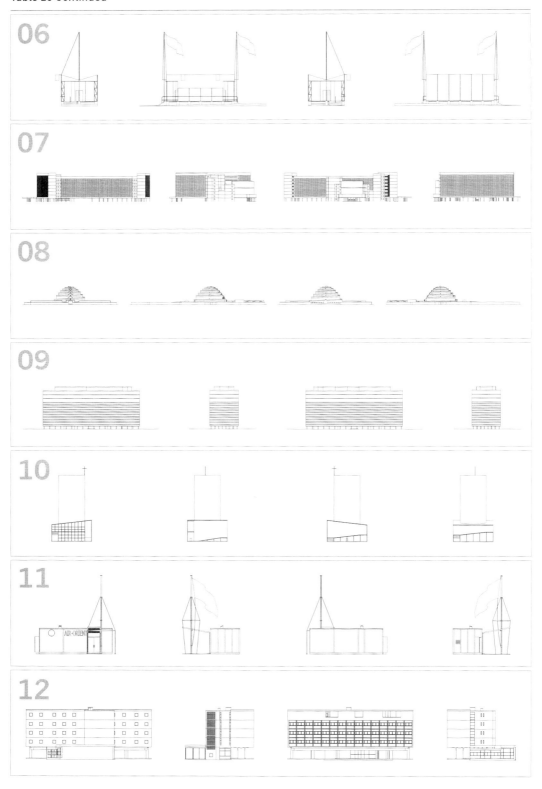

Table 20 Continued

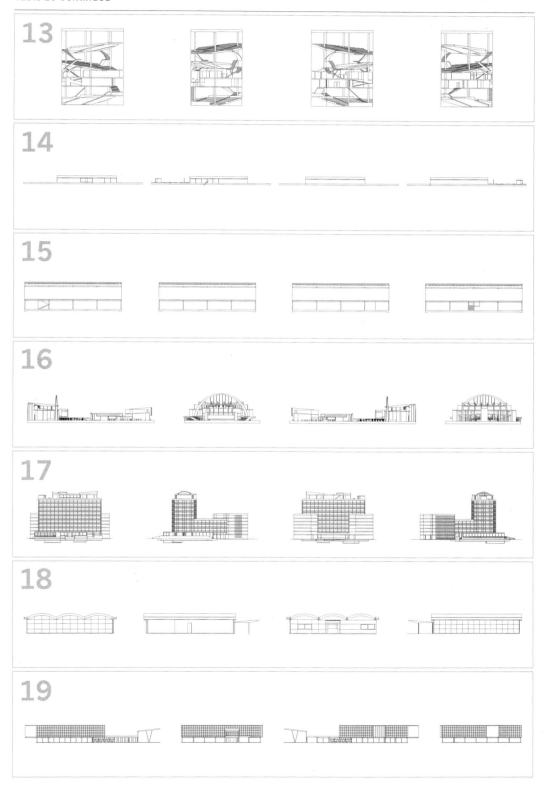

Table 20 Continued

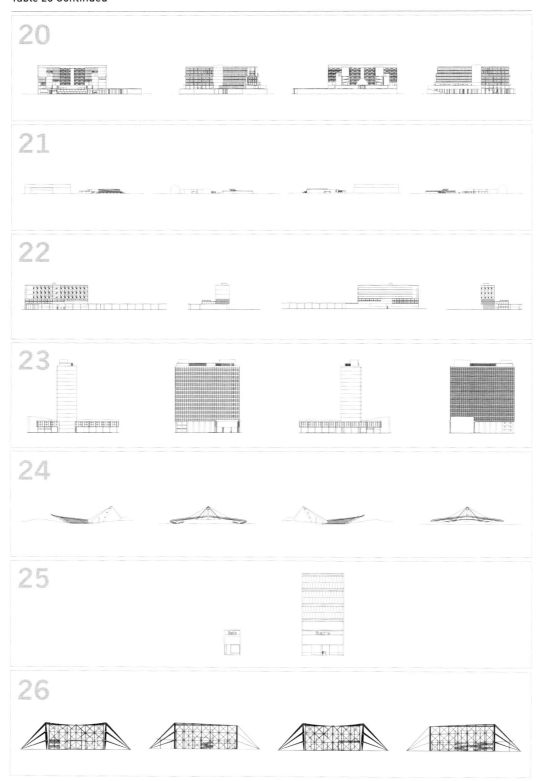

Table 20 Continued

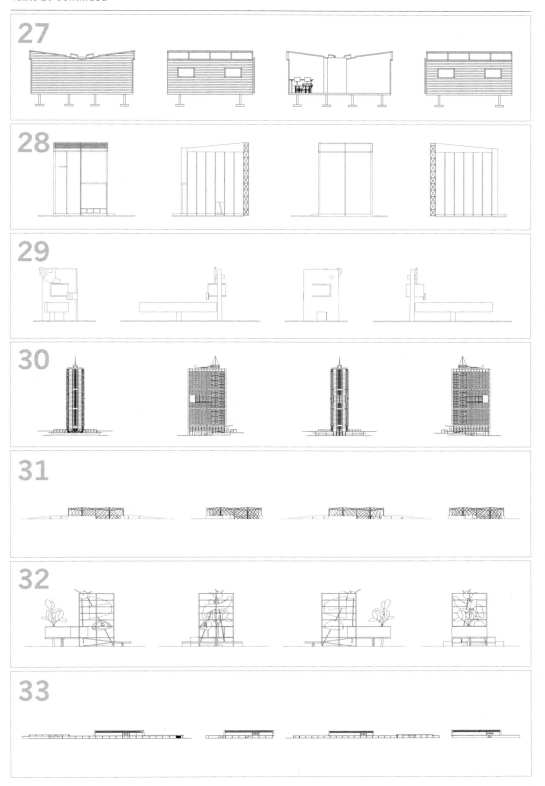

Table 20 Continued

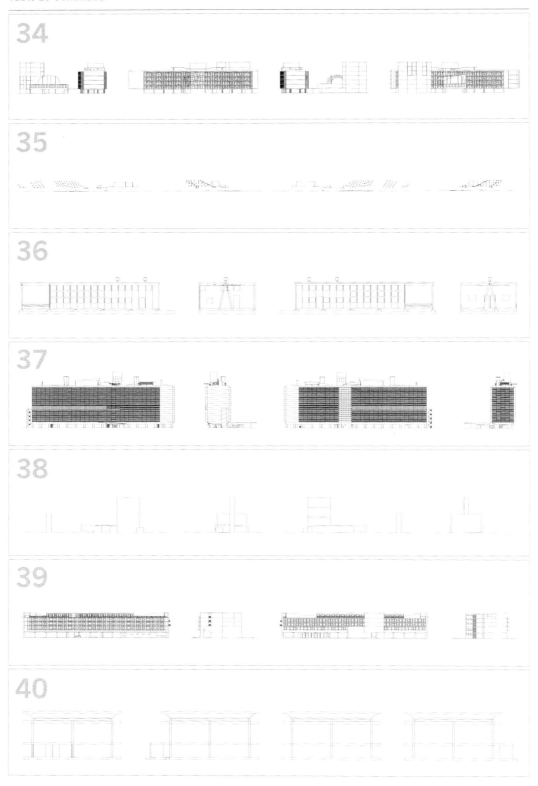

Table 20 Continued

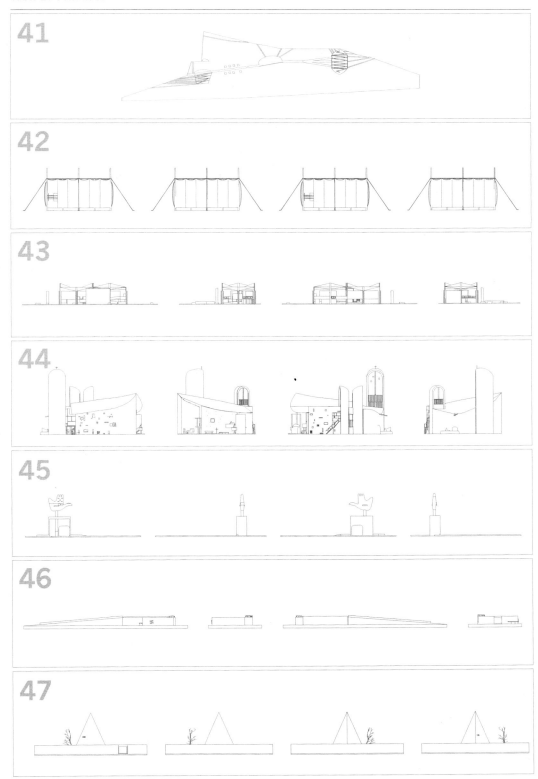

Table 20 Continued

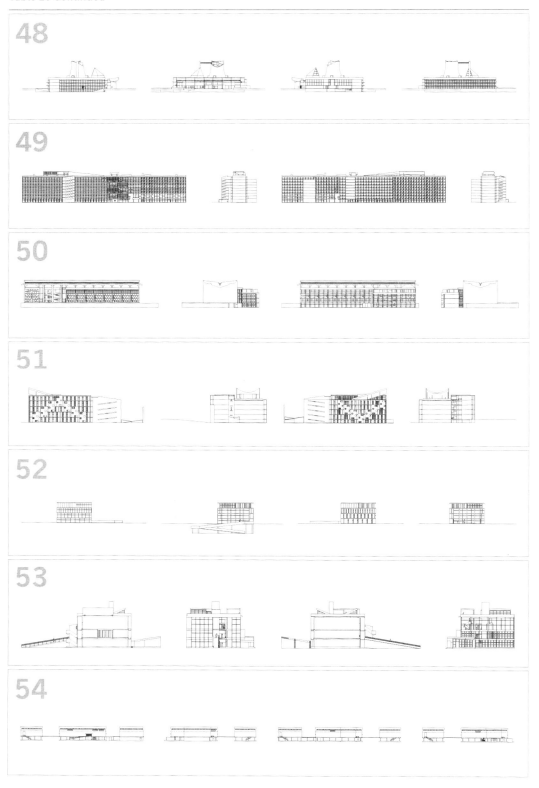

Table 20 Continued

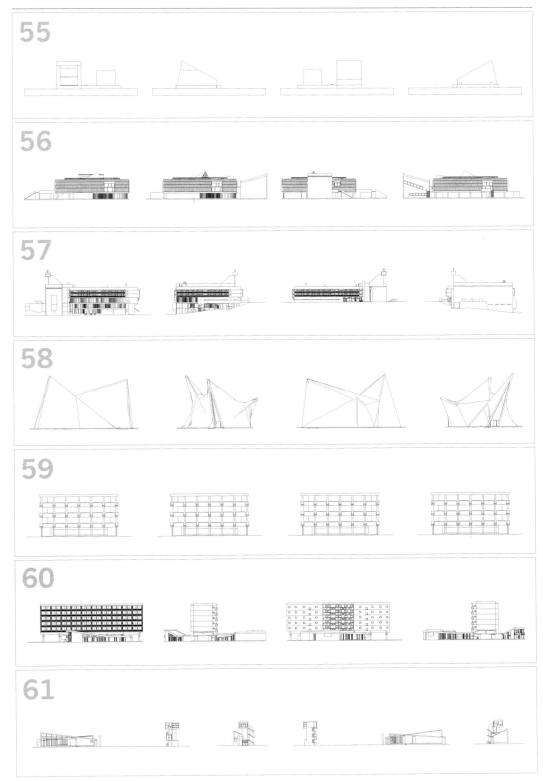

074

Table 20 Continued

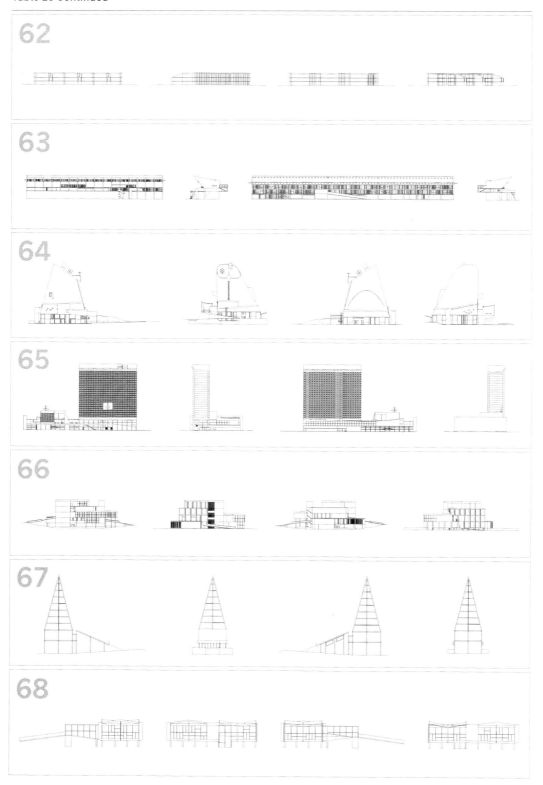

Façade Composition 075

Table 20 Continued

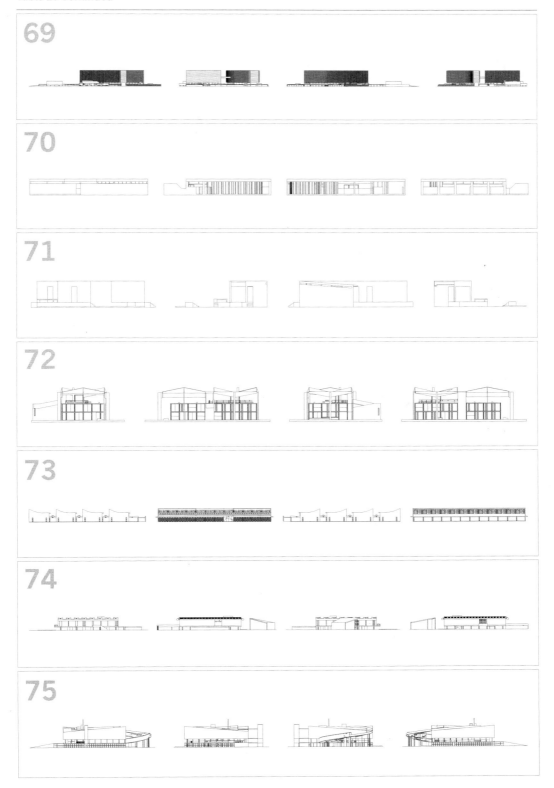

Table 20 Continued

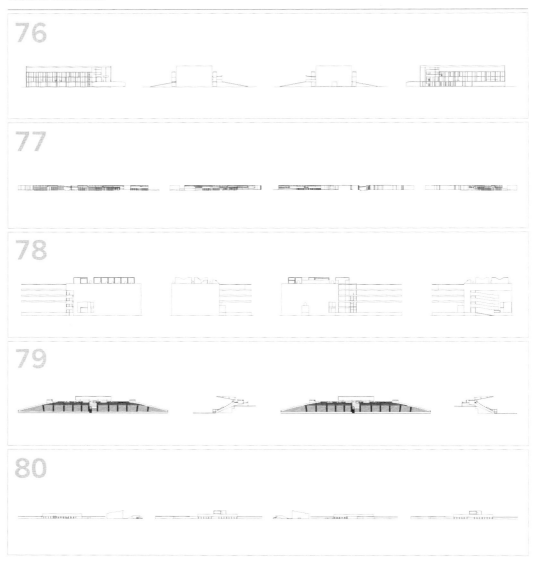

Façade Composition 077

As the the façade outline of most buildings is square, this section begins with the geometric composition of the façade and makes a two-step comparison: first, to abstract and summarize the composition schematism of the façade elements of each work and second, to make a horizontal comparison. Taking project 72, Pavillon d'Exposition ZHLC, Zurich as an example, we can extract two pieces of triangular roofs, two pillars supporting the roof, and two layers of the building walls (glass) and divide it into ten equal parts. The main components are extracted, while detail elements are removed—such as patio, windows, porches, stairs, and railings. Through this method, the extracted diagram is obtained, as shown in Figure 59.

Figure 59 Abstraction of façade composition

Table 21 Summary of abstracted façade compositions

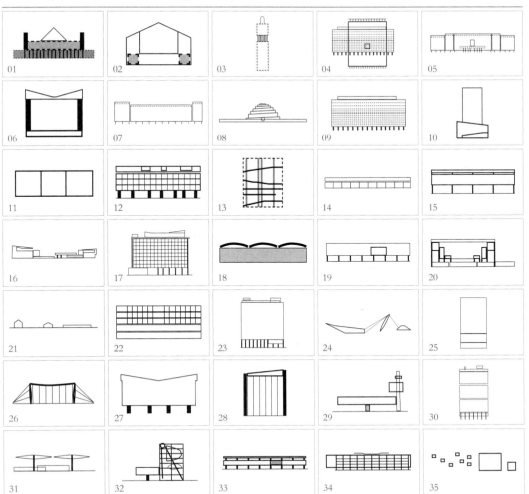

Table 21 Continued

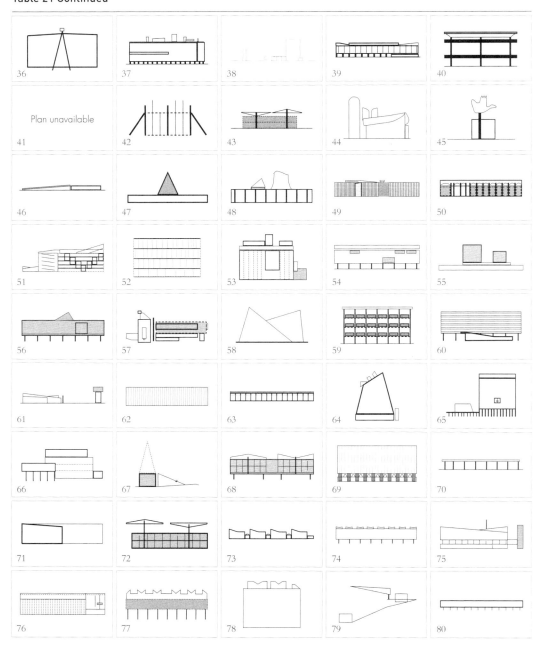

Based on Table 21, if you remove the scale, window, ramp and so on, and just look at the composition of the main elements, such as the roof, the wall, and the foundation support, the abstracted compositions can be divided into the following six categories (see pages 79 and 80).

Type A

Works of this category present a three-section composition on the façade, including the bottom pillar, the middle wall, and the roof. It is necessary to say that the wall and the roof belong to a complete square outline, not completely separated, but superimposed. They are projects 04, 05, 07, 09, 12, 14, 15, 17, 19, 23, 33, 34, 37, 39, 40, 54, 56, 60, 65, 74, 77, and 80 (totaling twenty-two works), as shown in Table 22.

Table 22 Summary of Type A works

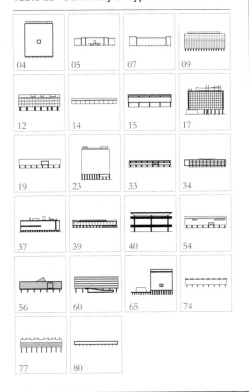

Type B

In this category, pillars hold the roof directly and are exposed, thus defining a complete frame outline. The roof is in the form of a one-piece or two-piece block, which is clearly separated from the walls. The form of the walls is weakened, mostly in small volumes with one or two layers. The works are projects 06, 26, 28, 31, 36, 42, 43, 68, and 72 (totaling nine works), as shown in Table 23.

Table 23 Summary of Type B works

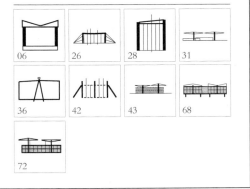

Type C

Here, columns as structural support in the façade disappear or degenerate. The whole composition is the superposition of two or more lumps and tends to shrink gradually on the vertical; the shape of the top is mostly in the form of a triangle or its variant. They are projects 01, 08, 10, 47, 48, 64, and 67 (totaling seven works), as shown in Table 24.

Table 24 Summary of Type C works

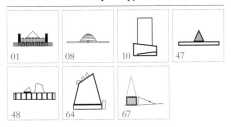

Type D

Works in this category have a façade that represents a repetitive rhythm separated into standard units. They are projects 18, 49, 50, 59, 62, 63, 69, 73, and 78 (totaling nine works), as shown in Table 25.

Table 25 Summary of Type D works

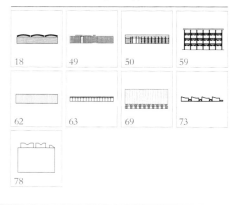

Type E

Here, walls are stratiform stacks, with obvious features in the horizontal layers. They are projects 20, 22, 51, 52, 57, 66, and 75 (totaling seven works), as shown in Table 26.

Table 26 Summary of Type E works

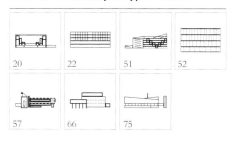

Type F

These works are composed of an independent column and an independent mass at the top, with a strong sculptural peculiarity. They are projects 29, 32, 45, and 61 (totaling four works), as shown in Table 27.

Table 27 Summary of Type F works

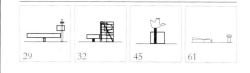

Other works lack commonality in the composition of the façade, such as Chapelle Notre Dame du Haut (project 44), and so the façade features will not be enumerated. Table 28 is obtained by categorizing the classes mentioned above.

· The façade composition of administration buildings falls within Types A, C, D, and E, with Type A accounting for forty-one percent, Type D accounting for twenty-four percent, and one work each of Types C and E.

· The façade composition of museums falls within Types A, C, and E, with Type A including the largest proportion at seventy-three percent, followed by Type E accounting for eighteen percent; there is only one Type C work.

· The façade composition of exhibition halls falls within Types A, B, and F, with Type B including the largest proportion at fifty-seven percent, followed by Types A and F with one work each.

· The façade composition of religious buildings falls within Types C, D, and E, with Type C including the largest proportion at fifty percent, followed by Types D and E with one work each.

· The façade composition of schools falls within Types A, B, C, D, and E, with Type A including the largest proportion at thirty-three percent, and the other categories containing one work each.

· Works in the categories of sports, public and commercial buildings have no obvious characteristics that show a common façade composition.

· The façade composition of complexes falls within Types A, D, and E, with Type A including the largest

proportion at fifty percent, followed by Types D and E, which contain one work each.
· Monuments mainly fall within Types E and F, with Type F containing a larger proportion at forty percent.
· Hospitals fall within Type A.

From the perspective of method, Type A is the most widely adopted—a three-segment composition form supported by columns, mainly used in administration buildings and museums. Type B is mainly used in exhibition halls; Type C is mainly used in religious buildings; and Type D is used most in administration buildings. Type E is not used much in buildings and Type F is used most in monument structures. From this, it can be seen that Le Corbusier tended to present a three-segment form with the column, the wall, and the roof in the façade composition of administration and museum buildings, while other functional buildings have their own façade composition characteristics. For example, all exhibition halls present a complete frame formed by the columns and roofs, with the walls weakened; religious buildings usually show a contraction of the geometric composition, completely different from the three-segment form, and in the outer façade of the church, the pillars disappear or are not represented.

Table 28 The 80 works categorized by function and façade composition

Function																	
Administration building	Work	05	07	09	16	17	23	34	38	39	50	48	49	53	62	69	75	76
	Type Code	A	A	A		A	A	A		A	D	C	D		D	D	E	
Museum	Work	08	14	15	20	33	40	51	54	56	74	80						
	Type Code	C	A	A	E	A	A	E	A	A	A	A						
Exhibition hall	Work	06	11	19	26	27	28	31	32	42	43	58	68	71	72			
	Type Code	B		A	B		B	B	F	B	B		B		B			
Religious building	Work	10	41	44	47	57	64	67	78									
	Type Code	C			C	E	C	C	D									
School	Work	01	12	36	60	66	73											
	Type Code	C	A	B	A	E	D											
Sports facility	Work	21	24	35	63	79												
	Type Code				D													
Public building (water conservancy)	Work	03	61															
	Type Code		F															
Complex	Work	04	18	22	30	37	65											
	Type Code	A	D	E		A	A											
Commercial building	Work	02	13	25	59	70												
	Type Code				D													
Monument	Work	29	45	46	52	55												
	Type Code	F	F		E													
Hospital	Work	77																
	Type Code	A																

3 Section Composition

The section, which reflects the inner space of the work can reflect the building's basic height, structural elements, internal organization of the space, and such. This part of the book conducts an overall survey and analysis of the sections of Le Corbusier's public works (Table 29).

Table 29 Sections of the 80 public works (cross-section and longitudinal section)

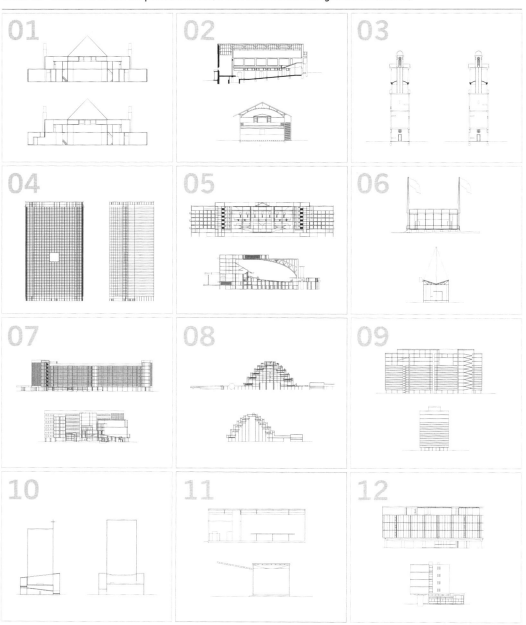

Table 29 Continued

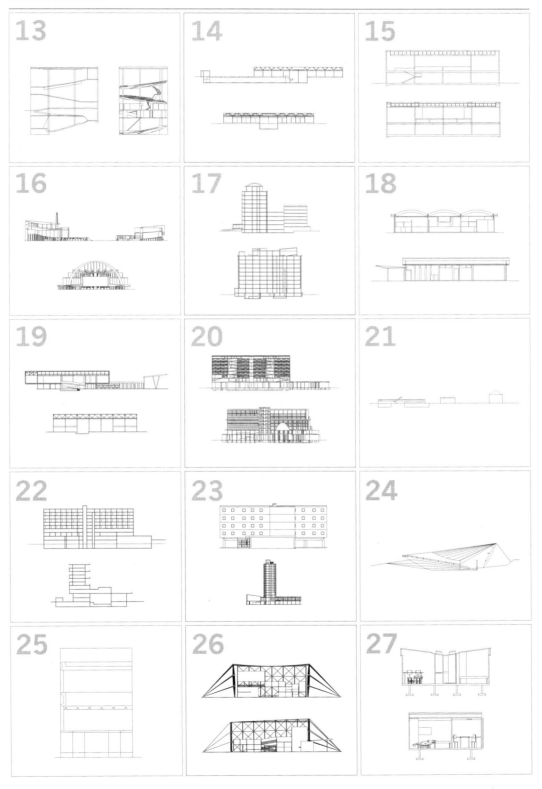

Table 29 Continued

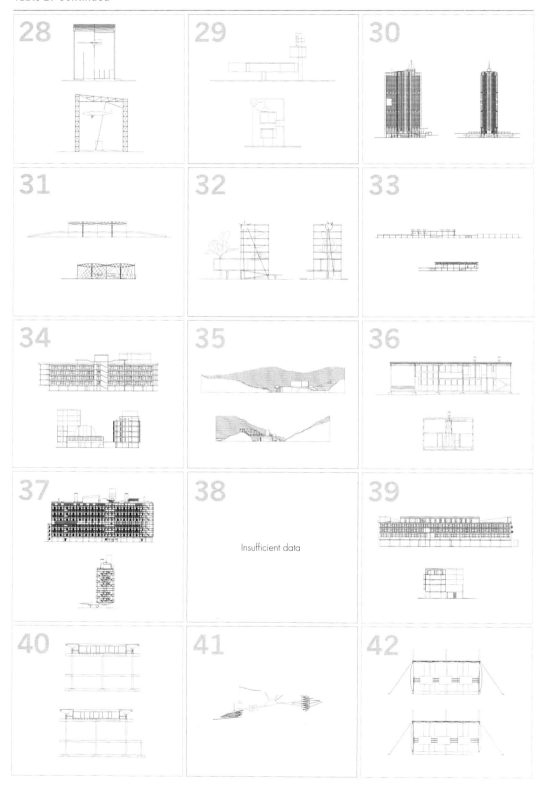

Table 29 Continued

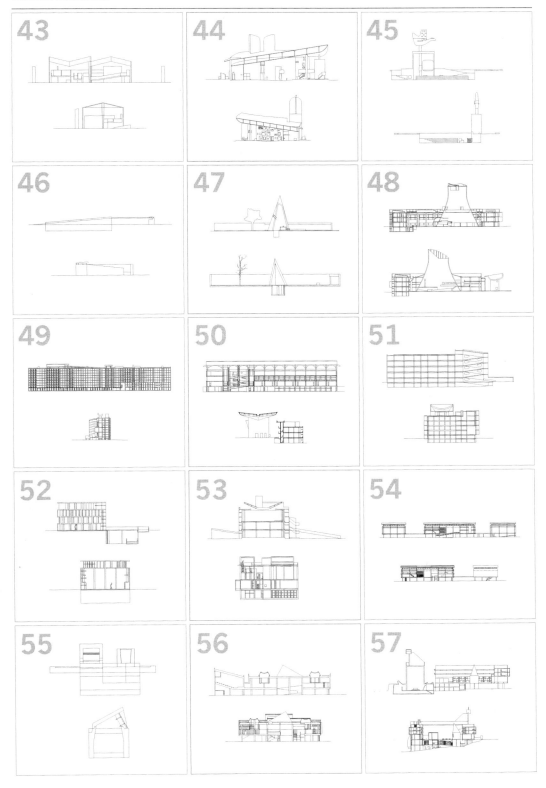

Table 29 Continued

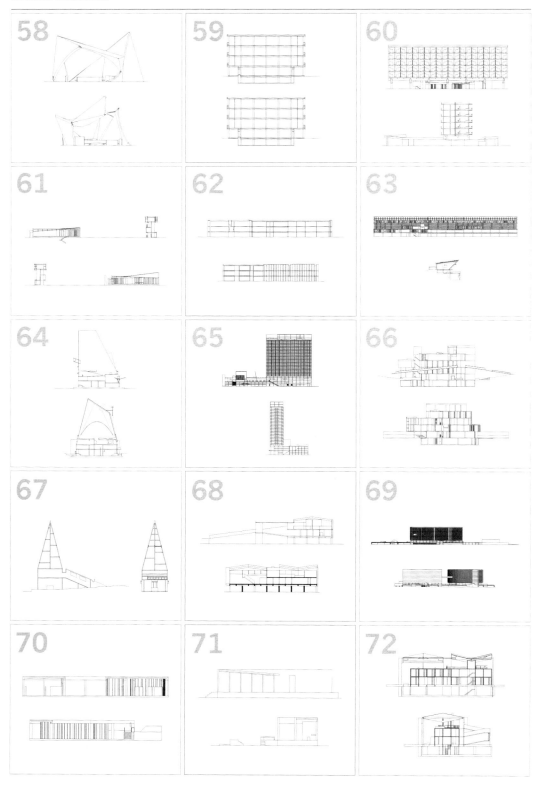

Table 29 Continued

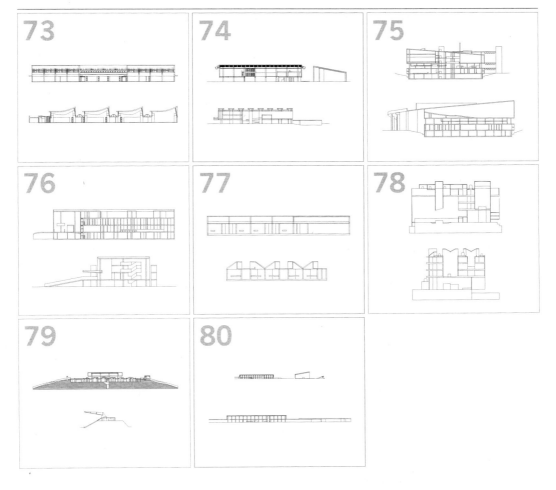

Because of the types of architecture, some works converge on the pattern of the façade and section composition, but compared with the façade, the section can reveal basic information about the building, such as the number of floors, the height of floors, the interior space, and the height difference between inside a room and outside. The sections of these works are extracted and shown in Table 30. Using project 02, Cinéma "La Scala," as an example (Figure 60), it can be seen from the cross-section and the longitudinal section that the horizontal section of the building can reveal the internal space of the building; the cross-section is, therefore, selected for processing. Processing consists of extracting three elements: each floor in the section of the building, the outline formed by the exterior wall and roof, and the indoor and outdoor terrace—that is, vertical from the ground to the interior, and then to the roof. These elements provide basic information of the extracted section.

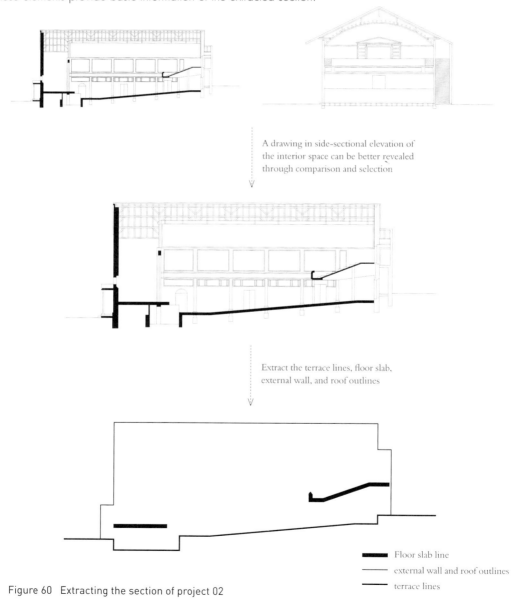

Figure 60 Extracting the section of project 02

Section Composition 089

Table 30 Extracting sections of the 80 works

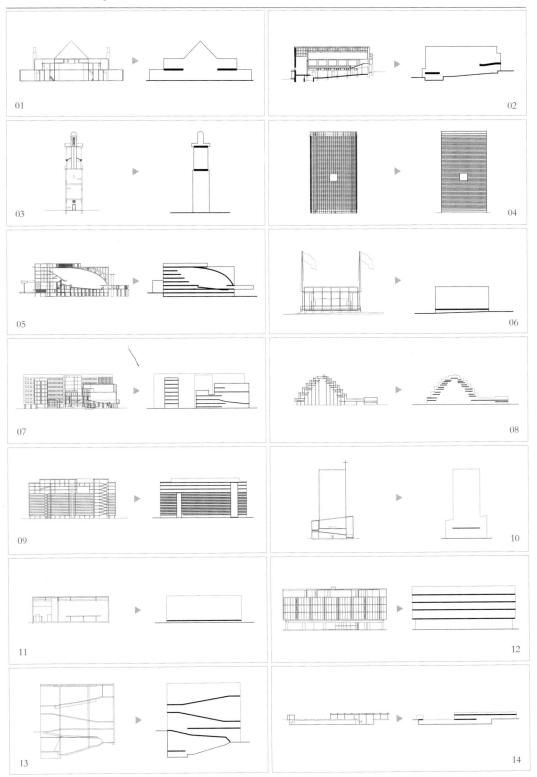

Table 30 Continued

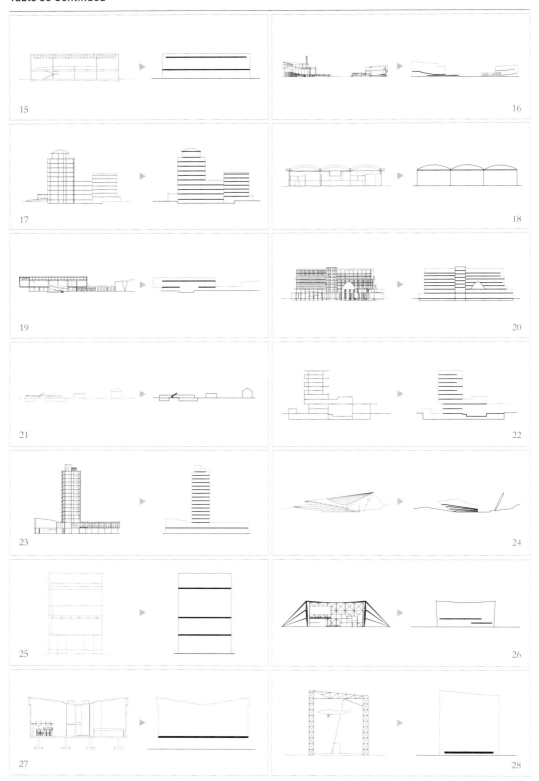

Table 30 Continued

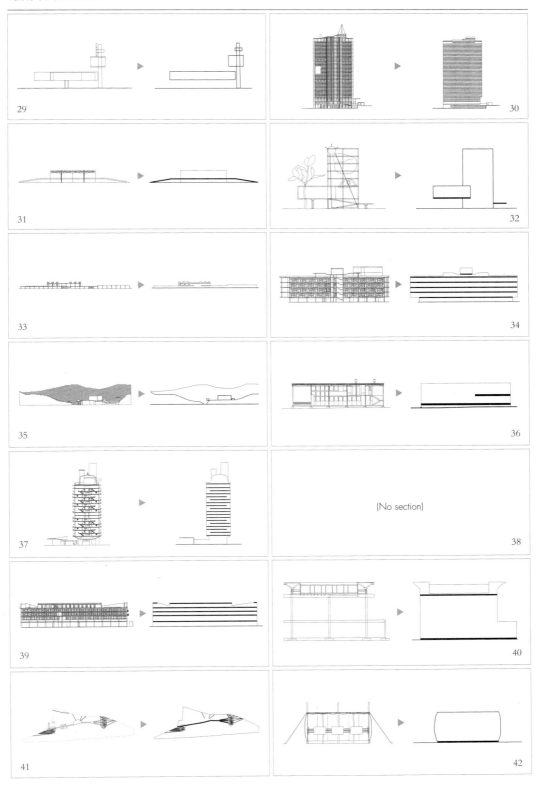

Table 30 Continued

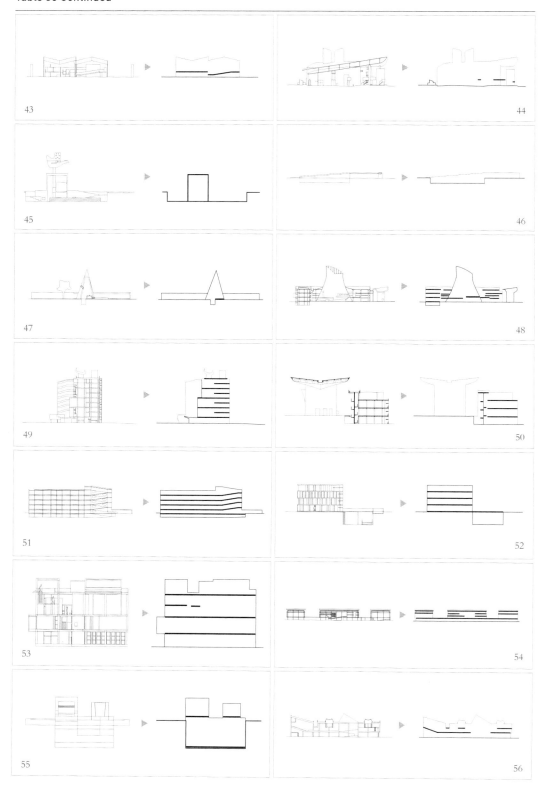

Table 30 Continued

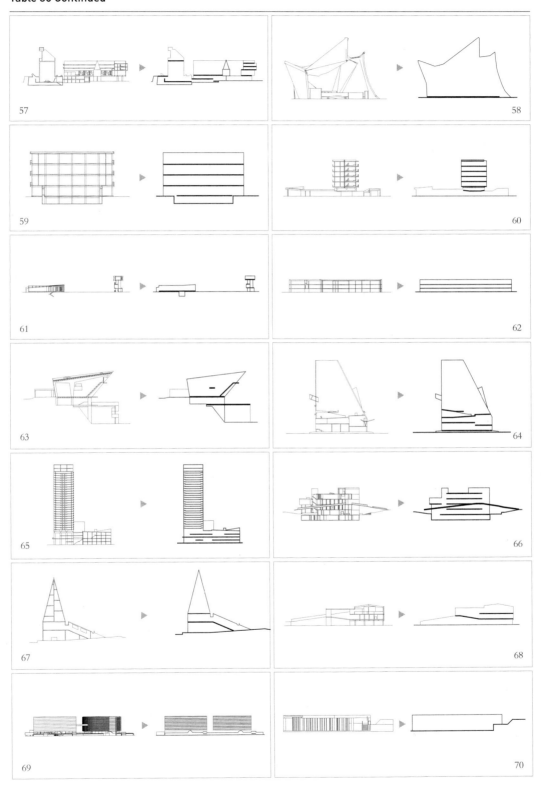

094

Table 30 Continued

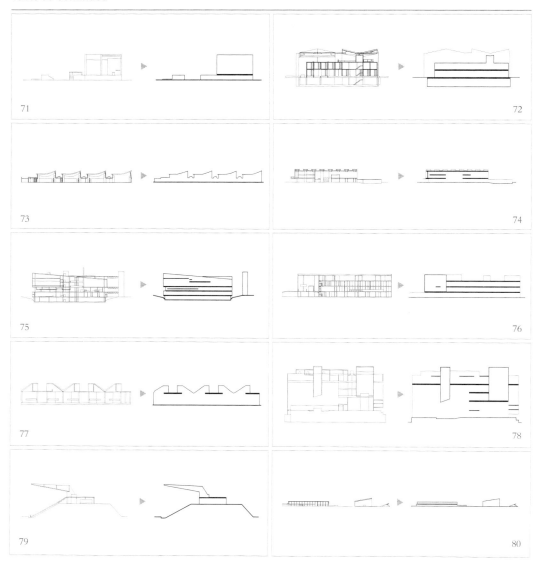

Table 31 Summary of extracted section composition

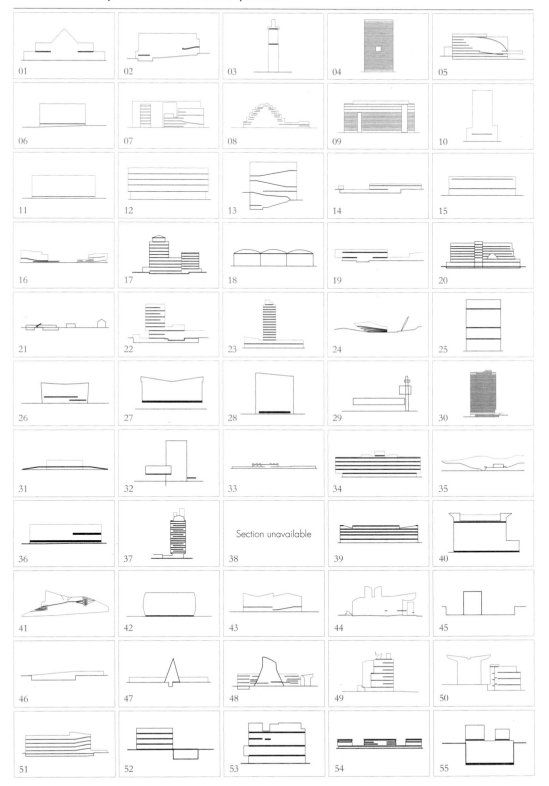

Table 31 Continued

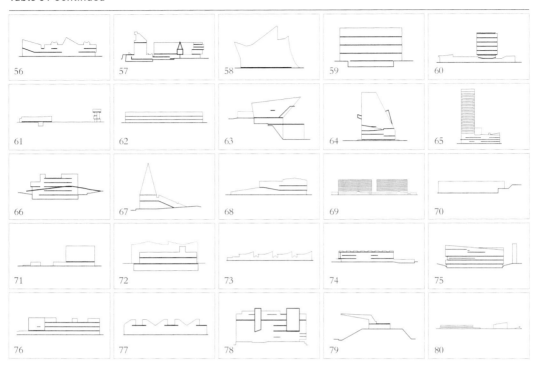

The extracted terrace, outline, and floor slab of each building section are combined to populate Table 31.

From the perspective of architectural topography, there are sixteen projects with a height difference in their base: projects 02, 06, 13, 24, 30, 44, 50, 52, 57, 63, 64, 66, 67, 70, 75, and 79.

Table 32 Summary of 16 projects with height difference in the base

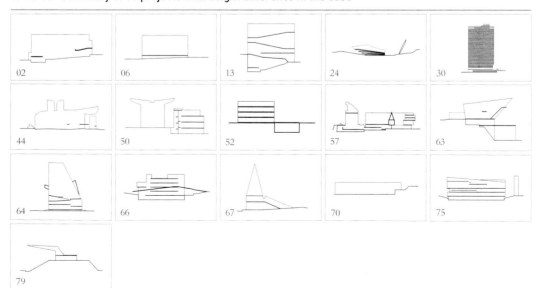

Based on the above analysis, three building methods can be determined:
1. The floor slab of the building itself is well connected to the terrain height difference of the base—that is, the floor slab is tilted with the gentle slope of the height difference. These works include projects 02, 13, 24, 44, 57, and 67, three of which are religious buildings (projects 44, 57, and 67).
2. The floor of the building is horizontal, and the height difference between the base and the terrain is balanced by the columns of the ground floor, such as in projects 06, 30, 50, 52, 63, 66, 70, and 75.
3. The building allows for the existence of the terrain height difference, which is represented by the fluctuation of the steps, while abandoning the mode to fill or tilt the floor, such as in projects 64 and 79.

Project 13, Cinéma à Montparnasse, is a special example. Its main entrance leads straight to the theater in the basement via a ramp, but can also go up to the ancillary function area on the first floor. In the basement space, the theater's own base is fitted to the ground; it uses the third method to respond to the height difference.

4 Form Composition

The form, which reflects the exterior outline of the work, is the third of the three memorandums that Le Corbusier put forth to architects.

In his 1936 speech titled *The Trend of Rational Architecture and the Cooperative Relationship between Painting and Sculpture*, published by the Royal Academy of Rome, Le Corbusier made it clear that the architecture of ancient Egypt, ancient Greece, and ancient Rome was architecture of basic geometry, such as the prism, the cube, the cylinder, and the trihedron, which is the first order. Gothic architecture did not have such basic geometry, creating an interior basic shape space, which is the second order. In order to facilitate comparison, we use the abstracted forms of the eighty public works. Figure 61 employs project 03 (Château d'Eau) as an example to show how the simplified form on the right is obtained by removing the detail elements such as windows, doors, railings and moldings, and crisperding, and only taking the volume formed by the outline of the periphery—which consists of a cylindrical body and a bell tower at the top. Using this method, the three-dimensional axonometric measurements are processed to obtain the abstracted forms in Table 33.

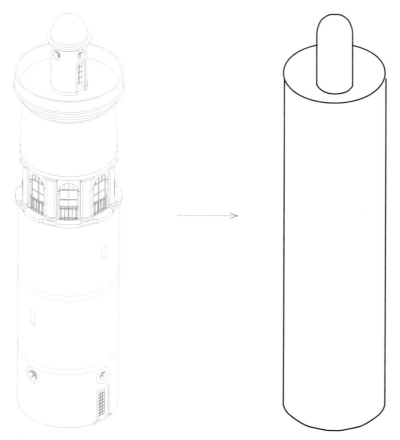

Figure 61　Form abstract of project 03

Table 33 Summary of abstracted form composition

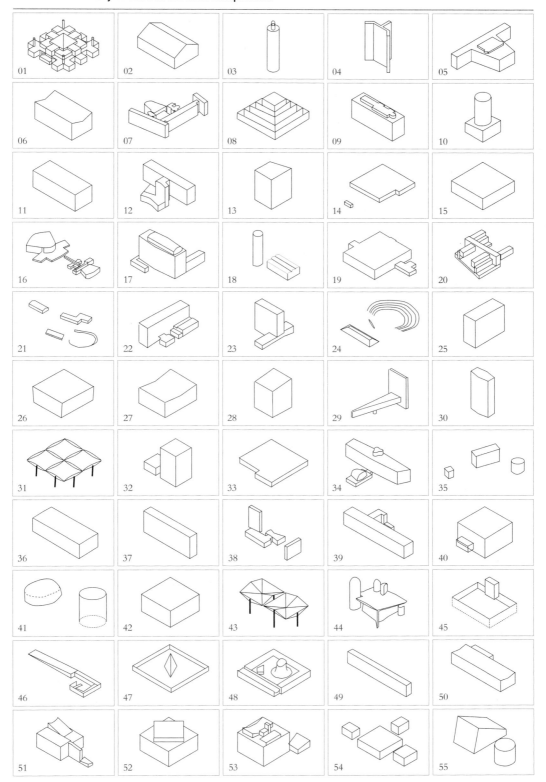

Table 33 Continued

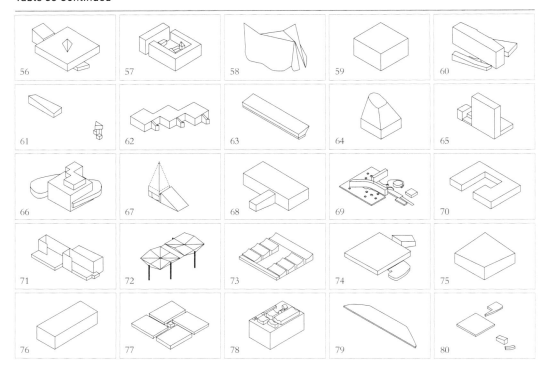

Le Corbusier's use of the form in his early practice tended toward numerous and miscellaneous block combinations, represented by projects 01, 05, 07, 16, and 20. Among them, project 20, Musée de la Ville et de l'État from 1935, is a demarcation point; later works developed toward the single geometry form (Figure 62). It should be noted that although works such as projects 48 and 57 also use a variety of geometries, they are all in the internal courtyard or roof; the external whole of the building still maintains a basic-dominated design, which is totally different from the external outlines of early works.

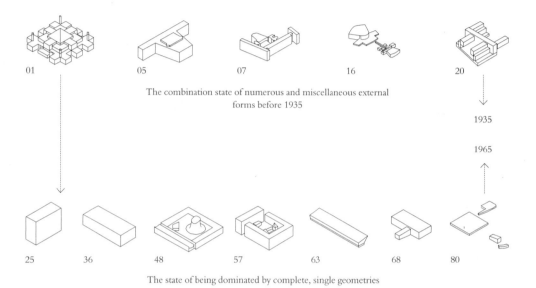

Figure 62 Evolution of external forms

From the way the forms are combined, it can be deduced that before the 1950s, the forms maintained the complete outlines of their respective blocks when they were combined. With the passing of time, and especially since Chapelle Notre Dame du Haut in the 1950s, the outlines among the forms began to show characteristics of fusion when they were combined (Figure 63). Projects 01 and 07 are used as representative works of the earlier period and projects 44, 64, and 69 are used as representative works of the later period.

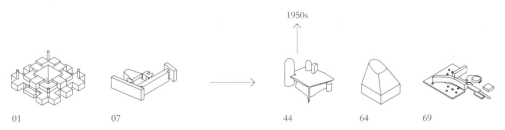

Figure 63 Evolution of combination forms

Part 2

Spatial Composition Analysis of Public Buildings from a Micro Perspective

A space is composed of building elements such as pillars, walls, and floors. These elements give the space a specific form. The space itself is not an element. Part 1 used a macro perspective to discuss the overall compositions of Le Corbusier's architectural works. Part 2 will now analyze the micro elements of his works' spatial composition, such as columns, windows, staircases, ramps, sunshade, and drainage.

1 Columns

Since Le Corbusier put forward the domino structure system in 1914, the fundamental structure, namely framework structure, has been widely used and public buildings are no exception.

Viewpoints Based on the Column Layout

Table 34 contains a summary of column layouts drawn from the plans of the eighty public building works.

Table 34 Column layout of the 80 public building works

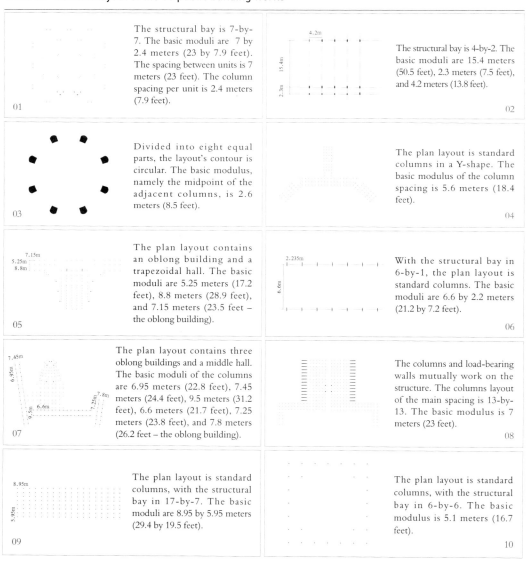

01 — The structural bay is 7-by-7. The basic moduli are 7 by 2.4 meters (23 by 7.9 feet). The spacing between units is 7 meters (23 feet). The column spacing per unit is 2.4 meters (7.9 feet).

02 — The structural bay is 4-by-2. The basic moduli are 15.4 meters (50.5 feet), 2.3 meters (7.5 feet), and 4.2 meters (13.8 feet).

03 — Divided into eight equal parts, the layout's contour is circular. The basic modulus, namely the midpoint of the adjacent columns, is 2.6 meters (8.5 feet).

04 — The plan layout is standard columns in a Y-shape. The basic modulus of the column spacing is 5.6 meters (18.4 feet).

05 — The plan layout contains an oblong building and a trapezoidal hall. The basic moduli are 5.25 meters (17.2 feet), 8.8 meters (28.9 feet), and 7.15 meters (23.5 feet – the oblong building).

06 — With the structural bay in 6-by-1, the plan layout is standard columns. The basic moduli are 6.6 by 2.2 meters (21.2 by 7.2 feet).

07 — The plan layout contains three oblong buildings and a middle hall. The basic moduli of the columns are 6.95 meters (22.8 feet), 7.45 meters (24.4 feet), 9.5 meters (31.2 feet), 6.6 meters (21.7 feet), 7.25 meters (23.8 feet), and 7.8 meters (26.2 feet – the oblong building).

08 — The columns and load-bearing walls mutually work on the structure. The columns layout of the main spacing is 13-by-13. The basic modulus is 7 meters (23 feet).

09 — The plan layout is standard columns, with the structural bay in 17-by-7. The basic moduli are 8.95 by 5.95 meters (29.4 by 19.5 feet).

10 — The plan layout is standard columns, with the structural bay in 6-by-6. The basic modulus is 5.1 meters (16.7 feet).

Table 34 Continued

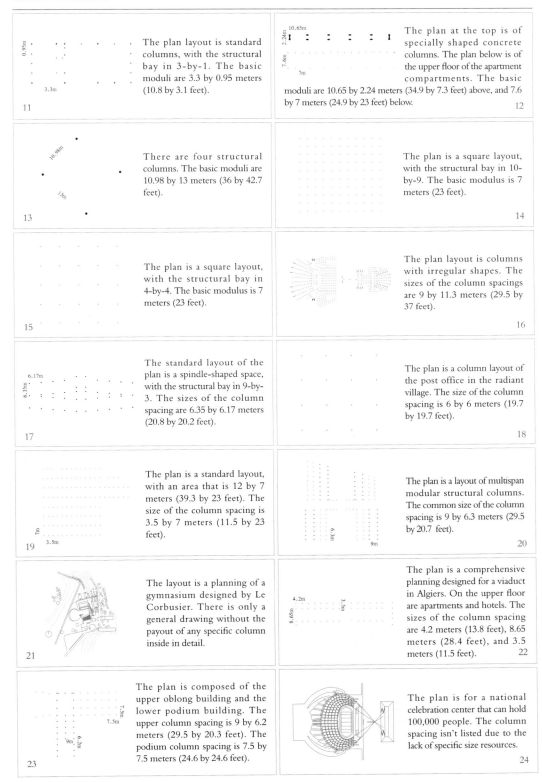

11	The plan layout is standard columns, with the structural bay in 3-by-1. The basic moduli are 3.3 by 0.95 meters (10.8 by 3.1 feet).	12 — The plan at the top is of specially shaped concrete columns. The plan below is of the upper floor of the apartment compartments. The basic moduli are 10.65 by 2.24 meters (34.9 by 7.3 feet) above, and 7.6 by 7 meters (24.9 by 23 feet) below.
13	There are four structural columns. The basic moduli are 10.98 by 13 meters (36 by 42.7 feet).	14 — The plan is a square layout, with the structural bay in 10-by-9. The basic modulus is 7 meters (23 feet).
15	The plan is a square layout, with the structural bay in 4-by-4. The basic modulus is 7 meters (23 feet).	16 — The plan layout is columns with irregular shapes. The sizes of the column spacings are 9 by 11.3 meters (29.5 by 37 feet).
17	The standard layout of the plan is a spindle-shaped space, with the structural bay in 9-by-3. The sizes of the column spacing are 6.35 by 6.17 meters (20.8 by 20.2 feet).	18 — The plan is a column layout of the post office in the radiant village. The size of the column spacing is 6 by 6 meters (19.7 by 19.7 feet).
19	The plan is a standard layout, with an area that is 12 by 7 meters (39.3 by 23 feet). The size of the column spacing is 3.5 by 7 meters (11.5 by 23 feet).	20 — The plan is a layout of multispan modular structural columns. The common size of the column spacing is 9 by 6.3 meters (29.5 by 20.7 feet).
21	The layout is a planning of a gymnasium designed by Le Corbusier. There is only a general drawing without the payout of any specific column inside in detail.	22 — The plan is a comprehensive planning designed for a viaduct in Algiers. On the upper floor are apartments and hotels. The sizes of the column spacing are 4.2 meters (13.8 feet), 8.65 meters (28.4 feet), and 3.5 meters (11.5 feet).
23	The plan is composed of the upper oblong building and the lower podium building. The upper column spacing is 9 by 6.2 meters (29.5 by 20.3 feet). The podium column spacing is 7.5 by 7.5 meters (24.6 by 24.6 feet).	24 — The plan is for a national celebration center that can hold 100,000 people. The column spacing isn't listed due to the lack of specific size resources.

105

Table 34 Continued

25	The plan is Le Corbusier's standard of displaying cabinets for businesses. The basic moduli are 1.92 meters (6.3 feet), 0.96 meters (3.1 feet), and 0.32 meters (1 foot).	26	The exterior structure is a steel truss column and the interior structure is a standard layout in I-steel. The outer column spacing is 5 by 5 meters (16.4 by 16.4 feet) and inner spacing is 3 by 3.3 meters (9.8 by 10.8 feet).
27	The plan is the standard oblong layout, with the structural bay in 3-by-1. The size of the column spacing is 3.6 by 1.75 meters (11.8 by 5.7 feet).	28	The structure is steel, same as project 26. The size of the column spacing is 6 by 2 meters (19.7 by 6.6 feet).
29	It's a sculpture structure. The main body is supported by a column and two load-bearing walls. The spacing is separately 14.45 meters (47.4 feet) and 16 meters (52.5 feet).	30	It is the standard column layout of the shuttle-shaped skyscraper. The column spacing is 7 meters (23 feet).
31	The building is composed of four square structural units. The pillars are made of I-beam, and the span between the two pillars at the end of each square structural unit is 45 meters (147.6 feet).	32	This is the framework of the Idéal Home – Londres (London Ideal Home) Show. The standard column spacing is 7 by 7 meters (23 by 23 feet).
33	The plan layout is a standard modulus, with the structural bay in 7-by-7. The column spacing is 7.6 by 7.6 meters (24.9 by 24.9 feet).	34	It is a column layout with shuttle-shaped administrative standard columns. The spacing is 5 meters (16.4 feet) and 8 meters (26.2 feet) separately.
35	The project is Aménagement Station de Sport d'Hiver et d'Été. Because of the limited resources, there is no detailed architectural layout.	36	The structural column is set in the middle of the plan. There are six arrayed trusses. The spacing is 3.8 by 1.7 meters (12.5 by 5.6 feet).
37	The plan at the top is of the specially shaped concrete column on the ground floor. The plan below is of the upper apartment compartments. The basic moduli are 8.4 by 12 meters (27.6 by 39.4 feet) above, and 4 by 4.2 meters (13.1 by 13.8 feet) below.	38	This work is the planning of the unfinished United Nations Headquarters. There is only a general drawing due to the lack of resources.

Table 34 Continued

39	The layout of the plan is standard columns, with the structural bay in 13-by-1. The column spacing is 6.25 by 6.7 meters (20.5 by 22 feet).
40	The plan is standard columns, with the structural bay in 2-by-2. There is a porch on the façade. The column spacing is 7 by 7 meters (23 by 23 feet).
41	The work is the planning of a basilica in the interior of a mountain. There is no other resource except a section plan.
42	The structure is the in-haul cable system, same as project 26. Both inner and outer structural columns have a structural bay in 2-by-2. The main spatial column spacing is 3.5 by 3.5 meters (11.5 by 11.5 feet).
43	The work is composed of two square structural frames, and each frame is composed of four steel columns around the square. The span between the columns is 15.55 meters (51 feet).
44	The columns of the work are in an irregular layout without standard modulus and spacing. The data isn't listed.
45	The work relates to the outdoor sculpture and square. It is composed of the structure's "hand," steps, stairs, and slopes, without standard structural columns.
46	Same as project 45, the work is an outdoor sculptural monument. It's composed of slopes and a sculpture, without standard columns.
47	The work is a combination of a pyramid-like auditorium and courtyard. On the one side of the square courtyard is a pavilion with a column spacing of 2.45 meters (8 feet).
48	The work is composed of three apartment buildings and an enclosing hall in the middle. The column spacing is 8.8 by 8.8 meters (28.9 by 28.9 feet), 6.2 by 4.4 meters (20.3 by 14.4 feet), and 6 by 4.4 meters (19.7 by 14.4 feet).
49	The standard column spacing is 4.1 by 6 meters (13.5 by 19.7 feet).
50	The bottom plan is the horizontal main space, with the structural bay in 13-by-5. The column spacing is 3.9 by 8.5 meters (12.8 by 27.9 feet).
51	The structure is the combination of columns and load-bearing walls. The column layout has a structural bay in 8-by-8. The basic column spacing is 5.35 meters (17.6 feet).
52	The plan is a square at an angle of 45 degrees, with the structural bay in 2-by-2. The column spacing is 5.5 by 5.5 meters (18.1 by 18.1 feet).

Table 34 Continued

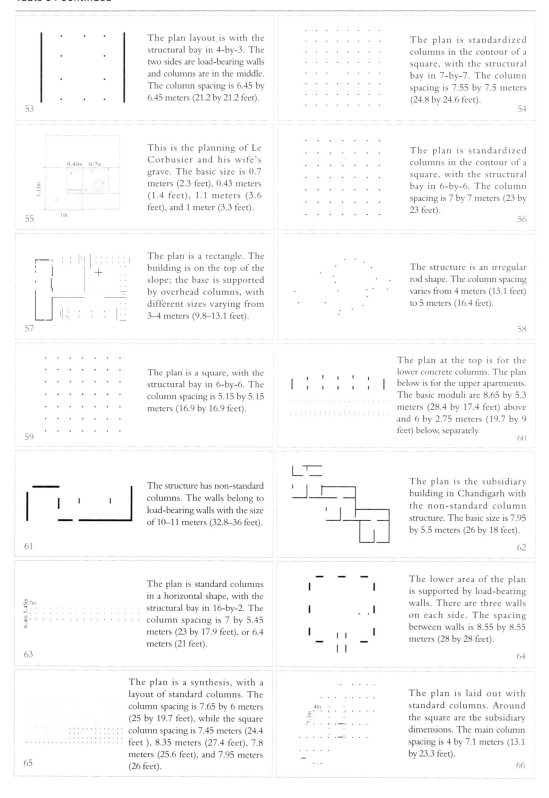

53	The plan layout is with the structural bay in 4-by-3. The two sides are load-bearing walls and columns are in the middle. The column spacing is 6.45 by 6.45 meters (21.2 by 21.2 feet).	54 — The plan is standardized columns in the contour of a square, with the structural bay in 7-by-7. The column spacing is 7.55 by 7.5 meters (24.8 by 24.6 feet).
55	This is the planning of Le Corbusier and his wife's grave. The basic size is 0.7 meters (2.3 feet), 0.43 meters (1.4 feet), 1.1 meters (3.6 feet), and 1 meter (3.3 feet).	56 — The plan is standardized columns in the contour of a square, with the structural bay in 6-by-6. The column spacing is 7 by 7 meters (23 by 23 feet).
57	The plan is a rectangle. The building is on the top of the slope; the base is supported by overhead columns, with different sizes varying from 3–4 meters (9.8–13.1 feet).	58 — The structure is an irregular rod shape. The column spacing varies from 4 meters (13.1 feet) to 5 meters (16.4 feet).
59	The plan is a square, with the structural bay in 6-by-6. The column spacing is 5.15 by 5.15 meters (16.9 by 16.9 feet).	60 — The plan at the top is for the lower concrete columns. The plan below is for the upper apartments. The basic moduli are 8.65 by 5.3 meters (28.4 by 17.4 feet) above and 6 by 2.75 meters (19.7 by 9 feet) below, separately.
61	The structure has non-standard columns. The walls belong to load-bearing walls with the size of 10–11 meters (32.8–36 feet).	62 — The plan is the subsidiary building in Chandigarh with the non-standard column structure. The basic size is 7.95 by 5.5 meters (26 by 18 feet).
63	The plan is standard columns in a horizontal shape, with the structural bay in 16-by-2. The column spacing is 7 by 5.45 meters (23 by 17.9 feet), or 6.4 meters (21 feet).	64 — The lower area of the plan is supported by load-bearing walls. There are three walls on each side. The spacing between walls is 8.55 by 8.55 meters (28 by 28 feet).
65	The plan is a synthesis, with a layout of standard columns. The column spacing is 7.65 by 6 meters (25 by 19.7 feet), while the square column spacing is 7.45 meters (24.4 feet), 8.35 meters (27.4 feet), 7.8 meters (25.6 feet), and 7.95 meters (26 feet).	66 — The plan is laid out with standard columns. Around the square are the subsidiary dimensions. The main column spacing is 4 by 7.1 meters (13.1 by 23.3 feet).

Table 34 Continued

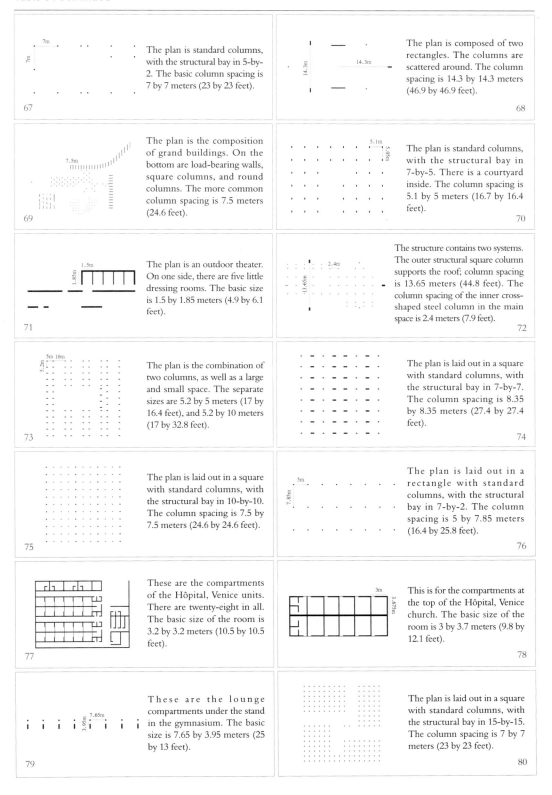

67. The plan is standard columns, with the structural bay in 5-by-2. The basic column spacing is 7 by 7 meters (23 by 23 feet).

68. The plan is composed of two rectangles. The columns are scattered around. The column spacing is 14.3 by 14.3 meters (46.9 by 46.9 feet).

69. The plan is the composition of grand buildings. On the bottom are load-bearing walls, square columns, and round columns. The more common column spacing is 7.5 meters (24.6 feet).

70. The plan is standard columns, with the structural bay in 7-by-5. There is a courtyard inside. The column spacing is 5.1 by 5 meters (16.7 by 16.4 feet).

71. The plan is an outdoor theater. On one side, there are five little dressing rooms. The basic size is 1.5 by 1.85 meters (4.9 by 6.1 feet).

72. The structure contains two systems. The outer structural square column supports the roof; column spacing is 13.65 meters (44.8 feet). The column spacing of the inner cross-shaped steel column in the main space is 2.4 meters (7.9 feet).

73. The plan is the combination of two columns, as well as a large and small space. The separate sizes are 5.2 by 5 meters (17 by 16.4 feet), and 5.2 by 10 meters (17 by 32.8 feet).

74. The plan is laid out in a square with standard columns, with the structural bay in 7-by-7. The column spacing is 8.35 by 8.35 meters (27.4 by 27.4 feet).

75. The plan is laid out in a square with standard columns, with the structural bay in 10-by-10. The column spacing is 7.5 by 7.5 meters (24.6 by 24.6 feet).

76. The plan is laid out in a rectangle with standard columns, with the structural bay in 7-by-2. The column spacing is 5 by 7.85 meters (16.4 by 25.8 feet).

77. These are the compartments of the Hôpital, Venice units. There are twenty-eight in all. The basic size of the room is 3.2 by 3.2 meters (10.5 by 10.5 feet).

78. This is for the compartments at the top of the Hôpital, Venice church. The basic size of the room is 3 by 3.7 meters (9.8 by 12.1 feet).

79. These are the lounge compartments under the stand in the gymnasium. The basic size is 7.65 by 3.95 meters (25 by 13 feet).

80. The plan is laid out in a square with standard columns, with the structural bay in 15-by-15. The column spacing is 7 by 7 meters (23 by 23 feet).

Among the eighty public building works, the layout of columns may be divided into five groups:
1. Lacking detailed plan resources—projects 21, 35, 38, and 41;
2. Sculptural works (without standard columns)—projects 29, 45, 46, 55, and 61;
3. Specially shaped structural works—projects 24, 44, and 58;
4. Non-standard structural works with basic units or structural size—projects 25, 71, 77, 78, and 79;
5. Standard structural works—which are the remaining sixty-three works.

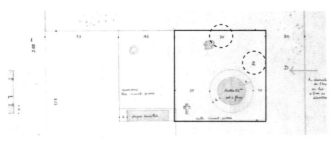

Figure 64   Plan of project 55

As the basic modulus, the measure of 7 meters (23 feet) appears twelve times in works that belong to the fifth group (standard structural and unit works), which makes up nearly twenty percent of the works in that group. They are projects 01, 08, 12, 14, 15, 19, 32, 40, 56, 63, 67, and 80. Of these works, six are museums. So, it can be deduced that the common column-spacing modulus in Le Corbusier's museum architectural works is 7 meters (23 feet). Le Corbusier even designed his wife's gravestone (project 55) to be 0.7 by 0.7 meters (2.30 by 2.30 feet); see Figure 64. This shows the importance of "7" in his public architectural works.

Viewpoints Based on the Column Forms

Table 35 presents the summary of column forms extracted from models of the eighty public architectural works. It is necessary to mention:
1. Not all the columns in the works are structural columns. The phrase "no column" indicates the lack of detailed resources and the lack of structural columns in the resource.
2. Some of the columns extracted from models are not standard "columns," but load-bearing walls. Some works in the list have several types of columns.
3. The ratios and heights of columns in some works are of little substantial meaning. One detail that is certain is the sectional form of columns. The type of columns used in most of the works is cylinder. However, the height of columns depends on layer and position, and some are thick while others are thin. Only specially shaped columns, such as those in Unité d'Habitation (project 37) and Couvent Sainte-Marie de la Tourette (project 57) are correct in ratio.
4. The form only analyzes the sectional form and outer appearance. There are no fake data statistics for the sectional column size.

Columns 111

Table 35 Summary of structural columns in the 80 works

Table 35 reveals that among the eighty works, there are twelve without structural columns. The other sixty-eight works with columns can be divided according to the six categories listed:

Type A

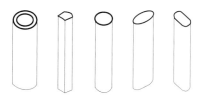

The column sections are varieties of circles, rings, ovals and other similar circular forms; the upper part of the column body should be the same as the lower part—projects 03, 04, 05, 07, 08, 09, 10, 12~20, 23, 27, 29, 30, 31, 33, 34, 39, 42, 45, 47~54, 56~60, 65, 66, 68, 69, 72, 74, 75, 76, and 80.

Type B

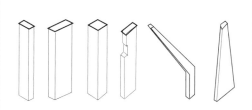

The column sections are squares, rectangles and similar forms; the upper part of the column body may or may not be the same as the lower part. The column should be upright or tilted—projects 01, 02, 05, 12, 20, 22, 28, 32, 34, 36, 37, 40, 43, 44, 50, 57, 60, 63, 65, 67~70, 72, 73, 74, 77, and 79.

Type C

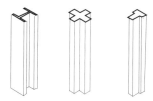

The column sections are I-shaped, cross-shaped, and T-shaped. Within the column body, the upper part should conform to the lower part. The body should be upright—projects 11, 26, 32, and 43.

Type D

The structural columns are steel trusses arranged in pairs—projects 06, 26, 28, and 31.

Type E

The structural column is a specially shaped column like a corbel column or shuttle mast—projects 24, 37, and 57.

Type F

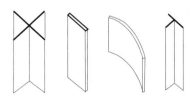

The column is essentially the support column or sheer wall in various shapes, such as a cross, square, as a curve, or in a T-shape—projects 05, 08, 57, 61, 64, 66, 68, 69, 72, and 79.

Type A, namely columns, is used most in Le Corbusier's public architectural works. These columns are presented in forty-nine projects through his whole design career. Type B, namely square and its variants, total twenty-seven projects—also through his entire design career. Both Type C and Type D appear four times, mostly mid-career, and Type E—the specially shaped constructional column—is used less; each of those instances was a unique case. Type F—the load-bearing column—is presented in ten projects, most often appearing later in his career.

2 Windows

Le Corbusier compared buildings to illuminated floors and is known for widely adopting horizontal French windows to maximize natural sunlight indoors. This section conducts an inspection and analysis of the windows (Table 36).

Table 36 Windows extracted from 80 public architectural works

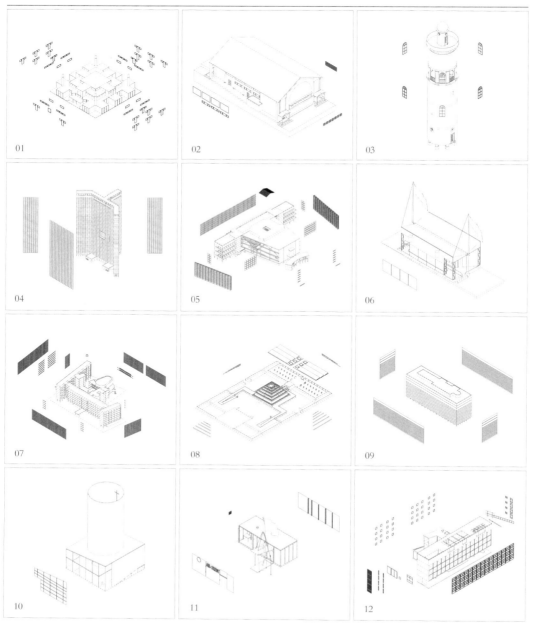

Table 36 Continued

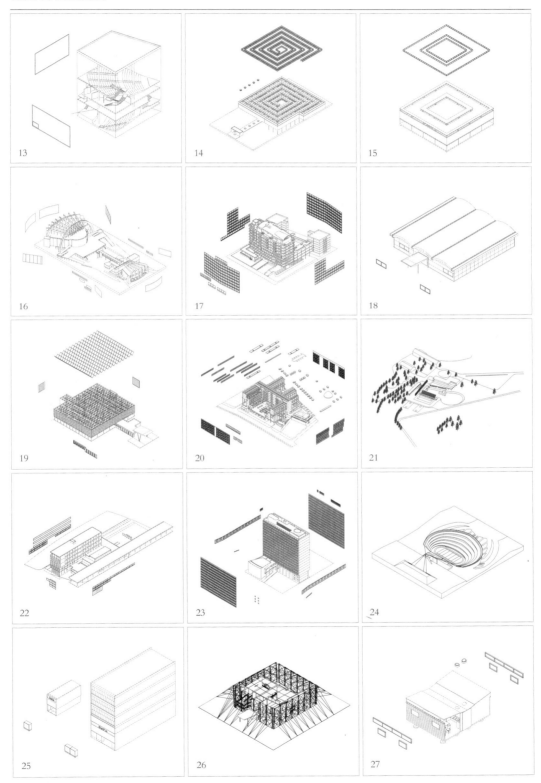

Table 36 Continued

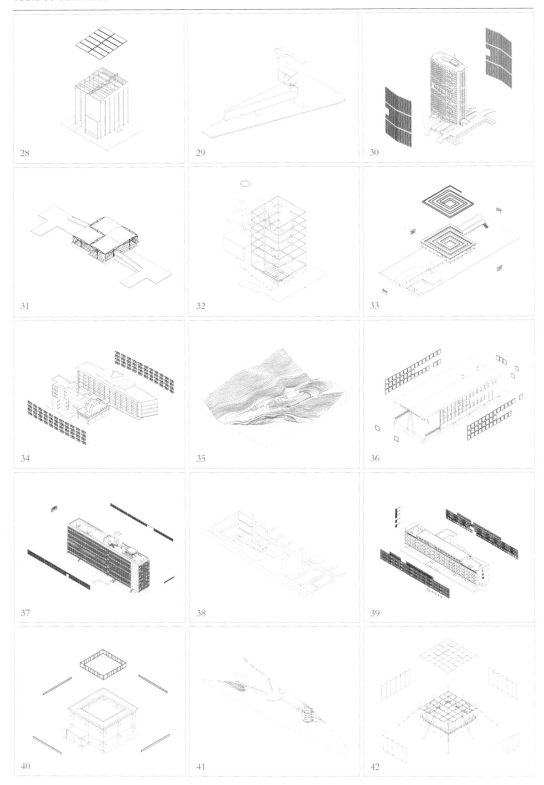

Table 36 Continued

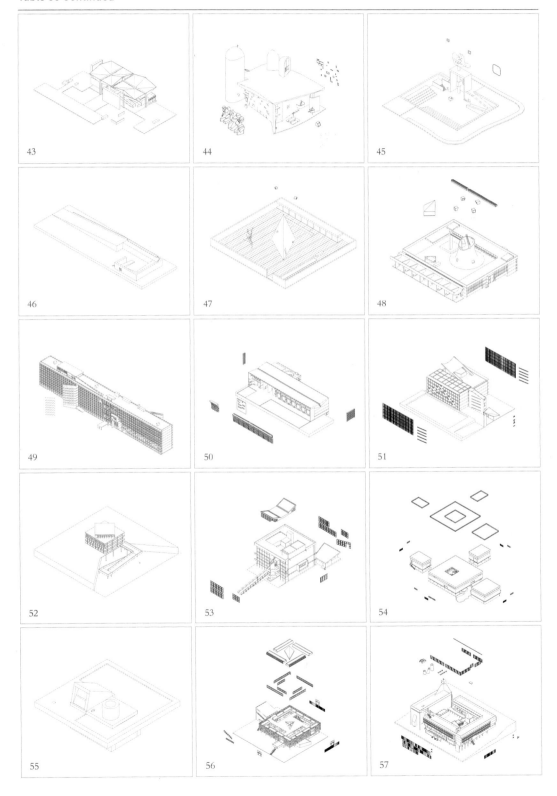

Table 36 Continued

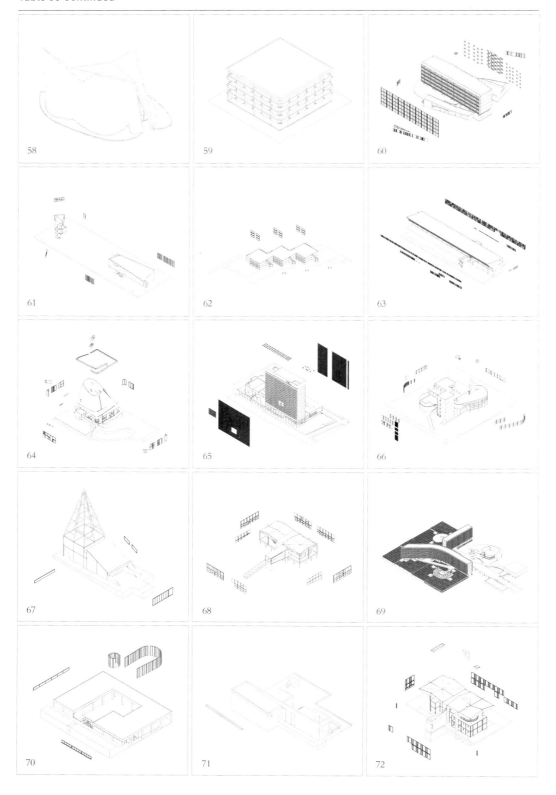

Table 36 Continued

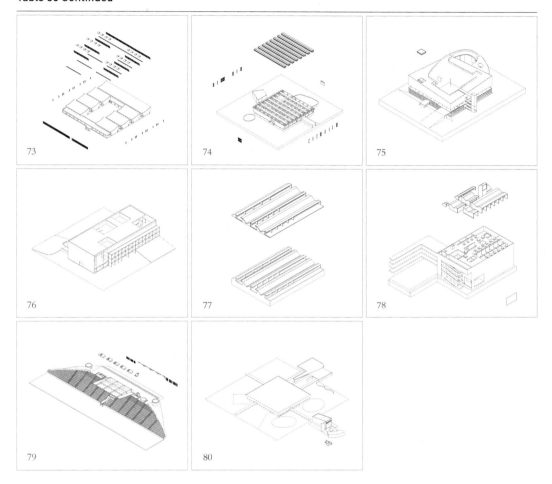

120

Excluding projects without detailed resources, as well as unfinished works without windows, leaves only sixty-four works for analysis.

Based on the placement/positioning of the windows in the architecture, three categories are determined:
1. Skylight—the window is set in the roof. There are fifteen works that feature skylights. A skylight also appears in the plan of the unfinished Palais de la Société des Nations (project 05).
2. Clerestory window—windows that are set above the sight line; appears in twenty works.
3. Sight-height window—windows that are set at the same sight height of the wall. There are sixty-four works that feature this type of windows; exceptions are projects 15, 40, and 71, and works without windows in the walls.

Figure 65 Classification based on window position

Sight-height windows can be further divided into subtypes:
1. Horizontal French window—projects 01, 02, 05, 08, 12, 16, 51, 56, 57, 67, 70, and 71; used less in public buildings than in private dwellings.
2. Glass wall or "window wall"—projects 04, 05, 06, 07, 09, 10, 11, 12, 13, 16, 17, 19, 20, 22, 23, 30, 34, 37, 39, 53, 56, 60, 64, 65, 66, 67, 68, and 72; widely used in public buildings.
3. Vertical strip window—projects 12, 39, 57, 62, 63, 72, 73, and 74.
4. Undulant grille glass wall—projects 51, 56, 57, 60, 61, 63, 66, 70, 73, and 79; used more in works that were taken on later in his career.
5. Trellis window—projects 01, 02, 05, 07, 12, 18, 27, 37, 39, 44, 45, 49, 60, and 64.
6. Round-corner window—projects 36, 45, and 50.
7. Others.

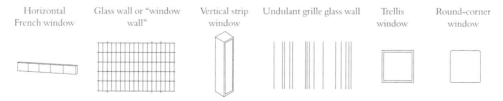

Figure 66 Sub-classification of sight-height window

The horizontal French windows that Le Corbusier used widely in housing design in his early years isn't used much. They appear in only twelve works, mostly in subsidiary functional rooms. The most widely used window type in Le Corbusier's public buildings is the second type, namely "window walls," which appear in twenty-eight works. The first time it was applied was in the double-glazed glass walls of the assembly hall in the Palais de la Société des Nations. Le Corbusier made it clear that windows are used for lighting rather than ventilation. Therefore, most of the glass walls he designed can't be opened and there is a separate indoor ventilation system that is approved by Le Corbusier as "correct breath." Trellis windows are equipped with separate fans, and appear in fourteen projects. Le Corbusier began using undulant grille glass walls in 1952 and they appear in ten works. Vertical strip windows appear in eight works while round-corner windows appear in three works. All the other window applications appear in small numbers. Next, is a comparison between the widely used skylight and clerestory window.

Skylight

Skylight here refers to windows set on the roof. The difference between a skylight and a clerestory window is that although the latter may belong to a part of the roof construction, it receives the light and then reflects it into the room. The first application of a skylight in Le Corbusier's public buildings was in Palais de la Société des Nations in 1927 (project 05) and the last application was in Palais des Congrès, Strasbourg in 1964 (project 75).

Table 37 Summary of skylight applications

Project name	Axonometric	Category	Window position	Window form
05 Palais de la Société des Nations		Administration building	Roof of assembly hall	
07 Centrosoyuz		Administration building	Top of the hall on the ground floor	
14 Musée d'Art Contemporain		Museum	Lighting on the ground floor	

Table 37 Continued

Project name	Axonometric	Category	Window position	Window form
20 Musée de la Ville et de l'État		Museum	Top of the hall on the ground floor	
27 TN-Wagon Maison Pavillon		Exhibition hall	Top of kitchen and bathroom	
47 Chapelle Funeraire Delgado-Chalbaud		Religious building	Roof and the wall	
48 Palais de l'Assemblée		Administration building	Top of the central hall	
56 Musée National d'Art Occidental		Museum	Top of the central hall	
57 Couvent Sainte-Marie de la Tourette		Religious building	Top of the sacristy, prayer room, and altar	
60 Maison du Brésil, Cité International Universitaire		School	Top of the hall on the ground floor	

Table 37 Continued

Project name	Axonometric	Category	Window position	Window form
64 Église Saint Pierre		Religious building	Top of the central hall	
65 Gare d'Orsay		Complex	Top of the hall on the ground floor	
66 Carpenter Center for Visual Arts, Harvard University		School	Top of the grand classroom on the ground floor	
72 Pavillon d'Exposition ZHLC, Zurich		Exhibition hall	Top of the umbrella-shaped roof	
75 Palais des Congrès, Strasbourg		Administration building	Top of the curved roof	

Table 37 shows that skylights are mostly used in administration and religious buildings and museums, and most of the forms are a cylinder, pyramid or cuboid. After Palais de l'Assemblée built in 1951 (project 48), the skylight varied from minimum independent geometry to external exhibition, to become more complex and difficult to identify, and had even been given an external mass figure, which enabled the skylight itself to become basic architecture.

Clerestory

There are twenty works that feature the clerestory window, as listed in Table 38.

Table 38 Summary of clerestory works

Project name	Axonometric	Window form
01 Ateliers d'Artistes		
08 Mundaneum, Musée Mondial (museum)		
12 Pavillon Suisse, Cité Internationale Universitaire		
14 Musée d'Art Contemporain		
15 Musée des Artistes Vivants		
19 Centre d'Esthetique Contemporaine		

Table 38 Continued

Project name	Axonometric	Window form
27 TN-Wagon Maison Pavillon		
33 Musée à Croissance Illimitée		
40 Musée et Lotissement Delaunay		
44 Chapelle Notre Dame du Haut		
48 Palais de l'Assemblée		
53 Palais des Filateurs		
56 Musée National d'Art Occidental		

Table 38 Continued

Project name	Axonometric	Window form
57 Couvent Sainte-Marie de la Tourette		
64 Église Saint Pierre		
71 Centre d'Art International		
73 École d'Art et d'Architecture		
74 Musée, Chandigarh		
77 Hôpital, Venice		
78 Église, Venice		

According to Table 38, when Le Corbusier designed the first public building in 1910, he paid attention to enabling lighting through the use of clerestory windows. And until he designed the plan of Hôpital, Venice (project 77) in 1965 before he died, the clerestory was still in use. On the top of Ateliers d'Artistes (project 01), the cross shape not only highlights the center and shows the cross's flank, but also forms the gap to receive the sidelight (Figure 67). This way of receiving natural light is similar to the light belt on the upper part of the mosque dome.

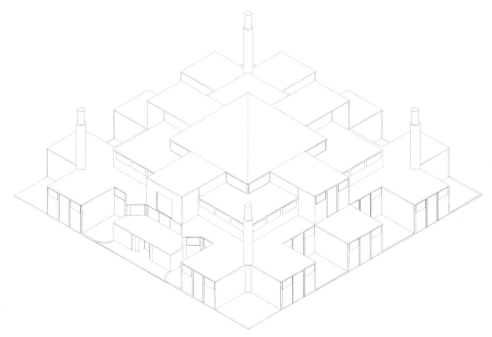

Figure 67   Axonometric drawing of project 01

Since working on Musée d'Art Contemporain in 1931 (project 14), Le Corbusier tried to take advantage of the staggered movement between a raised mass and an adjacent roof slab to let light in through the two sides. This method was used in projects 15, 19, 33, 40, 53, 56, 74, 77, and 78, which makes up almost fifty percent of the works listed above that use clerestory lighting. There exists a seam between the roof and the top of the wall in projects 01, 08, 12, 27, 44, 48, 57, 71, and 73, which is forty-five percent of the works that use clerestory lighting. The third type of clerestory lighting is seen in project 64, Église Saint Pierre. Le Corbusier made a linear notch on the wall of the church and covered it with a board on the outside, which was also the conduit for the drainage system of the house. The design is also applied on the south wall of Chapelle Notre Dame du Haut (project 44) and the flank of Couvent Sainte-Marie de la Tourette (project 57). Although there is some difference in the application, the light comes from a notch on the interior or exterior wall. The size and height of the walls differ, thus forming a unique indoor lighting atmosphere. This method is used in fifteen percent of the works, and in all religious buildings.

128

③ **Staircases**

There are fifty-three works with stairs. They are projects 01, 02, 03, 04, 05, 07, 08, 09, 12, 13, 14, 15, 16, 17, 18, 19, 20, 22, 23, 30, 33, 34, 36, 37, 39, 43, 44, 45, 48, 49, 50, 51, 53, 54, 56, 57, 60, 61, 62, 63, 64, 65, 66, 67, 68, 69, 70, 72, 74, 75, 76, 78, and 79.

Table 39 The 53 public buildings with staircases

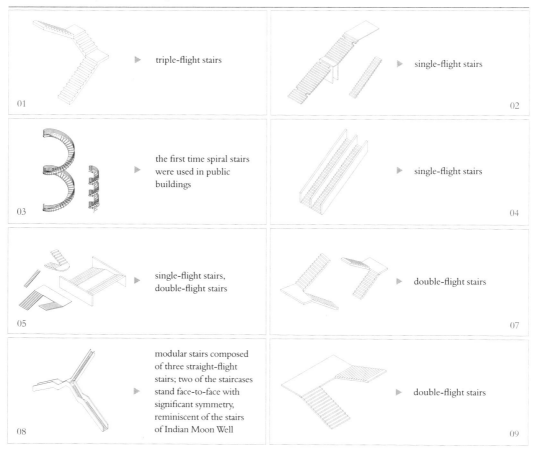

01	▶ triple-flight stairs	
02	▶ single-flight stairs	
03	▶ the first time spiral stairs were used in public buildings	
04	▶ single-flight stairs	
05	▶ single-flight stairs, double-flight stairs	
07	▶ double-flight stairs	
08	▶ modular stairs composed of three straight-flight stairs; two of the staircases stand face-to-face with significant symmetry, reminiscent of the stairs of Indian Moon Well	
09	▶ double-flight stairs	

Table 39 Continued

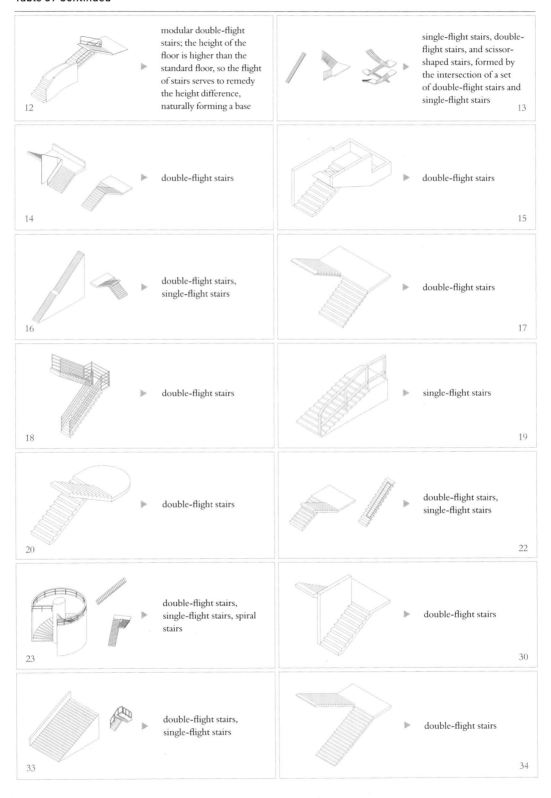

12	modular double-flight stairs; the height of the floor is higher than the standard floor, so the flight of stairs serves to remedy the height difference, naturally forming a base
13	single-flight stairs, double-flight stairs, and scissor-shaped stairs, formed by the intersection of a set of double-flight stairs and single-flight stairs
14	double-flight stairs
15	double-flight stairs
16	double-flight stairs, single-flight stairs
17	double-flight stairs
18	double-flight stairs
19	single-flight stairs
20	double-flight stairs
22	double-flight stairs, single-flight stairs
23	double-flight stairs, single-flight stairs, spiral stairs
30	double-flight stairs
33	double-flight stairs, single-flight stairs
34	double-flight stairs

Table 39 Continued

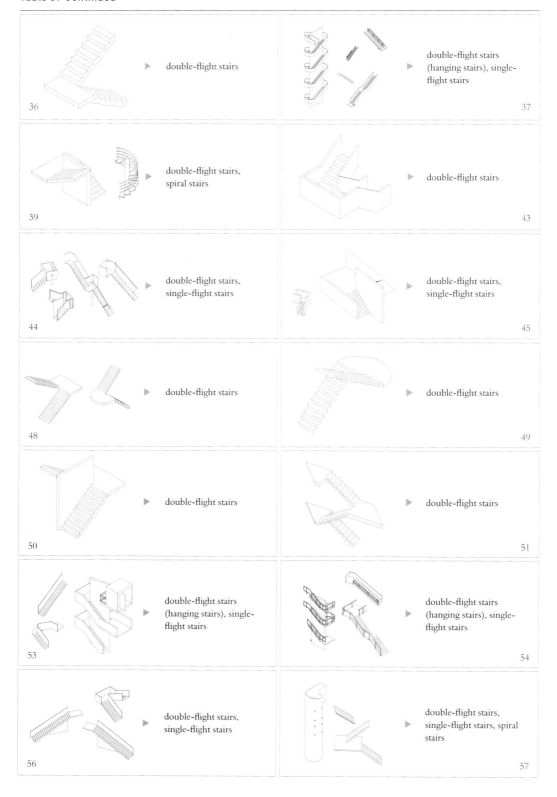

Staircases 131

Table 39 Continued

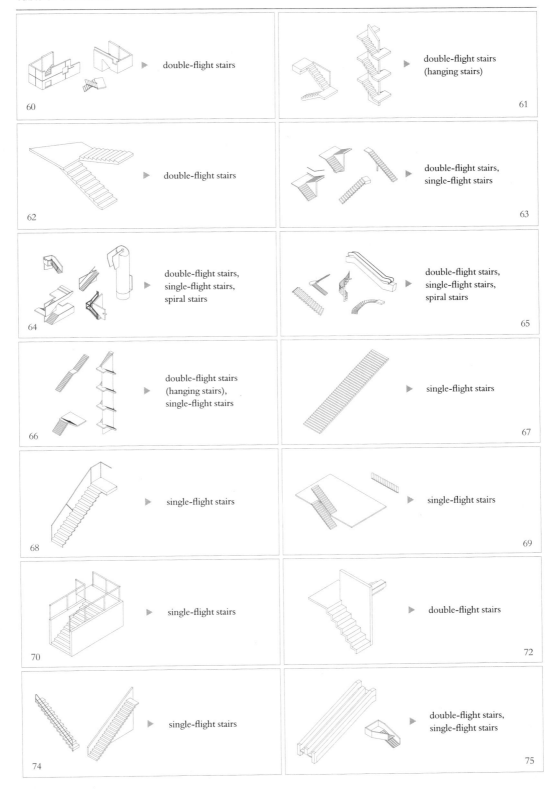

60	double-flight stairs
61	double-flight stairs (hanging stairs)
62	double-flight stairs
63	double-flight stairs, single-flight stairs
64	double-flight stairs, single-flight stairs, spiral stairs
65	double-flight stairs, single-flight stairs, spiral stairs
66	double-flight stairs (hanging stairs), single-flight stairs
67	single-flight stairs
68	single-flight stairs
69	single-flight stairs
70	single-flight stairs
72	double-flight stairs
74	single-flight stairs
75	double-flight stairs, single-flight stairs

Table 39 Continued

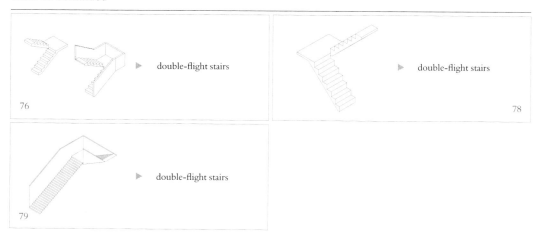

The works listed in Table 39 can be divided into works with single-flight stairs and double-flight stairs: twenty-six works have single-flight stairs, forty-two have double-flight stairs, one features a set of three-flight stairs (project 01), and six have spiral stairs (projects 03, 23, 39, 57, 64, and 65). From the perspective of construction features, it is seen that Le Corbusier usually adopts a type of unique cantilevered stairs. The load-bearing board of stairs is located in the middle, and the flight of steps is cantilevered. This appears in projects 37, 53, 54, 61, 66, and 72.

Spiral Stairs

Le Corbusier used spiral stairs for the first time in project 03, Château d'Eau. Figure 68 shows that there are two sets of spiral stairs. The stairs at the bottom of the building are close to the exterior wall, leaving the middle high space for stairs. After people arrive at the viewing platform floor by way of the first spiral stairs, the second spiral stairs are presented in the middle of the plane; through that they can reach the top floor—this leaves the surrounding space for viewing. The spiral stairs in this work have completed a transformation vertically. The transformation between traffic-space and use-space is completed in a limited plane.

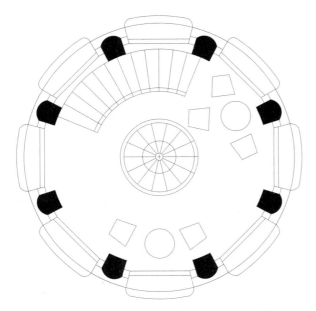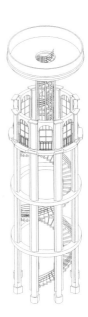

Figure 68 Plan and axonometric drawing of project 03

The second time that spiral stairs were used is in Ministère de l'Education Nationale et de la Santé (project 23). The plan shows that the spiral stairs are located in the middle of a podium on the ground floor, occupying the whole space. It also serves as the focus of the whole space while solving circulation problems (Figure 69).

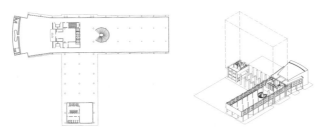

Figure 69 Plan, axonometric drawing, and photo of project 23

134

The third time that spiral stairs were used is in Usine Claude et Duval (project 39), where the stairs are located in the middle of the three-story plane. Compared with project 23, the stairs are smaller and play an auxiliary role in transportation (Figure 70).

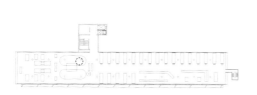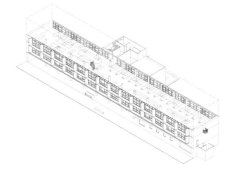

Figure 70   Plan and axonometric drawing of project 39

The fourth time was in Couvent Sainte-Marie de la Tourette (project 57). The difference is that the spiral stairs were now presented in a separate mass outside the building. As shown in Figure 71, they are located on one side of the middle courtyard. As a kind of auxiliary vertical transportation, they enable access directly from the first floor to the third floor. The spiral stairs here remove the function of the stairs in Château d'Eau (project 03), but adopt its vertical mass feature.

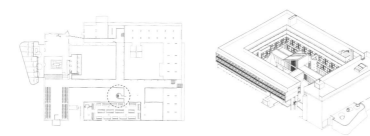

Figure 71   Plan, axonometric drawing and photo of project 57

The fifth time was in Église Saint Pierre (project 64), and in a similar style to project 57. The spiral stairs appear on one side of the main body of the church as an independent appendage, which enables direct access to the hall of the church from the ground floor, playing a role of hidden and affiliated traffic connection (Figure 72). The last project to adopt spiral stairs was Gare d'Orsay (project 65), where the stairs are placed indoors, just like in project 39.

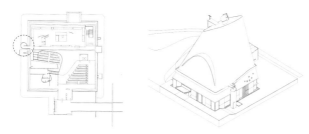

Figure 72   Plan, axonometric drawing and photo of project 64

Cantilevered stairs

Table 40 shows six works use cantilevered stairs with a special structure.

Table 40 Axonometric diagram, plans, and photo of works using cantilevered stairs

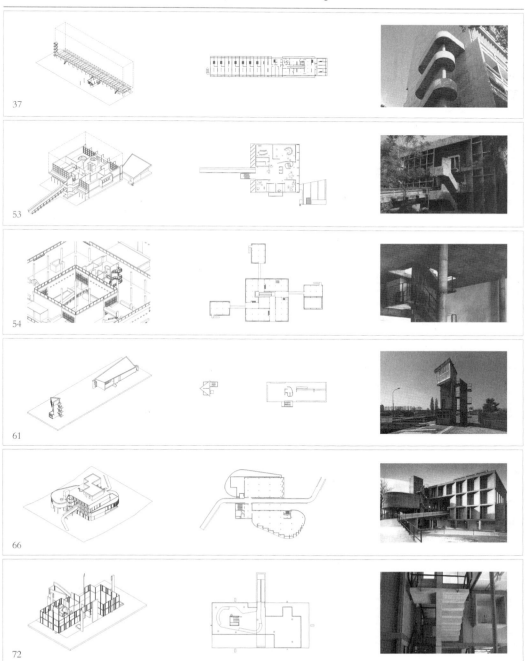

4 Ramps

There are forty-two works that include designed ramps. They are projects 07, 08, 09, 10, 13, 16, 17, 18, 19, 20, 26, 28, 30, 31, 32, 33, 37, 41, 43, 45, 46, 48, 49, 50, 51, 52, 53, 54, 56, 57, 63, 64, 65, 66, 68, 69, 72, 74, 75, 76, 77, and 78.

Table 41 Axonometric drawing of 42 works with ramps

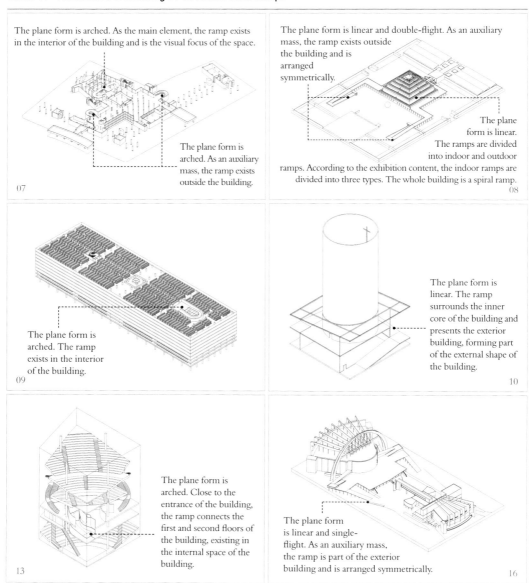

The plane form is arched. As the main element, the ramp exists in the interior of the building and is the visual focus of the space.

The plane form is arched. As an auxiliary mass, the ramp exists outside the building.

07

The plane form is linear and double-flight. As an auxiliary mass, the ramp exists outside the building and is arranged symmetrically.

The plane form is linear. The ramps are divided into indoor and outdoor ramps. According to the exhibition content, the indoor ramps are divided into three types. The whole building is a spiral ramp.

08

The plane form is arched. The ramp exists in the interior of the building.

09

The plane form is linear. The ramp surrounds the inner core of the building and presents the exterior building, forming part of the external shape of the building.

10

The plane form is arched. Close to the entrance of the building, the ramp connects the first and second floors of the building, existing in the internal space of the building.

13

The plane form is linear and single-flight. As an auxiliary mass, the ramp is part of the exterior building and is arranged symmetrically.

16

Table 41 Continued

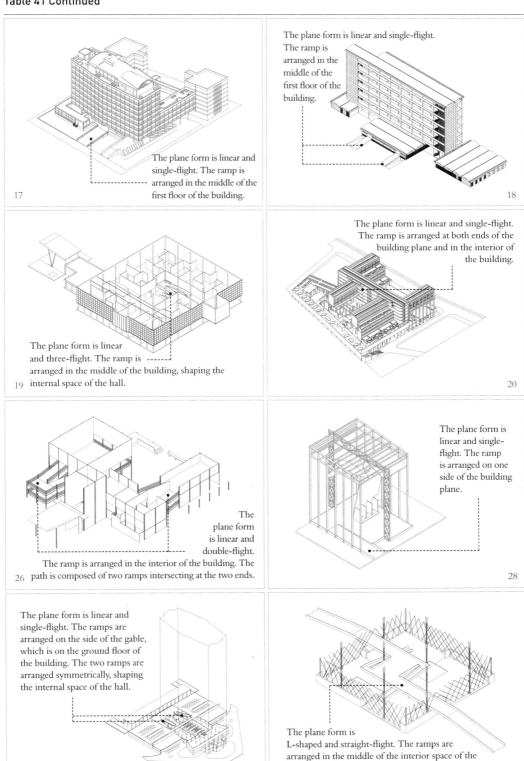

Table 41 Continued

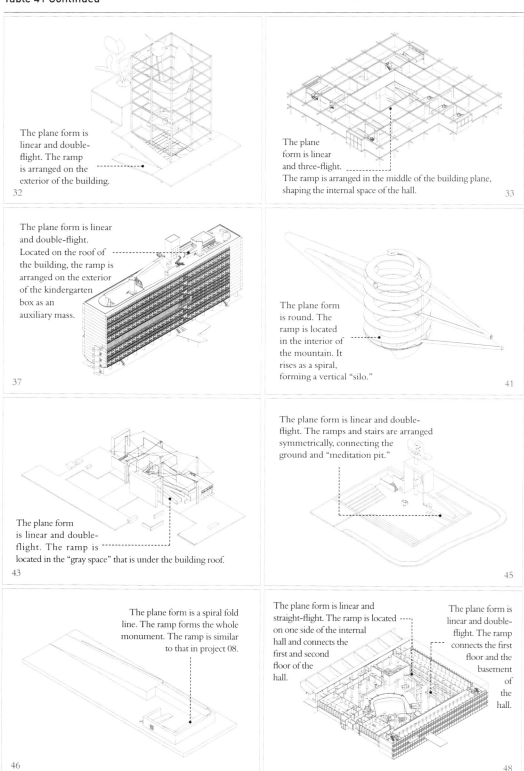

Table 41 Continued

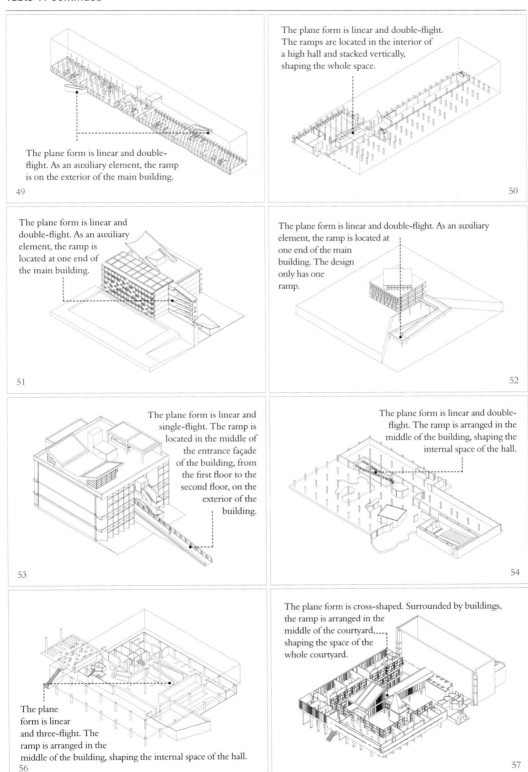

Table 41 Continued

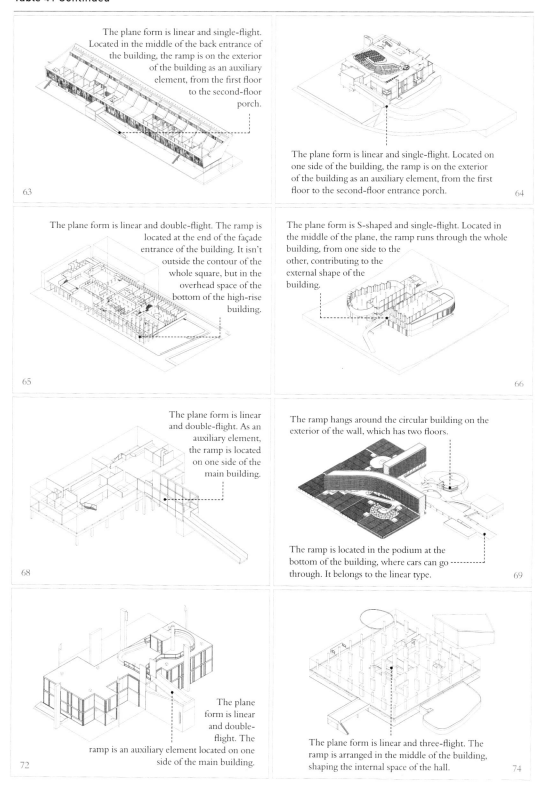

63 — The plane form is linear and single-flight. Located in the middle of the back entrance of the building, the ramp is on the exterior of the building as an auxiliary element, from the first floor to the second-floor porch.

64 — The plane form is linear and single-flight. Located on one side of the building, the ramp is on the exterior of the building as an auxiliary element, from the first floor to the second-floor entrance porch.

65 — The plane form is linear and double-flight. The ramp is located at the end of the façade entrance of the building. It isn't outside the contour of the whole square, but in the overhead space of the bottom of the high-rise building.

66 — The plane form is S-shaped and single-flight. Located in the middle of the plane, the ramp runs through the whole building, from one side to the other, contributing to the external shape of the building.

68 — The plane form is linear and double-flight. As an auxiliary element, the ramp is located on one side of the main building.

69 — The ramp hangs around the circular building on the exterior of the wall, which has two floors. The ramp is located in the podium at the bottom of the building, where cars can go through. It belongs to the linear type.

72 — The plane form is linear and double-flight. The ramp is an auxiliary element located on one side of the main building.

74 — The plane form is linear and three-flight. The ramp is arranged in the middle of the building, shaping the internal space of the hall.

Table 41 Continued

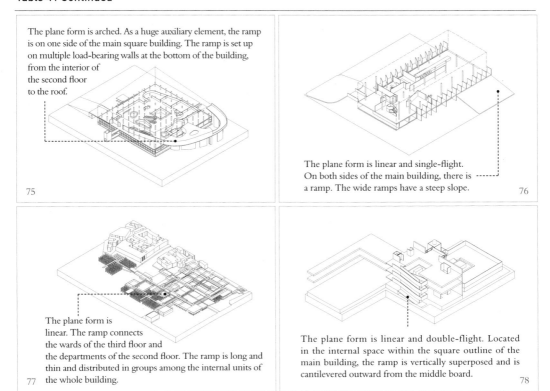

75 The plane form is arched. As a huge auxiliary element, the ramp is on one side of the main square building. The ramp is set up on multiple load-bearing walls at the bottom of the building, from the interior of the second floor to the roof.

76 The plane form is linear and single-flight. On both sides of the main building, there is a ramp. The wide ramps have a steep slope.

77 The plane form is linear. The ramp connects the wards of the third floor and the departments of the second floor. The ramp is long and thin and distributed in groups among the internal units of the whole building.

78 The plane form is linear and double-flight. Located in the internal space within the square outline of the main building, the ramp is vertically superposed and is cantilevered outward from the middle board.

As can be seen from Table 41, buildings with ramps account for 52.5 percent of the public buildings. The first use of a ramp was in project 07, Centrosoyuz. The function of the ramp itself was transportation, but what form a ramp takes and how it participates in the space of the building is quite different. These can be divided into six categories:

Type A—as the transportation core of the interior building, the ramp belongs to vertical superposition with standard units. The ramp is spiral or double-flight.

Type B—the ramp is located in the interior of the building. Some are three-flight ramps and others are vertically superposed double-flight ramps.

Type C—the ramp is a rising spiral. It is exactly the "building" itself, and the interior and exterior of the building are consistent.

Type D—the ramp is located on one side of the main building and is on the exterior as an auxiliary element.

Type E—located in the middle of the building façade, the ramp connects the ground and the main entrance of the building in a long linear corridor. There are two ways to design ramps entering the building: one is perpendicular to the building façade, while the other is parallel.

Type F—as the main transportation element connection block, the ramp is located in the courtyard enclosed by the building.

Table 42 The six ways that ramps fit into the building composition

Type	Diagram	Formation	Feature	Project
A		Vertical internal transportation core	Strong functionality	07, 09, 20
B		Indoor focus of hall	Shaping the internal space	19, 33, 43, 48, 50, 54, 56, 65, 74, 78
C		The ramp is exactly the "building" itself and presented on the exterior	Consistent in interior and exterior	08, 10, 41, 46
D		Attached to the main building in auxiliary mass	Represented in mass externally	32, 37, 49, 51, 52, 63, 64, 68, 72
E		Entering the main entrance of the building through the corridor	Represented in linear externally	17, 18, 28, 30, 31, 53, 66, 75, 76
F		Connecting blocks in a courtyard	A horizontal element displayed inside	57, 77

There are five works—projects 13, 16, 26, 45, and 69—that cannot be classified into these six categories. The ramp of project 13 (Cinéma à Montparnasse) is indoors, connecting the first and second floor, neither in the center of the plane nor in the cantilevered hall. The ramps of projects 16 (Palais des Soviets) and 69 (Olivetti, Centre de Calculs Électroniques) are outdoors, which is only a small component of the large buildings. The ramp of project 26 (Pavillon des Temps Nouveaux) is a part of the path of the exhibition space. Project 45 (Main Ouverte, Chandigarh) is an outdoor sculpture. The ramp is opposite the stairs, connecting the floor and the sunken space.

5 Sunshading

Among the eighty public architecture works, there are nineteen works with shade facilities. They are projects 23, 30, 34, 37, 39, 47, 48, 49, 51, 52, 53, 54, 59, 62, 65, 66, 69, 75, and 76.

Table 43 Axonometric drawings of the 19 public buildings with sunshading

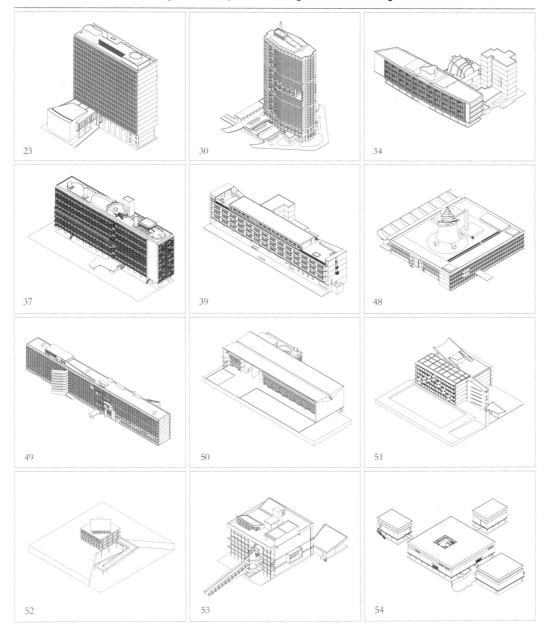

Table 43 Continued

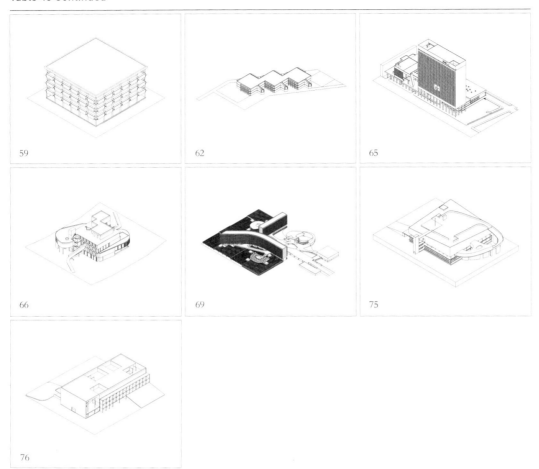

Based on Table 43, sunshading techniques can be divided into three distinctions: sun visor, sunken balcony, and wall plants. The earliest work to use a sun visor was project 23. In general, sun visor adaptations were used mainly in Le Corbusier's later practice.

Sunken Balcony

There are four works that adopt this technique: projects 30, 49, 59, and 65. In project 30, Gratte-Ciel, Quartier de la Marine, Cité des Affaires (Figure 73), the building is shuttle-shaped, with a transportation core in the middle, open office spaces on both sides, a sunken balcony around the building, and a standard floor of 2.2 meters (7.2 feet) in height. The balcony is divided into equal-sized compartments by partition walls, and the columns are exposed in the middle of the single-span balcony. The balcony of project 49 (Secrétariat, Chandigarh) is the same as that of project 59 (City Center, Chandigarh). As shown in Figure 74, the balcony is also divided into equal compartments. The railing measures about 1.1 meters (3.6 feet) high and is located in the middle of the balcony unit, and is separated from the walls on both sides to form a uniform façade pattern. There are two forms of sunken balconies in project 65, Gare d'Orsay (Figure 75). One is the square grid while the other is the plane inclined to a certain angle and extended outward.

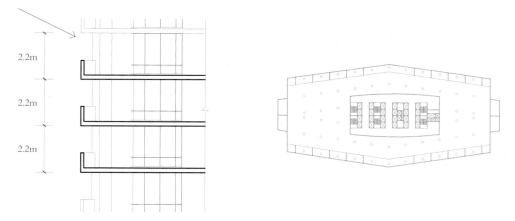

Figure 73 Sectional part and standard floor plan of project 30

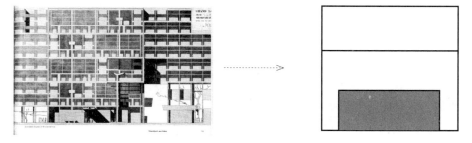

Figure 74 Form extract of sunken balcony in projects 49 and 59

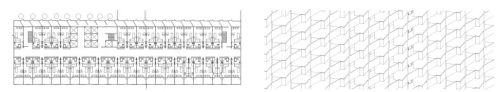

Figure 75 Standard floor plan and partial axonometric drawing of project 65

Wall Plants

There is only one example of this technique—project 54, Musée, Ahmedabad. Le Corbusier designed a ring of concrete grooves surrounding the façade of the pavilion. In summer, plants like vines can be planted along the grooves. Figure 76 shows that green plants climb up along the wall, offering cooling and protection from light. This strategy combines the outline treatment of the façade, which not only plays a functional role, but also conforms to the composition rules of the building.

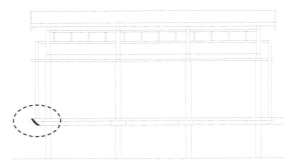

Figure 76 Photo and partial section of project 54

Sun Visor

This technique is the most widely used technique and is used in fifteen works. Project 65 uses a sunken balcony, as well a a sun visor in the bottom podium.

Table 44 Summary of sun visor forms used in 15 works

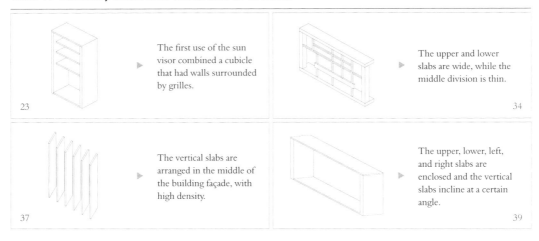

Table 44 Continued

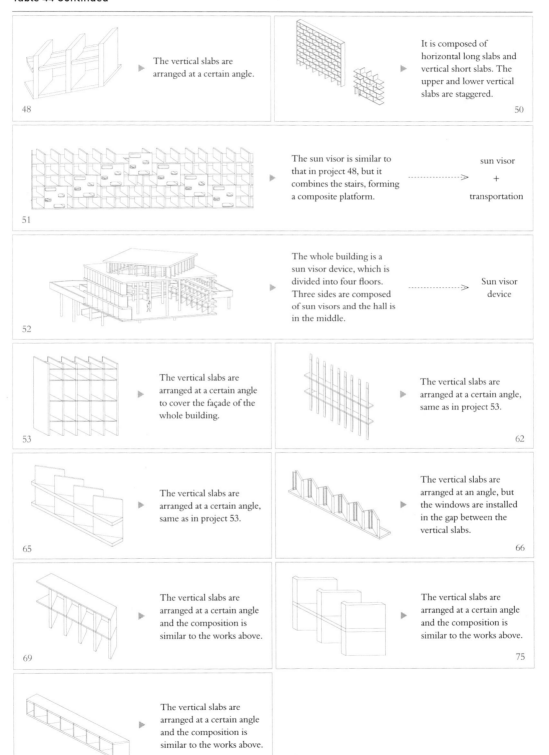

It can be seen from Table 44 that projects 51 (Musée de la Connaissance) and 52 (Tour d'Ombres) are relatively special examples. Although sunshades are used, the sunshade facilities of project 51 combine with the stairs to form a platform with composite functions (Figure 77), which can not only block the sunlight, but also connect the upper and lower floors. In addition, there is a vertical board around the location of the double-flight stairs connecting the five floors, so that people can't see it outside. Holes are opened on the board and seven boards are arranged on the façade, which adds a layer to the building façade. Project 52 is similarly distinct because the whole building is a sunshade device. The three sides of the building are surrounded by sunshades. One side is hollowed out and a transparent high hall is set in the middle, arranged south–to–north. The angle of the sunshade keeps a certain relationship with the incident angle of the sun throughout the four seasons.

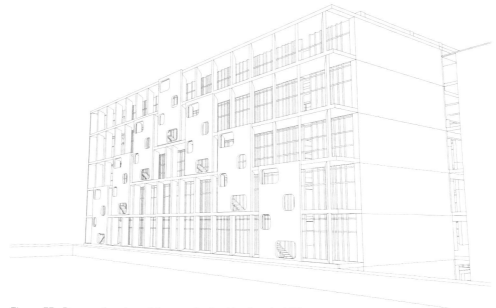

Figure 77   Perspective view of the sunshade side of project 51

6 Drainage Structures

The basic construction of architecture dictates that any building being constructed will face the challenge of drainage; however, not all drainage parts are "expressed" by Le Corbusier. For example, in the plan of Palais de la Société des Nations (project 05), the drainage section is not mentioned in the statement of the whole building scheme. Therefore, this section only selects the cases that show the drainage on the exterior of the building, mainly projects 06, 27, 44, 48, 50, 53, 54, 57, 61, 63, 64, 67, 69, 71, 73, and 74.

Table 45 Axonometric drawings of 16 works with drainage

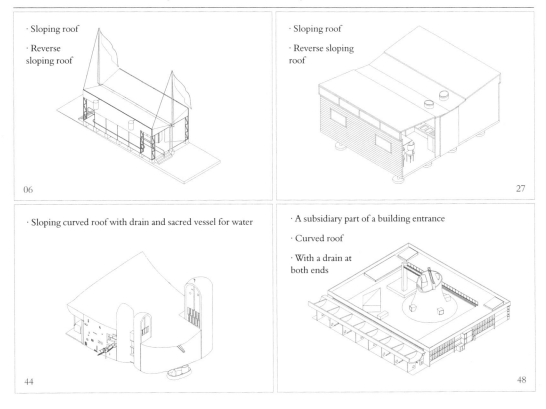

Table 45 Continued

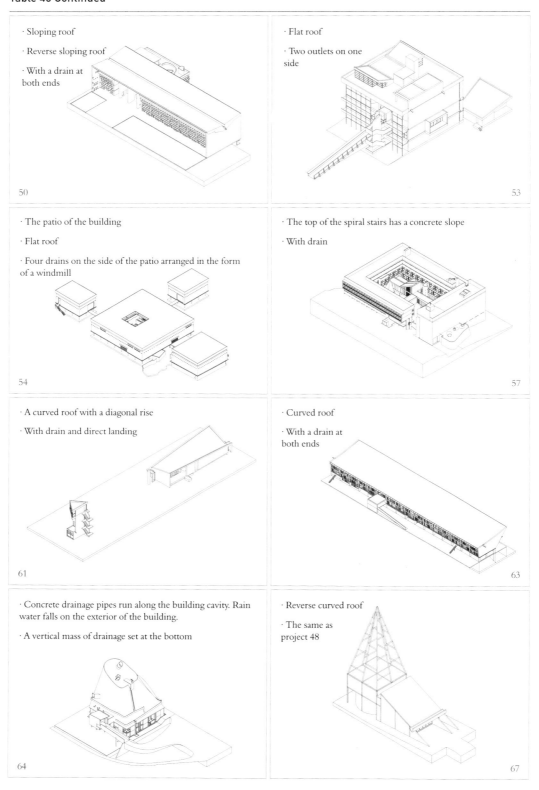

- Sloping roof
- Reverse sloping roof
- With a drain at both ends

50

- Flat roof
- Two outlets on one side

53

- The patio of the building
- Flat roof
- Four drains on the side of the patio arranged in the form of a windmill

54

- The top of the spiral stairs has a concrete slope
- With drain

57

- A curved roof with a diagonal rise
- With drain and direct landing

61

- Curved roof
- With a drain at both ends

63

- Concrete drainage pipes run along the building cavity. Rain water falls on the exterior of the building.
- A vertical mass of drainage set at the bottom

64

- Reverse curved roof
- The same as project 48

67

Table 45 Continued

· On the workshop floor at the bottom, the roof is composed of an inverted trapezoid concrete reservoir arranged in a row; grooves are installed at the edge of the building to receive rainwater 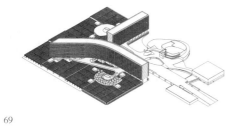 69	· Single sloping roof · With a drain at the end 71
· From the curved roof to the low spatial mass roof, there is a drain at both ends 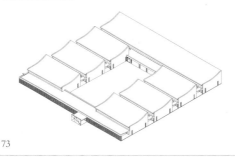 73	· The roof is composed of a series of units on the opposite slope arranged in rows; grooves are installed along the edge of the building to receive rain, similar to project 69  74

There are seven types of drainage forms identified (Figure 78):

1. The structural form of the reverse sloping roof renders the ridge lower than the eave, and the rainwater gathers at the ridge line and drains along one or both sides. (Seen in projects 06, 27, and 50.)
2. The roof itself is a reservoir, which is drained from both sides after collection. (Seen in projects 48, 63, and 67.)
3. The two corners of the roof are raised to form a warped roof and the rainwater is drained along the slope. (Seen in project 61.)
4. A flat roof that has a drain. (Seen in projects 53, 54, and 73.)
5. A roof that slopes in one direction. (Seen in projects 44, 57, and 71.)
6. The roof is composed of a row of reservoirs and a water collector is arranged at the end to collect and drain. (Seen in projects 69 and 74.)
7. The drainage pipe runs along the exterior of the building and then lands with a vertical waterfall-shaped groove. (Seen in project 64.)

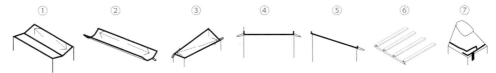

Figure 78 Classification of drainage types

Part 3
Case Studies

Administration Building —————— A
Museum ————————————— B
Exhibition Hall ————————— C
Religious Building ———————— D
School ————————————— E
Sports Facility ————————— F
Public Building (Water Conservancy) ——— G
Complex ————————————— H
Commercial Building ———————— I
Monument ————————————— J
Hospital ————————————— K

A-05
Palais de la Société des Nations

Design period: 1927–29
Location: Geneva, Switzerland
Status: Unbuilt

Although the project won the first prize in a large international competition in 1927, it was never realized. The site is located in Geneva. One side of the palace faces a lake, while the other side faces a road. Palais de la Société des Nations houses a library, an office building, a meeting hall, and an assembly hall. The library and the office building are close to the road while the assembly hall is near the lake. The assembly hall is selected as the featured work in this project. The whole structure is composed of a slab-type building in the shape of a rectangle and includes a trapezoidal hall near the lake. Two semi-arches, fixed by three horizontal trusses, support the roof. Apart from the brilliant ideas displayed in the structure, the hall design, with a capacity to hold a large number of people, also takes acoustics into consideration, enabling the audience to listen to the speaker's voice clearly from any location.

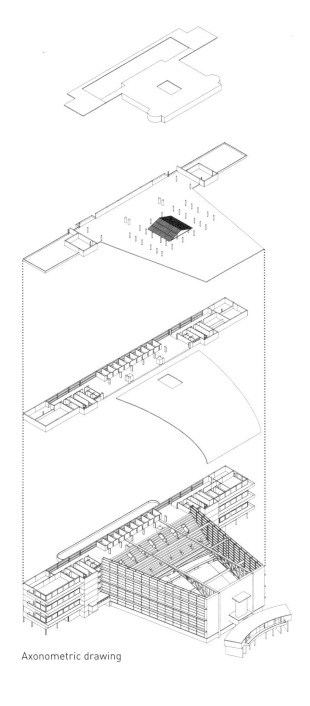

Axonometric drawing

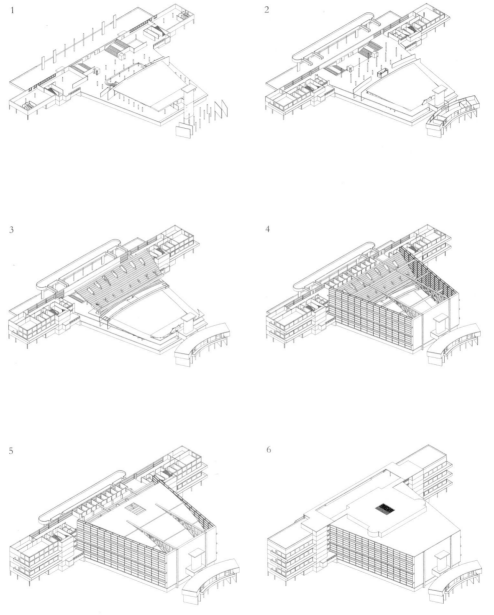

Exploded axonometric drawing

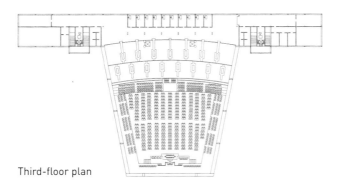

Third-floor plan

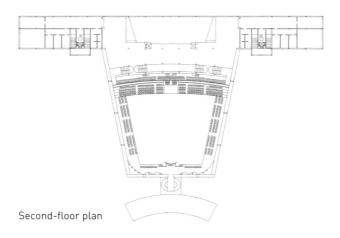

Second-floor plan

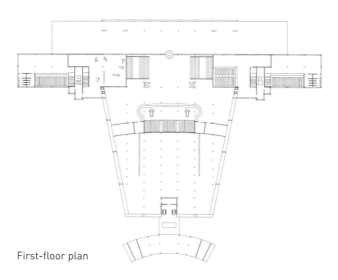

First-floor plan

Administration Building 157

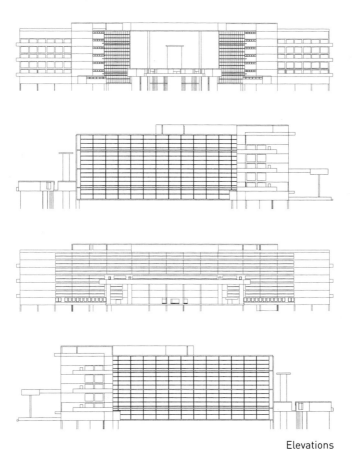

Elevations

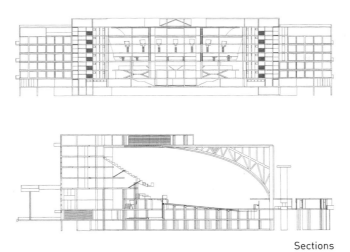

Sections

A-07
Centrosoyuz

Design period: 1928
Location: Moscow, Russia
Status: Built

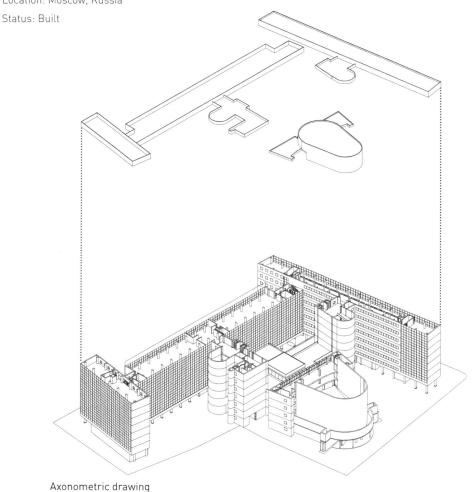

Axonometric drawing

This modern office for 2,500 employees required the most advanced modern technologies. Le Corbusier's plan was chosen from an extensive competition. Centrosoyuz has four parts, including three slab-type buildings and a club in the middle. In this project, Le Corbusier puts forward a heating and ventilating design known as "accurate breath system." Concerned about the cold conditions in Moscow, he made the whole building airtight. Through the air-conditioner and "neutralization wall" heat insulation, the internal temperature can be constantly maintained at about 18 °C (64.4 °F).

Administration Building 159

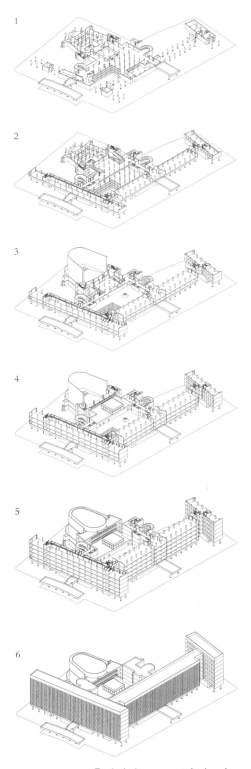

Exploded axonometric drawing

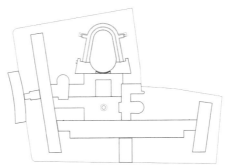

Roof plan

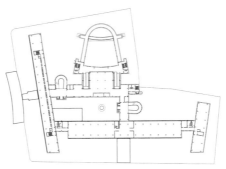

Third-floor plan

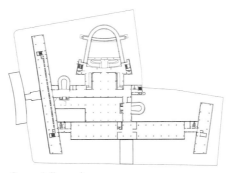

Second-floor plan

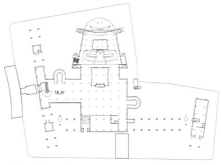

First-floor plan

Administration Building 161

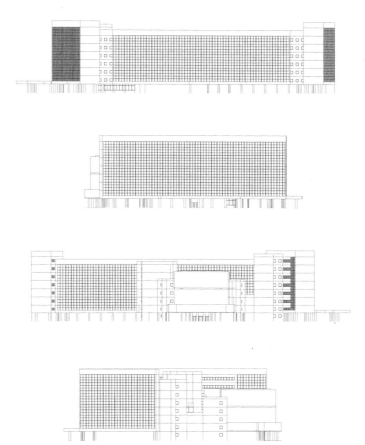

Elevations

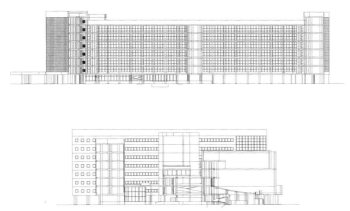

Sections

A-09
Mundaneum, Musée Mondial (administration building)

Design period: 1929
Location: Geneva, Switzerland
Status: Unbuilt

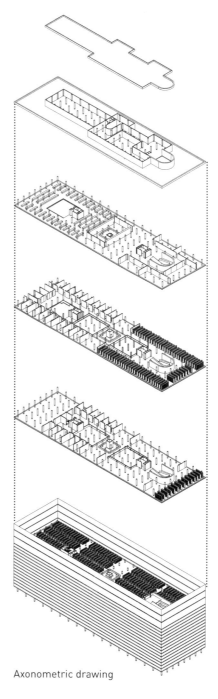

Project Mundaneum aimed to build in Geneva, a branch of the Mundaneum international center in Brussels, to be a world-class scientific, documentary, and educational center. It is supported by stilts at the bottom and the turning flow lines of automobile transportation are set below. There are two halls on the ground floor. One is a loading hall while the other is a visitor entry hall. The plan is a rectangle; the traffic core is located at the center; the bookshelves are set around the hall; and it is a totally translucent building.

Axonometric drawing

Administration Building 163

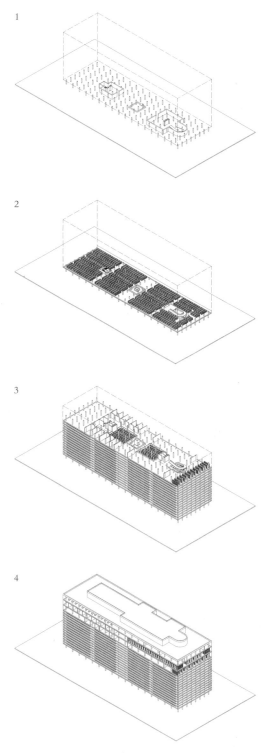

1

2

3

4

Exploded axonometric drawing

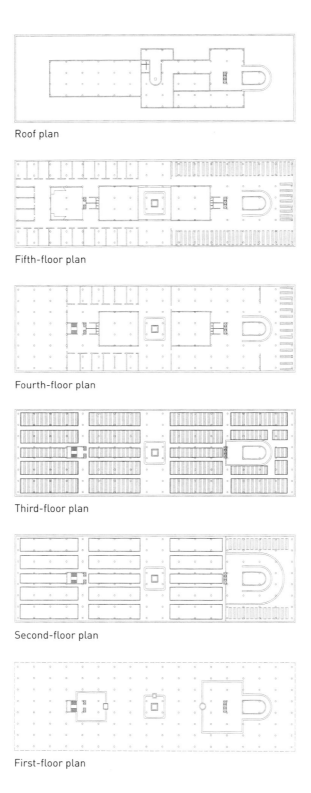

Roof plan

Fifth-floor plan

Fourth-floor plan

Third-floor plan

Second-floor plan

First-floor plan

Administration Building   165

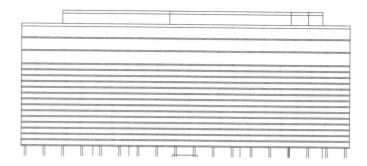

Elevations

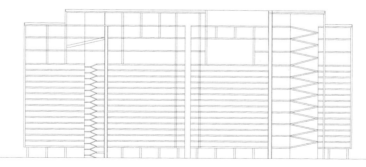

Section

A-16
Palais des Soviets

Design period: 1931
Location: Moscow, Russia
Status: Unbuilt

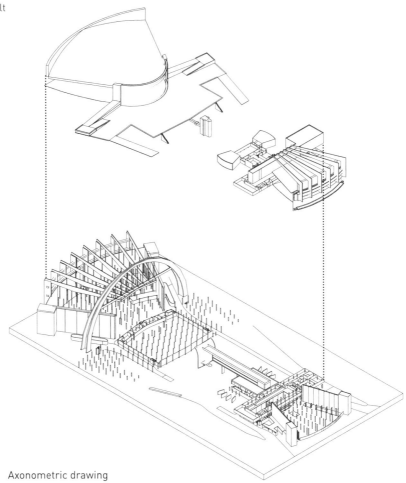

Axonometric drawing

A competition held by the Soviet government tasked participants to design a gigantic complex that includes a hall to hold 15,000 people, offices, a library, a restaurant, and other similar facilities. The hall is placed on one end, while the multifunction hall, able to hold 50,000, is used as a roof terrace. The project mainly focuses on solving transportation problems with human traffic flow and connections between city roads. It was never built due to differing opinions.

Administration Building 167

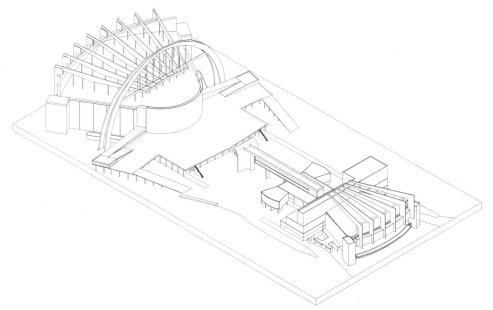

Exploded axonometric drawing

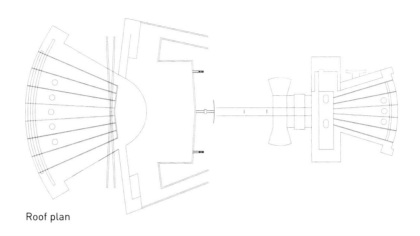

Roof plan

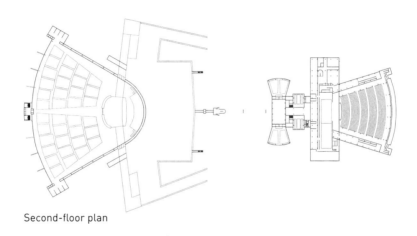

Second-floor plan

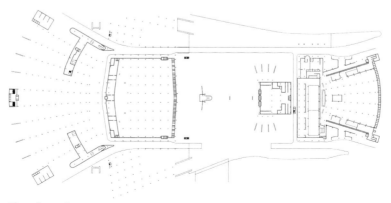

First-floor plan

Administration Building 169

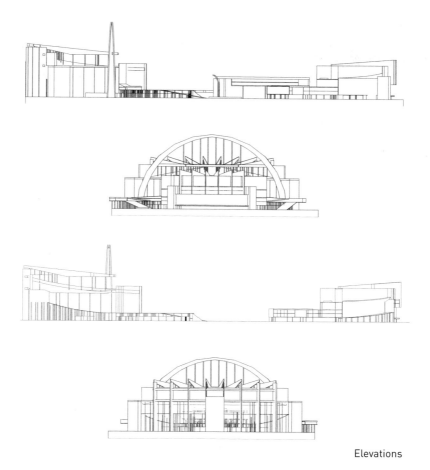

Elevations

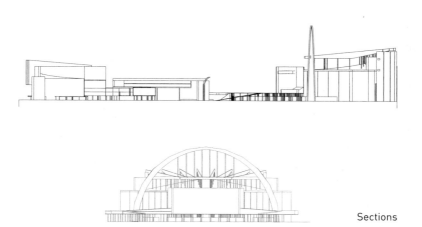

Sections

A-17
Immeuble Rentenanstalt

Design period: 1933
Location: Zurich, Switzerland
Status: Unbuilt

The building was submitted for a 1933 competition in Zurich, but it was never built. The project that Le Corbusier put forward on the plan is a shuttle building; on the north of the base, are the reserved residential buildings. The transportation facilities center and restrooms are located in the center of the plan. The office space is divided by the surrounding partition walls. The two axes are symmetrical and the exterior surface of the building is a glass wall. The bottom is supported by stilts. The columns aren't wrapped in the interior of the building. Instead, they are situated at the exterior the building.

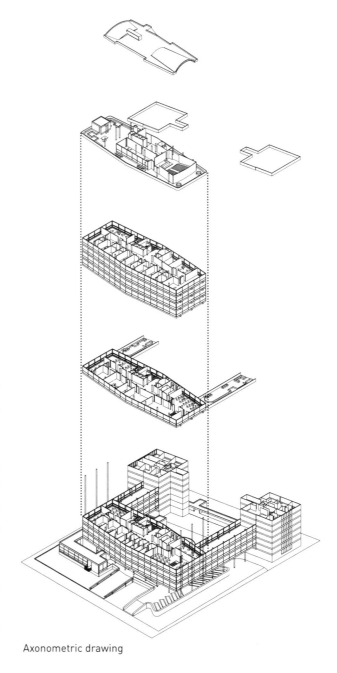

Axonometric drawing

Administration Building 171

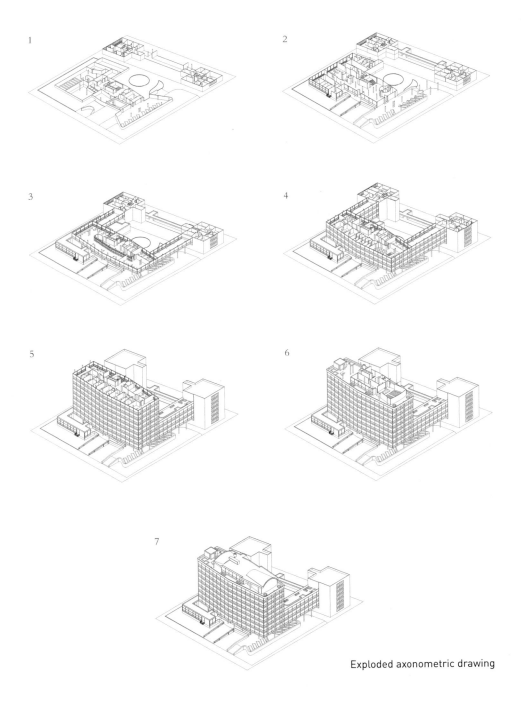

Exploded axonometric drawing

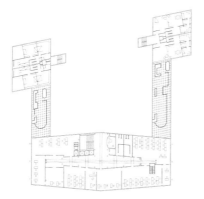
Fourth-floor plan

Roof plan

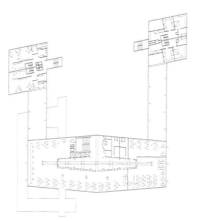
Second-floor plan

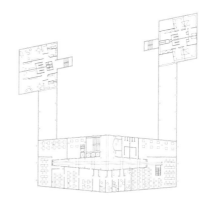
Third-floor plan

Typical floor plan

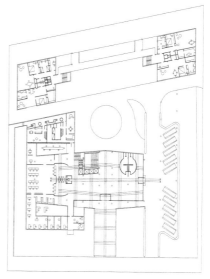
First-floor plan

Administration Building   173

Elevations

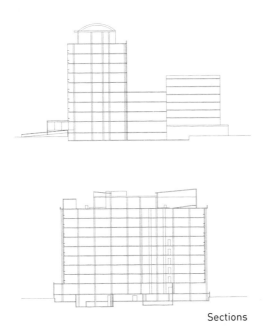

Sections

A-23
Ministère de l'Education Nationale et de la Santé

Design period: 1936
Location: Rio de Janeiro, Brazil
Status: Built

The designer is the architecture committee represented by Oscar Niemeyer. Le Corbusier participated in the project as an advisor. It relies on the sunshade system on the surface and stilts at the bottom to solve sunshade problems. The first floor of the building incorporates the entrance and makeshift parking lots. The second floor houses exhibition halls, the auditorium, executive halls, and other areas. The whole building is a slab-type building supported by stilts. In the process of Brazil's modern architecture development, Le Corbusier—as an advisor—played an enormous role in designing this architecture.

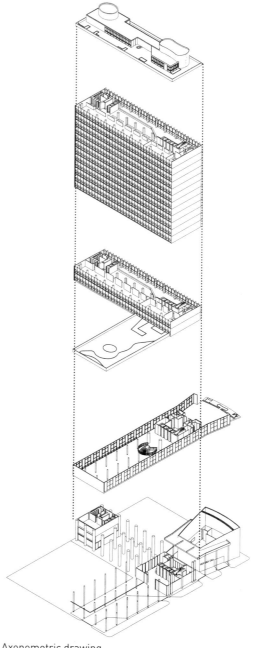

Axonometric drawing

Administration Building 175

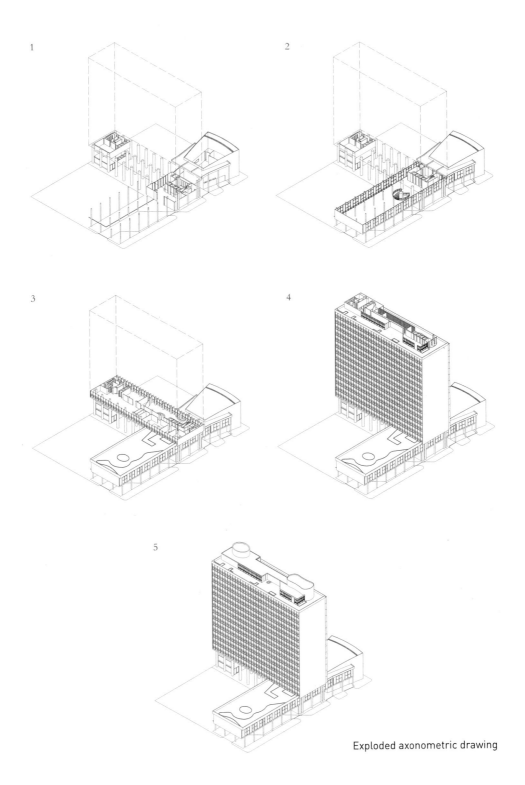

Exploded axonometric drawing

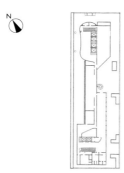

Roof plan

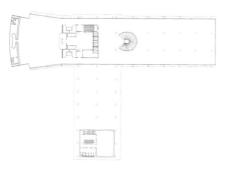

Second-floor plan

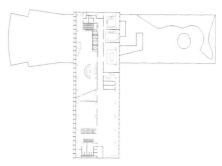

Third-floor plan

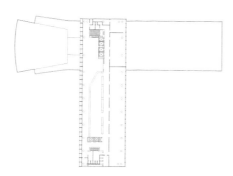

Typical floor plan

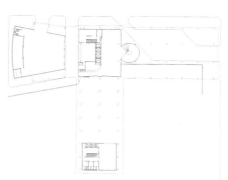

First-floor plan

Administration Building 177

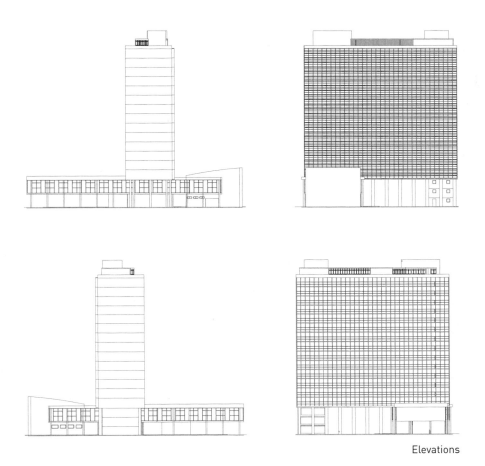

Elevations

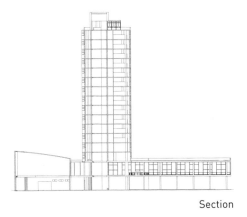

Section

A-34
Station Biologique

Design period: 1939
Location: Roscoff, France
Status: Unbuilt

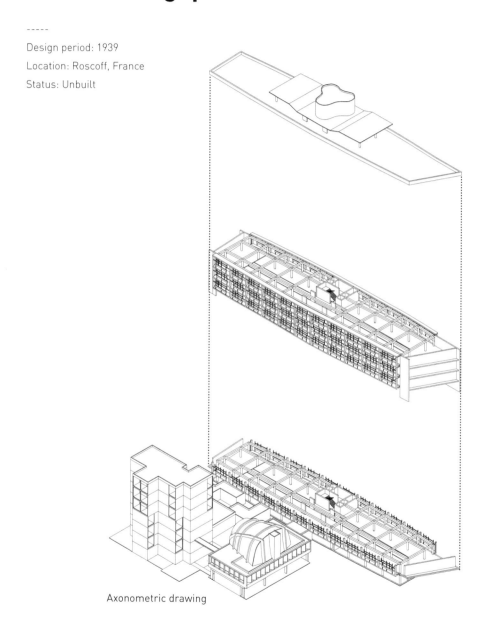

Axonometric drawing

The project includes an aquarium, a studio, and specialist housing. The building at the bottom includes the entrance, a trapezoidal auditorium, and a club. On the right corner of the plan, are the ancient residential buildings on the original base. Le Corbusier designed a slab-type building with a shading system, including facilities like hives, a vertical slim board, and a sunken terrace.

Administration Building 179

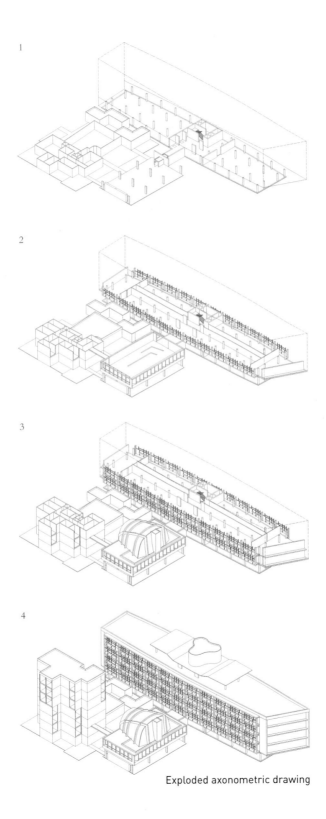

Exploded axonometric drawing

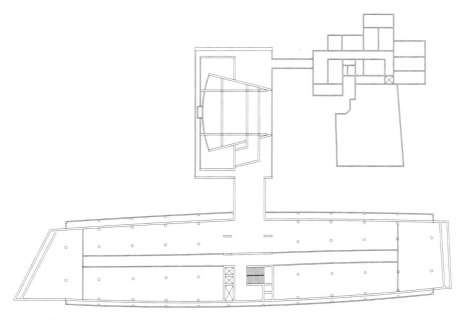

Second-floor plan

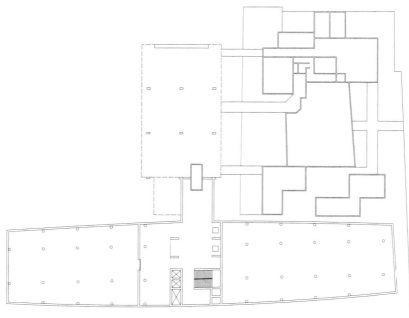

First-floor plan

Administration Building 181

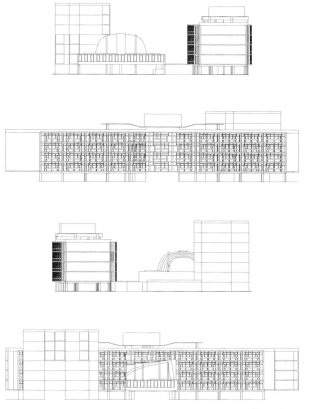

Elevations

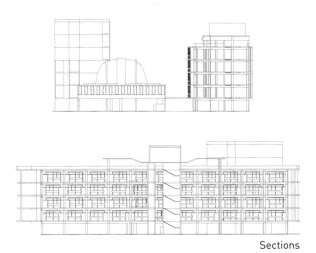

Sections

A-38
Palais des Nations Unies

Design period: 1946
Location: New York, United States
Status: Built

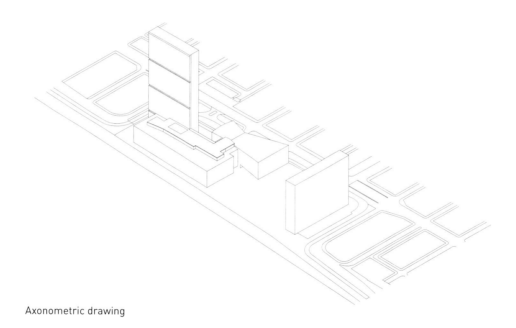

Axonometric drawing

In 1946, architects representing ten countries were invited to participate in the design of Palais des Nations Unies in New York. Liang Sicheng, who was the representative for China, and Le Corbusier, the representative for France, proposed this scheme. The location—gridlike, urban Manhattan. Here, Le Corbusier tried to realize his vision of "La Ville Radiuse" in New York City. The scheme is composed of a high-rise building, namely "Cartesian Skyscraper"—proposed by Le Corbusier—and the attached podium. Its design aims to leave as much space as possible on the ground through vertical development.

Administration Building 183

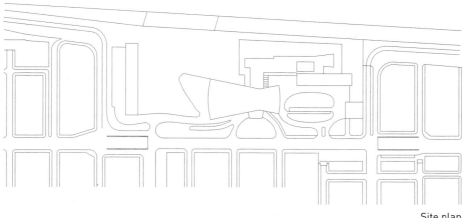
Site plan

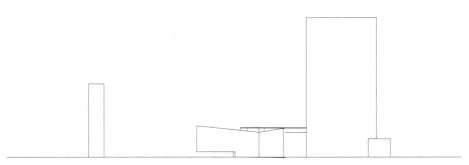
Elevation

A-39
Usine Claude et Duval

Design period: 1946–51
Location: Saint-Dié, France
Status: Built

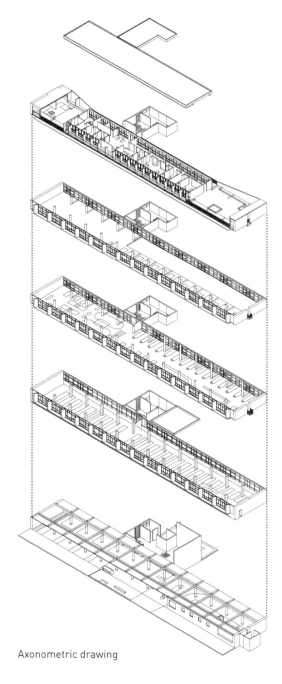

Entrusted by an entrepreneur in Saint-Dié, Le Corbusier built this new factory where he experimented with three architectural techniques. First, the modular system was applied to the façade's concrete sunshade grid, the concrete columns, and the window lattice of the glass walls; the accurate numerical design was carried out according to the "Corbusier red and blue ruler." Second, the garment workshop hall, with partial height, was designed on the section, so that each process of garment making was accommodated reasonably and efficiently. Third, the ceiling, the pipe well, and other places adopted bright and strong colors, which formed a contrast with the concrete texture of the building itself. The main body of the building is above the elevated bottom column and the entrance is located in the middle of the plane. At the two ends of the building are located a garage and a bicycle garage. The gables at both ends of the building were constructed with sandstones reused from the previous building.

Axonometric drawing

Administration Building   185

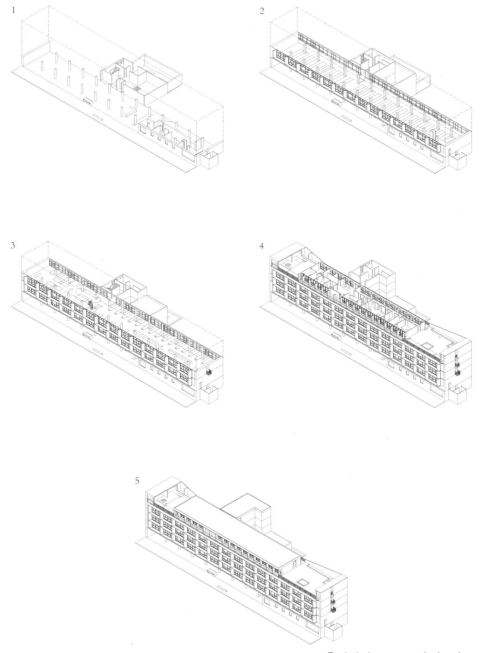

Exploded axonometric drawing

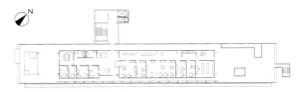

Fifth-floor plan

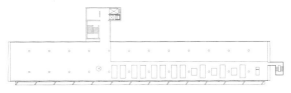

Fourth-floor plan

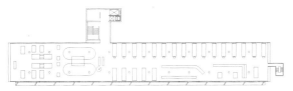

Third-floor plan

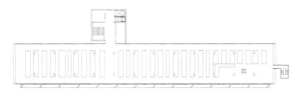

Second-floor plan

First-floor plan

Administration Building

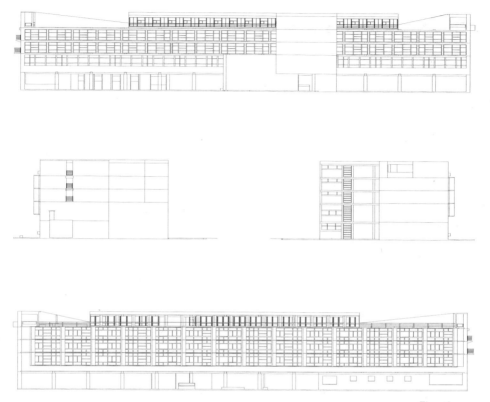

Elevations

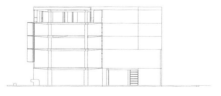

Section

A-48
Palais de l'Assemblée

Design period: 1951–57
Location: Chandigarh, India
Status: Built

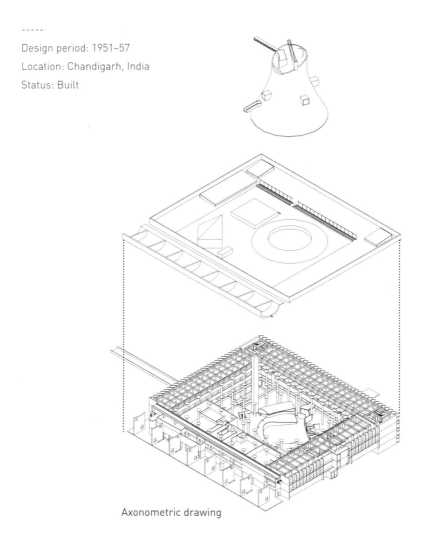

Axonometric drawing

Palais de l'Assemblée has one floor underground and three floors aboveground. The plane is surrounded by a U-shaped office block and a detached porch. The "square" in the middle is the assembly hall of the House of Representatives and the Senate. Le Corbusier deliberately broke from the traditional layout of a large room in the parliament building; through such a design, people from different political parties were provided with a place to gather for mutual consultation and discussion of political affairs. The assembly hall of the House of Representatives is a "tower" composed of a huge circular hyperbolic thin shell. Le Corbusier introduced the prototype of an industrial cooling tower into the parliament building, reflecting his design concept of creatively applying the ideas of existing elements in nature.

Administration Building 189

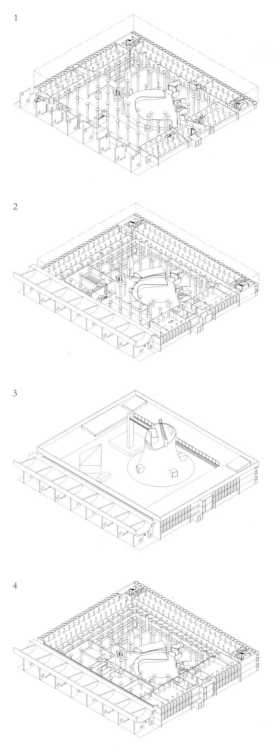

Exploded axonometric drawing

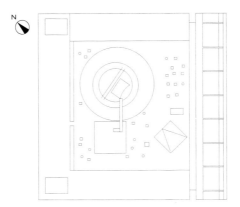

Roof plan

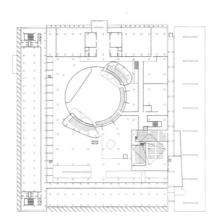

Second-floor plan

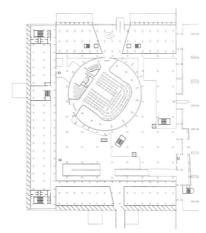

First-floor plan

Administration Building 191

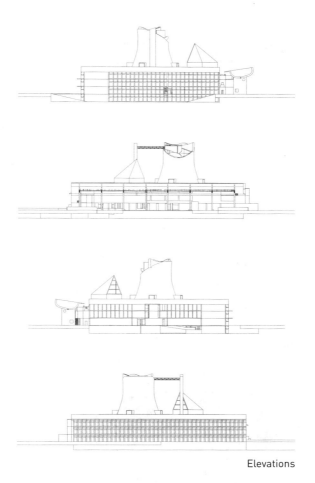

Elevations

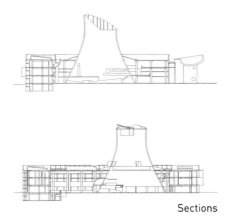

Sections

A-49
Secrétariat, Chandigarh

Design period: 1952–56
Location: Chandigarh, India
Status: Built

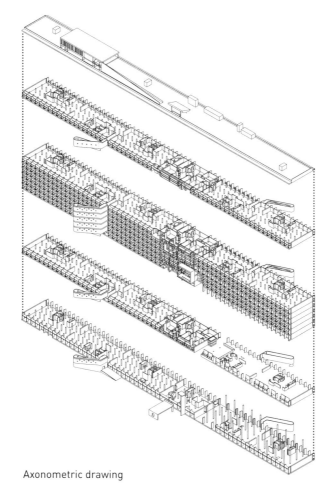

Axonometric drawing

This was a "giant ship" in Chandigarh. The secrétariat has a length of 254 meters (833 feet) and a height of 42 meters (138 feet), which can accommodate more than 3,000 civil servants. The plane is in a thin rectangular shape and is divided into several districts. In the middle, is the ministers' area, and in the northeast and southwest area, are the offices. There are two vertical ramps outside the rectangular plane, which were the passageways for mules to transport materials during construction. The façade of the building has a concrete sunshade grille and a concave balcony to resist the strong local sunshine.

Administration Building 193

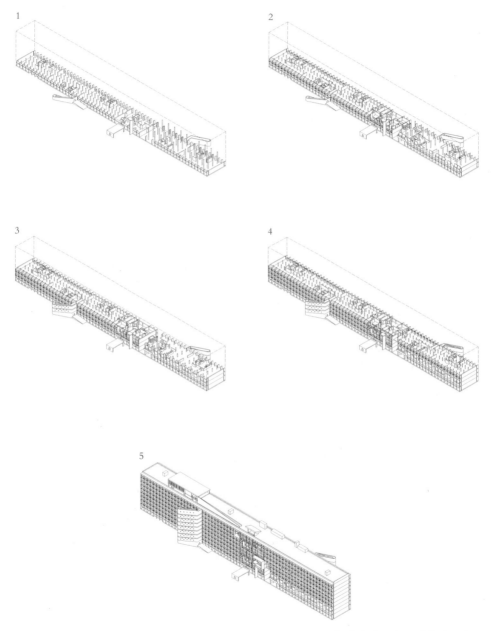

Exploded axonometric drawing

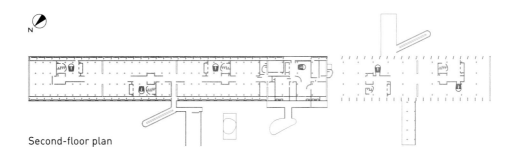

Second-floor plan

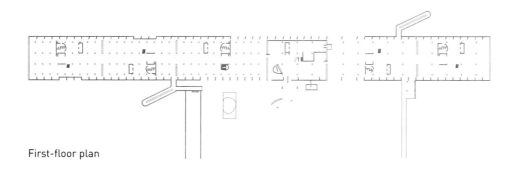

First-floor plan

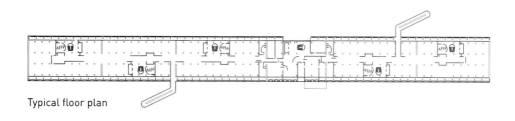

Typical floor plan

Administration Building 195

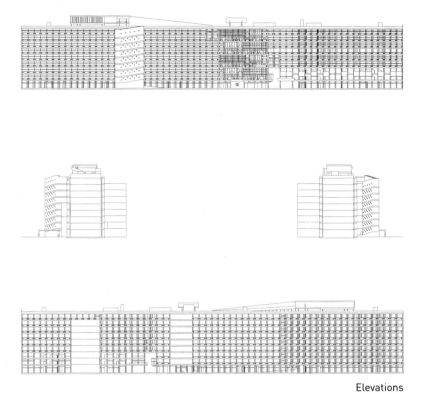

Elevations

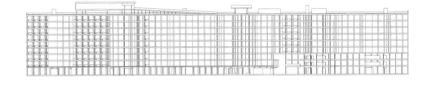

Sections

A-50
Haute Cour

Design period: 1952–56
Location: Chandigarh, India
Status: Built

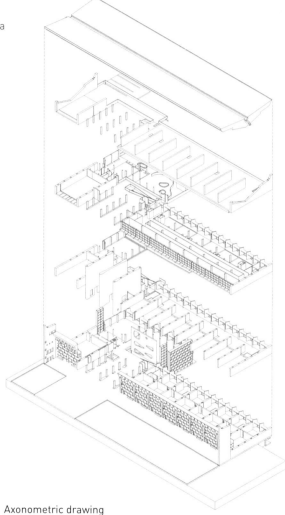

Axonometric drawing

The building has one floor underground and four floors aboveground. It is covered by a huge, concrete inverted-arch roof. The entrance porch of the underground floor is composed of three partition walls covered with shotcrete and the deep part denotes the ramp leading to the upper floor. The dimensions of each concrete grid on the façade are designed according to the modular system, which ensures the unity of all parts in the overall composition. The first floor is for the grand court and open hall; the second floor is for the lawyers' and judges' offices (in small compartments); the third floor is for offices, archives, and the dining room; and the fourth floor, with an umbrella roof, has a terrace.

Administration Building   197

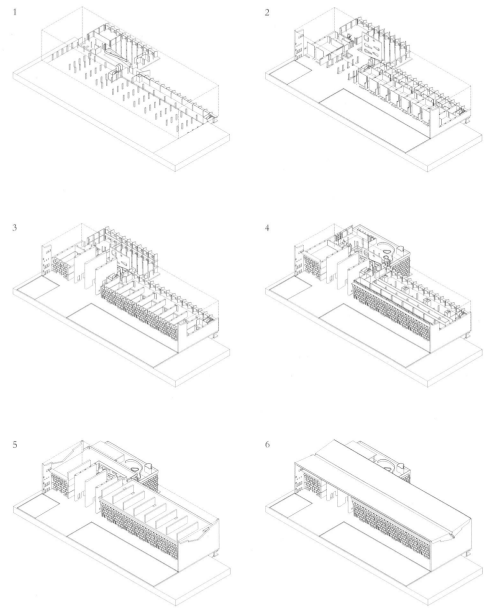

Exploded axonometric drawing

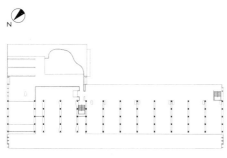

Fourth-floor plan

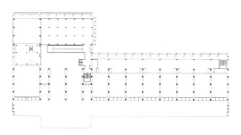

Second-floor plan

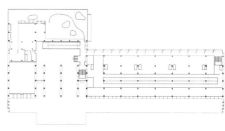

Third-floor plan

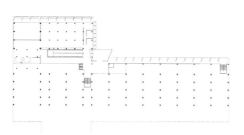

Basement floor plan

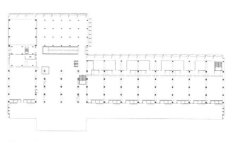

First-floor plan

Administration Building 199

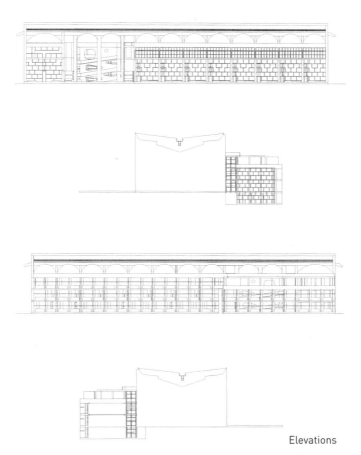

Elevations

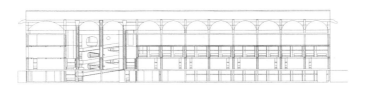

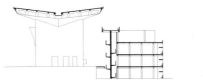

Sections

A-53
Palais des Filateurs

Design period: 1954–57
Location: Ahmedabad, India
Status: Built

The building base is located in a garden near the river. A long ramp on the west façade leads pedestrians directly to the office floor. There are almost no windows on the north and south façades of the building and the east and west façades utilize sunshade grids. In the middle of the plane, is the elevator, and the concrete frame structure enables the indoor space to be freely arranged. The first floor stipulates the entrance, office, dining room, and kitchen, among other areas. The dining room and kitchen are outside the square plane of the main body and are located in the southeast area. The second floor contains the offices and meeting rooms, and the third floor is sectioned for the open hall and the assembly hall.

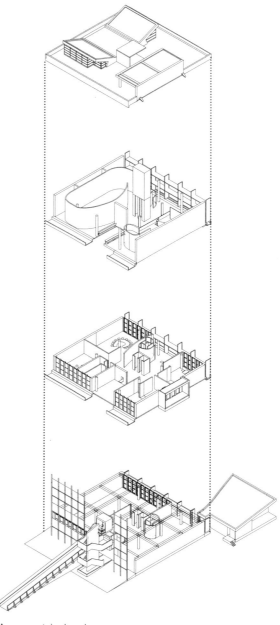

Axonometric drawing

Administration Building 201

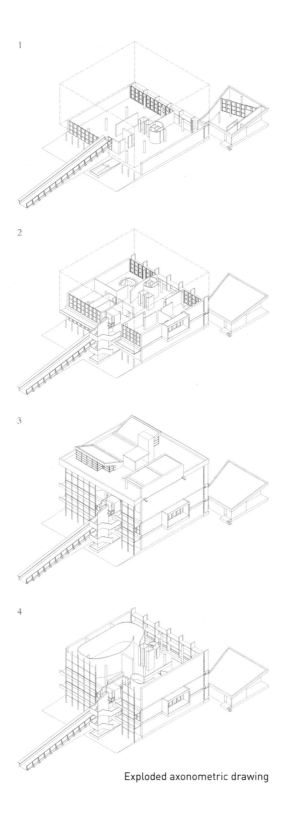

Exploded axonometric drawing

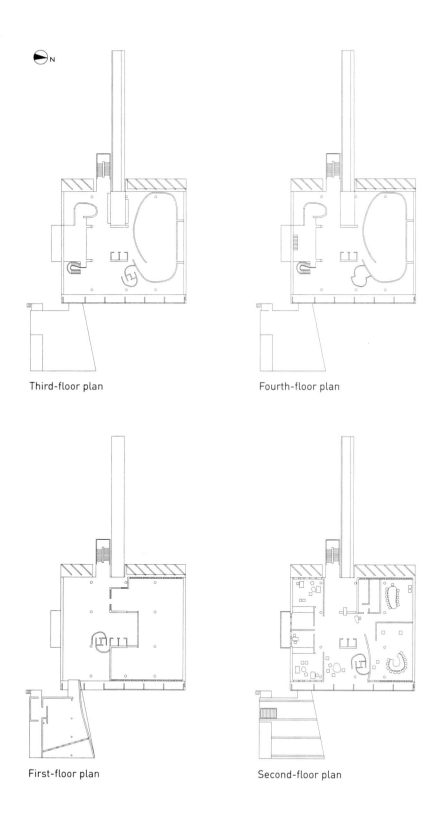

Administration Building 203

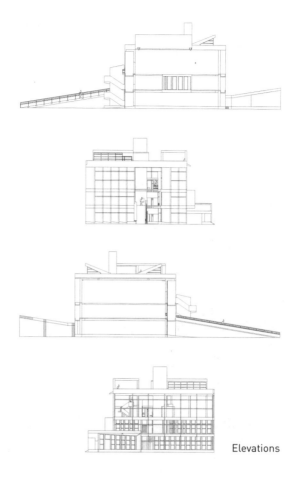

Elevations

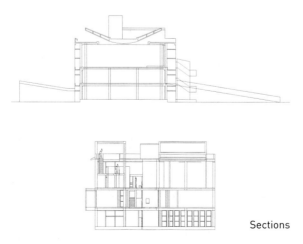

Sections

A-62
Extensions of Haute Cour

Design period: 1960–65
Location: Chandigarh, India
Status: Built

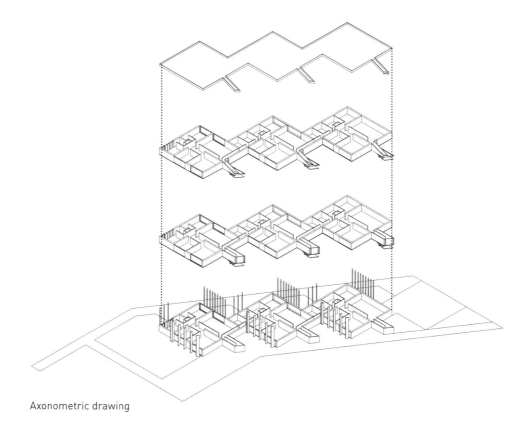

Axonometric drawing

The base is located on the east of the grand court of Chandigarh, with an archives repository and offices. Le Corbusier paid more attention to the design of these subsidiary buildings in order to maintain a unified relationship with the whole building group as much as possible. The building adopts a standard, square plane that can extend to the north. The partition walls in four directions divide the space into several main compartments and connect with the adjacent units through one corner of the building. The staircase is outside the square plane and a small courtyard is enclosed between the two standard units.

Administration Building 205

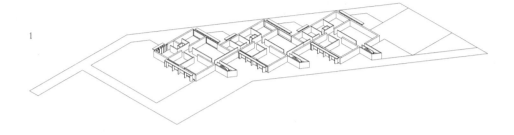

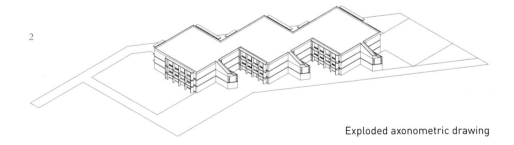

Exploded axonometric drawing

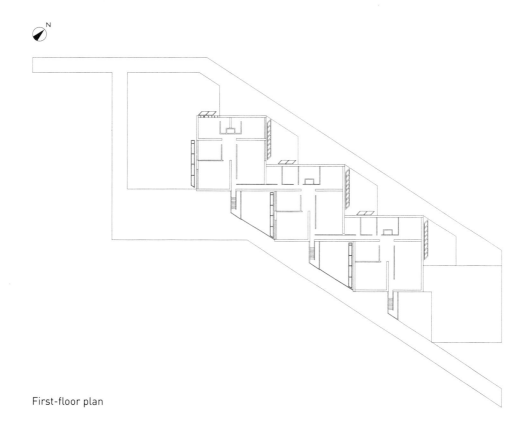

First-floor plan

Administration Building 207

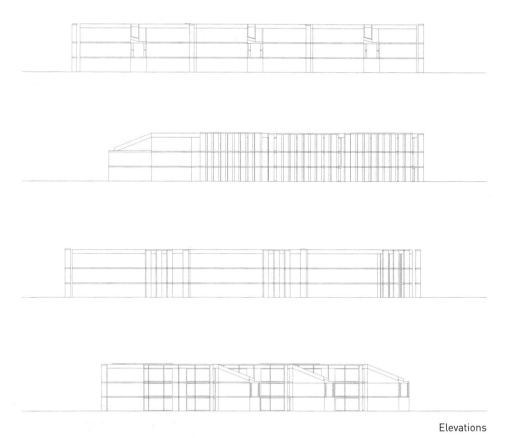

Elevations

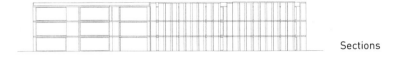

Sections

A-69
Olivetti, Centre de Calculs Électroniques

Design period: 1963–64
Location: Rho, Italy
Status: Unbuilt

This is a building complex that can accommodate more than 4,000 staff, consisting of two scientific research buildings and a workshop on the ground floor. The workshop is divided into three standard square planes. From the roof plane, the internal units are arranged in a square spiral, and four internal staircases are connected to the upper and lower floors. On the top of the workshop, are the roof garden and restroom facilities. This was an experiment on the use of the square spiral layout that was also used in Musée à Croissance Illimitée (project 33); they share a common theme that can be standardized along the existing framework.

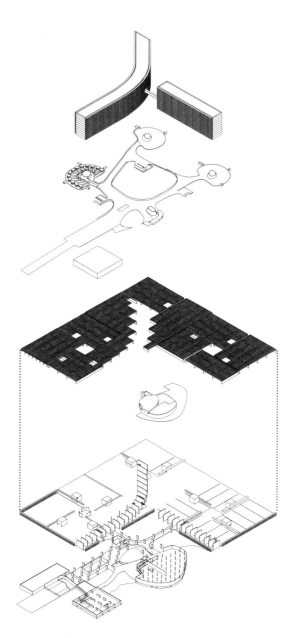

Axonometric drawing

Administration Building 209

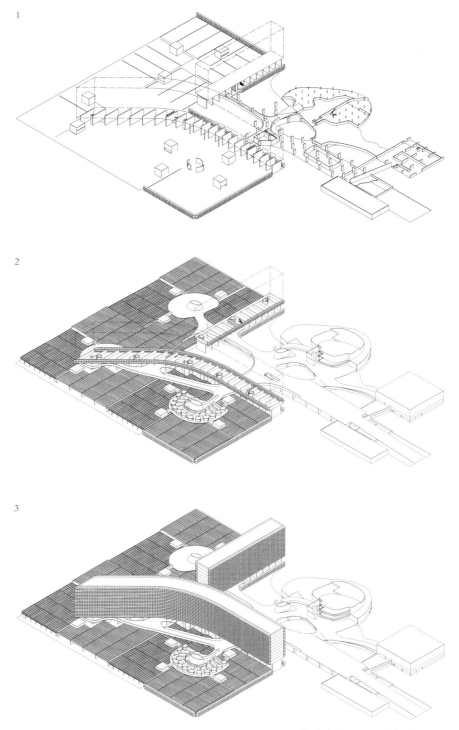

Exploded axonometric drawing

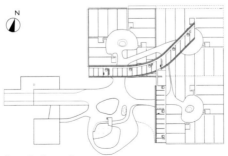

Fourth-floor plan

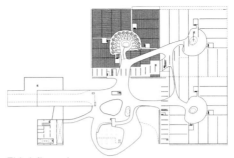

Third-floor plan

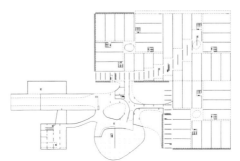

Second-floor plan

First-floor plan

Administration Building 211

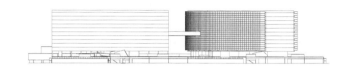

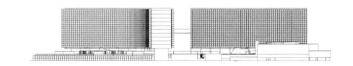

Elevations

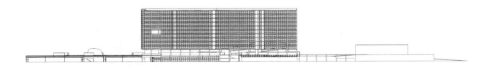

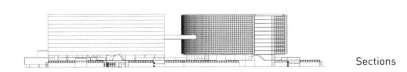

Sections

A-75
Palais des Congrès, Strasbourg

Design period: 1964
Location: Strasbourg, France
Status: Unbuilt

The whole building is composed of a square block and a large ramp running directly from the second floor to the roof. The first floor is for the conference halls, entrance reception areas, and offices of different sizes. The second floor is for leisure and entertainment spaces, such as a library, bar, and salon. The third floor is for the assembly hall, designed to accommodate a large number of people. An escalator connects each floor. The overall composition is based on the free plane brought about by the framework. The large ramp on the north of the building is supported by a concrete load-bearing wall on the ground floor, connecting the second floor, the third floor, and the roof. This was a common method used by Le Corbusier in public buildings—that is, apart from the vertical transportation center in the center of the building, a ramp or stairs is designed for the outside of the building, such as the ramps at Secrétariat, Chandigarh (project 49), and Pavillon d'Exposition ZHLC, Zurich (project 72).

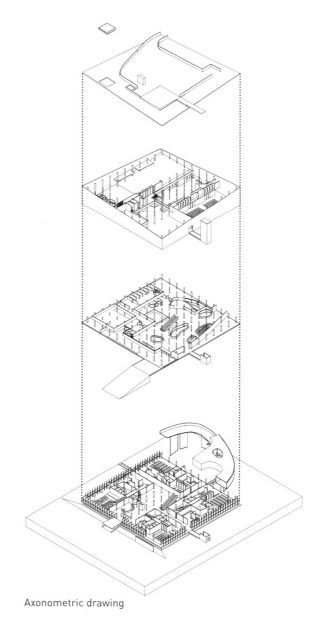

Axonometric drawing

Administration Building 213

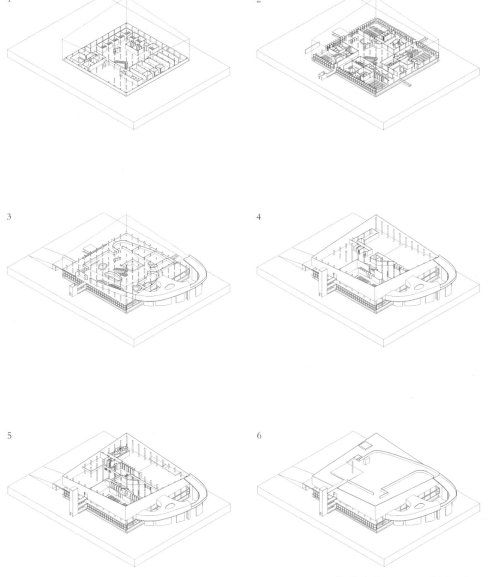

Exploded axonometric drawing

214

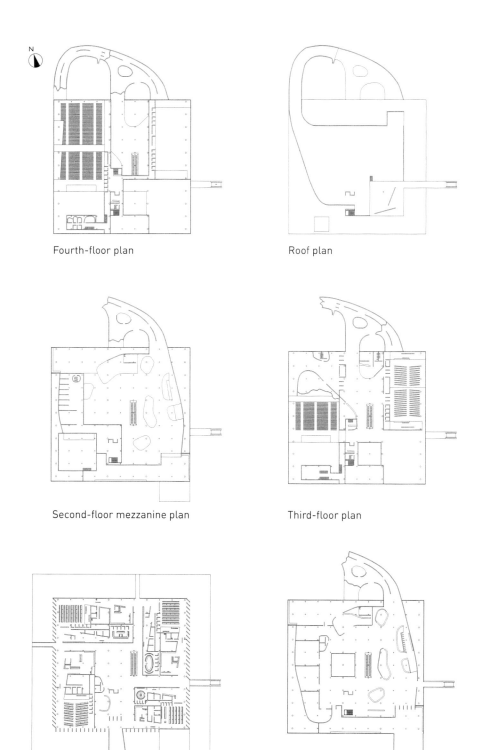

Fourth-floor plan

Roof plan

Second-floor mezzanine plan

Third-floor plan

First-floor plan

Second-floor plan

Administration Building 215

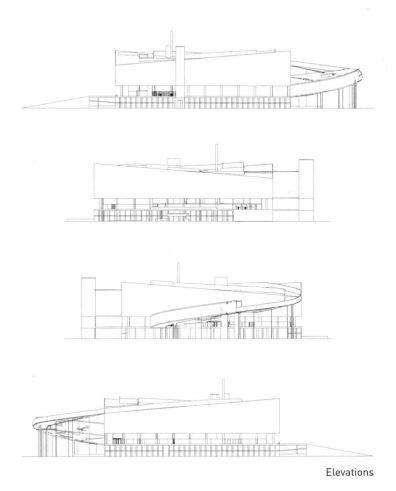

Elevations

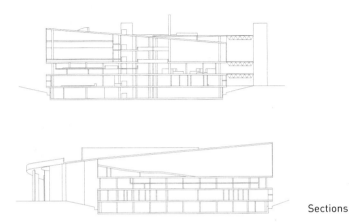

Sections

A-76
Ambassade de France, Brasilia

Design period: 1964–65
Location: Brasilia, Brazil
Status: Unbuilt

The project is a building complex, mainly composed of embassy residences and embassy office buildings. The selected project details the ambassador's residence. The first floor locates the entrance, kitchen, front hall, and servant room; the second floor stages the dining room and living room; the third floor locates the bedroom suite; and the fourth floor hosts the entertainment room, children's room, and study. The plane is square. The east and west façades of the building are equipped with sunshade grids, which are integrated into a square block. There is a large ramp on the east side, which directly connects the first floor and the second floor.

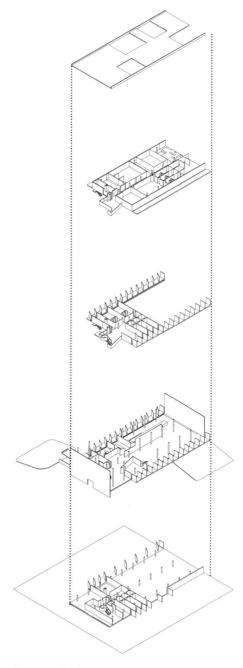

Axonometric drawing

Administration Building 217

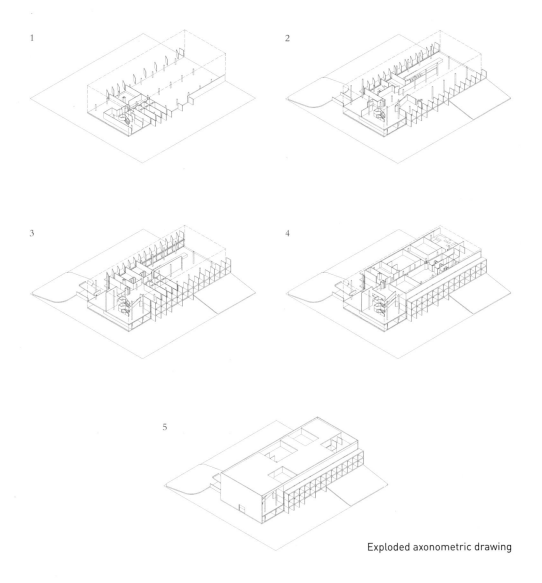

Exploded axonometric drawing

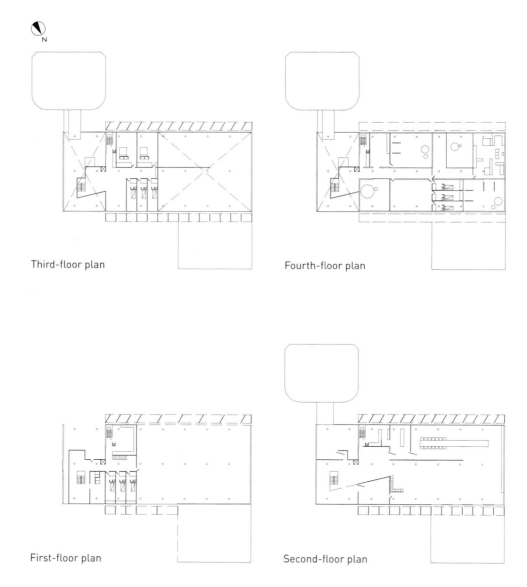

Third-floor plan

Fourth-floor plan

First-floor plan

Second-floor plan

Administration Building 219

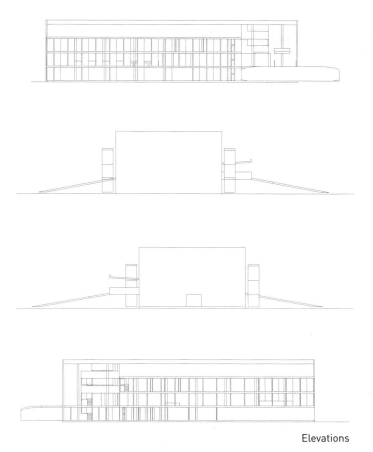

Elevations

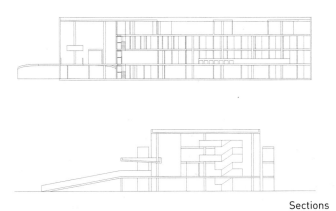

Sections

MUSEUM

B-08
Mundaneum, Musée Mondial (museum)

Design period: 1929
Location: Geneva, Switzerland
Status: Unbuilt

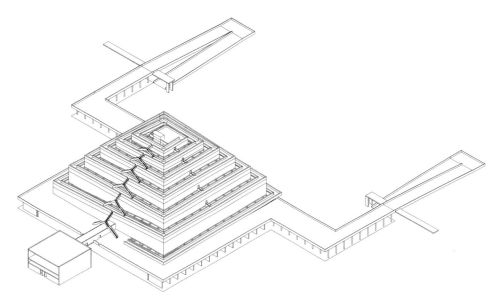

Partial axonometric drawing

This design is for the plan of Mundaneum, Musée Mondial (museum). As a branch of the Mundaneum in Brussels, Belgium, the museum is a world-class scientific statelessness exhibition center designed for the people of the world. It hosts displays on famous people from every era, as well as their works. The three focal elements of this center are works, time, and place. In order to present these three elements simultaneously, Le Corbusier designed three corridors with no partition, but instead, with a ramp that rises in a spiral. People take the elevator to the top directly, then enter into the museum along the ramp. The concept of the unfinished museum is the ideal "Babel Tower" that Le Corbusier designed in the twentieth century, but it too was not completed. The key words of the plan are "spiral" and "ramp." Le Corbusier creatively used the spiral in his design of museums, particularly in his series associated with the Musée à Croissance Illimitée (project 33).

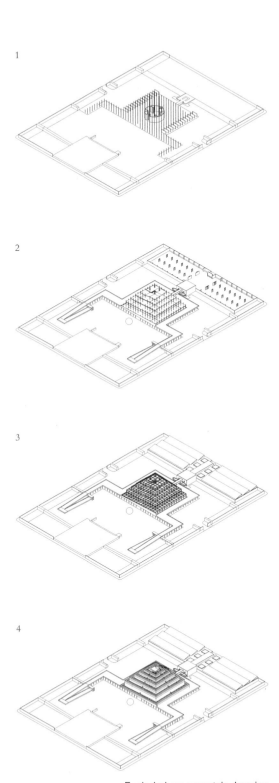

Exploded axonometric drawing

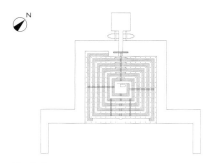

Roof plan

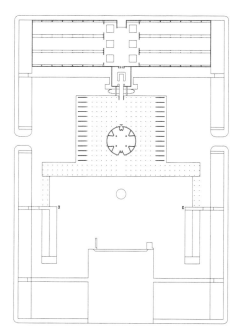

First-floor plan

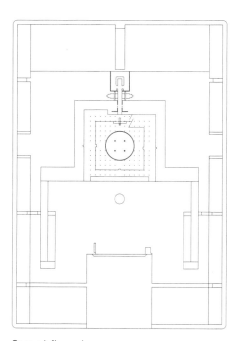

Second-floor plan

Museum 223

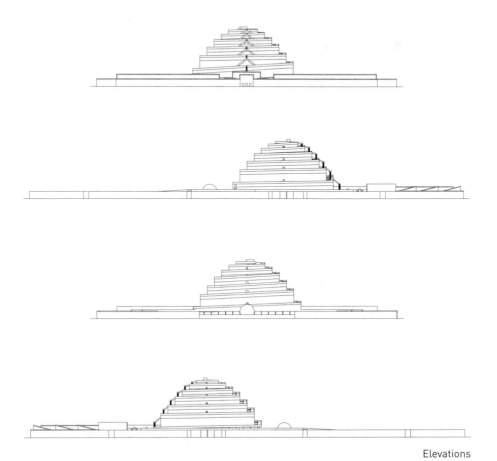

Elevations

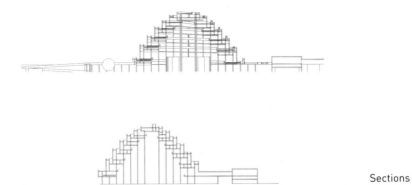

Sections

B-14
Musée d'Art Contemporain

Design period: 1931
Location: Paris, France
Status: Unbuilt

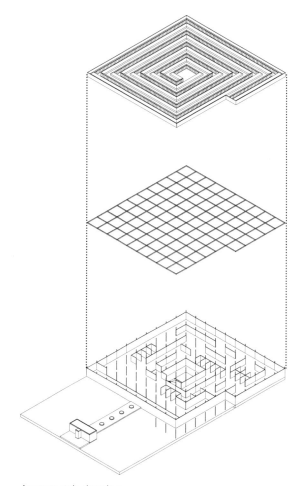

Axonometric drawing

Designed in 1931, Musée d'Art Contemporain was intended for Paris, but was never built. And like in Le Corbusier's other museum projects, one of the core topics was the typical challenge created by the needs of an expandable exhibition hall, and an organization of the exhibition space beyond a technical level. The solution: 7-by-7 standard columns and spiral lines—Le Corbusier designed a long underground corridor. As Le Corbusier highlighted, people don't usually see the façade of a museum, but what they *do* see will always usually be the exhibition walls, and the exhibition space expanded by the spiral lines— as shown in the roof plan, these exhibition halls spiral outward from the center. The incident angle of the skylight can be adjusted, thus controlling lighting.

Museum 225

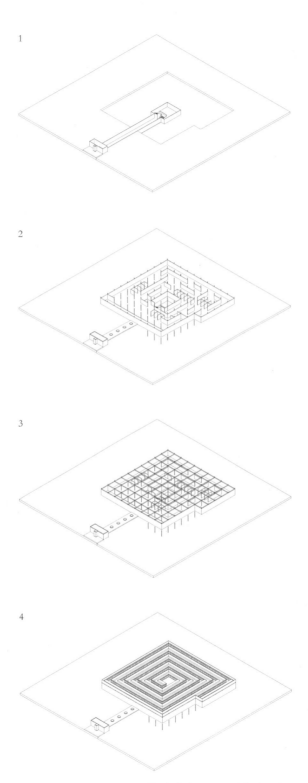

Exploded axonometric drawing

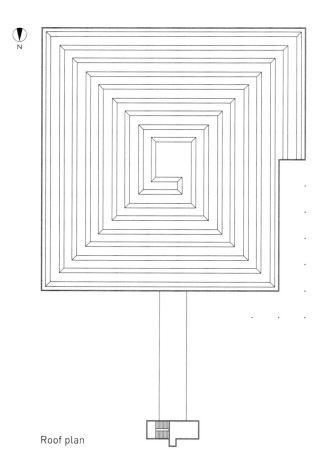

Roof plan

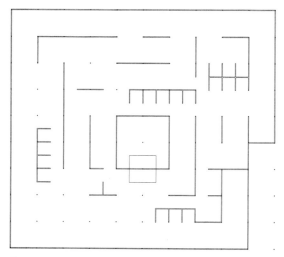

First-floor plan

Museum 227

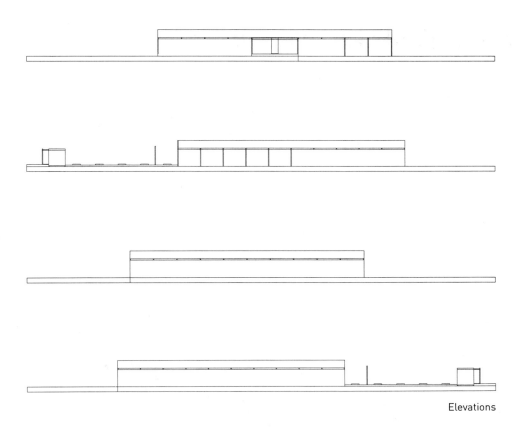

Elevations

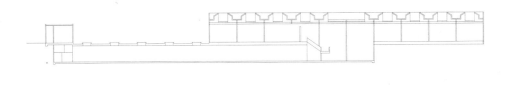

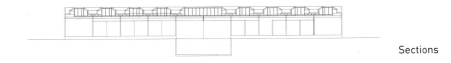

Sections

B-15
Musée des Artistes Vivants

Design period: 1931
Location: Paris, France
Status: Unbuilt

This is an unbuilt museum plan that isn't in *Le Corbusier Complete Works*. The building has two layers, with a four-by-four pattern. With a double-flight staircase on one side, the middle hall is a square, cantilevered space surrounded by exhibition walls. The appearance of the museum reflects the style of the works in his later career, such as Musée National d'Art Occidental (project 56). Both are a floating box supported by stilts.

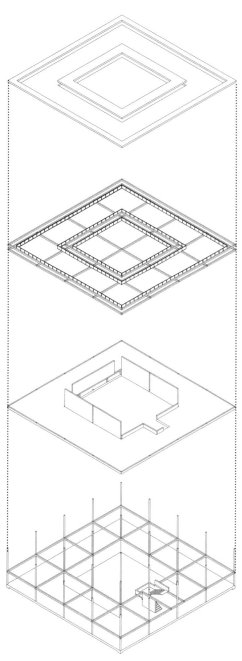

Axonometric drawing

Museum 229

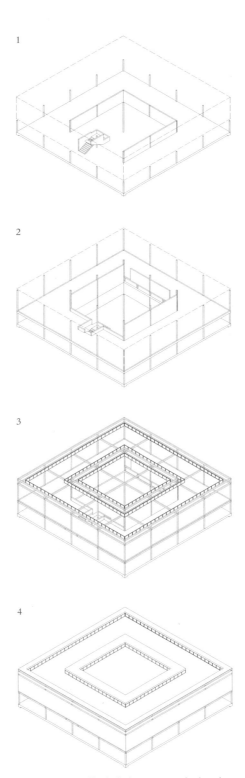

Exploded axonometric drawing

Roof plan

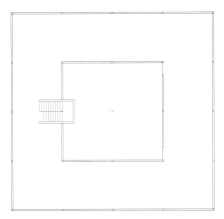

Second-floor plan

First-floor plan

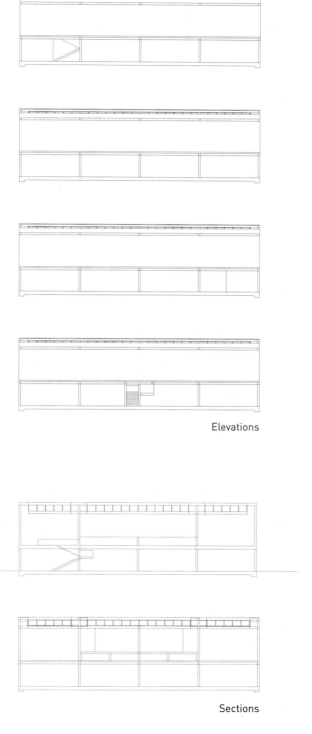

Elevations

Sections

B-20
Musée de la Ville et de l'État

Design period: 1935
Location: Paris, France
Status: Unbuilt

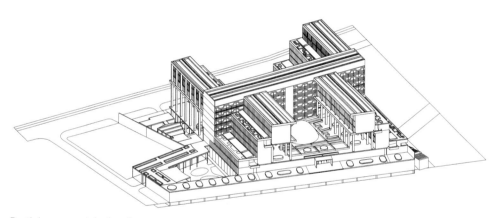

Partial axonometric drawing

Le Corbusier participated in a competition held by the Expo Preparatory Committee. The project required designing a national museum and a Paris city museum on the same site. With a thin building in the middle, the plan relies on the slab-type building with elevators and ramps to design two museums, as required by the competition. In the plan, the north situates the Paris city museum (Musée de la Ville), while the south locates the national museum (Musée de l'État). The two museums are deliberately separate, with separate entrances. Each museum uses cascading blocks to organize the hall. Compared with other museum projects, this work is a serious recognition of Paris's city status; the competition requirements regarding compositions of mass and space were also complex.

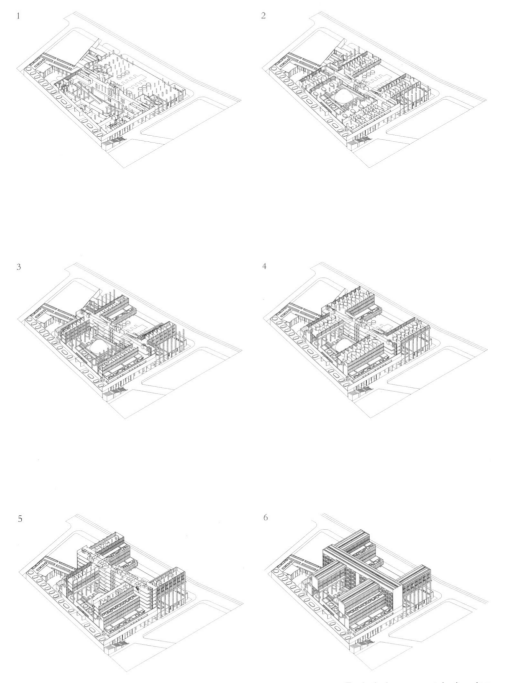

Exploded axonometric drawing

234

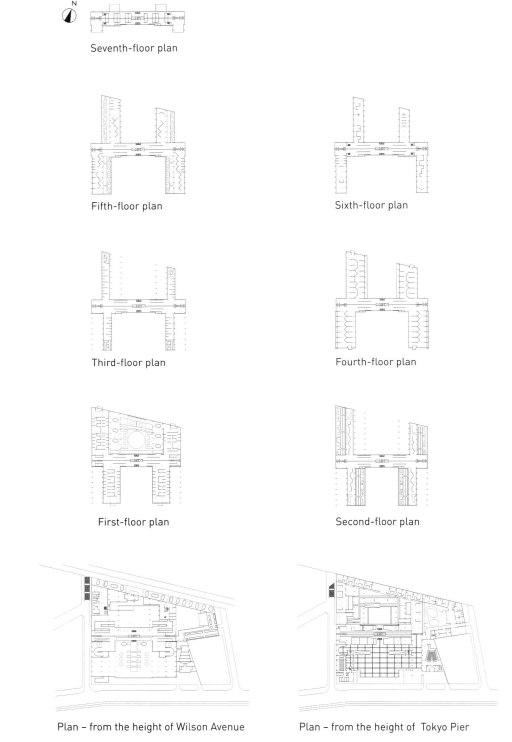

Seventh-floor plan

Fifth-floor plan

Sixth-floor plan

Third-floor plan

Fourth-floor plan

First-floor plan

Second-floor plan

Plan – from the height of Wilson Avenue

Plan – from the height of Tokyo Pier

Museum 235

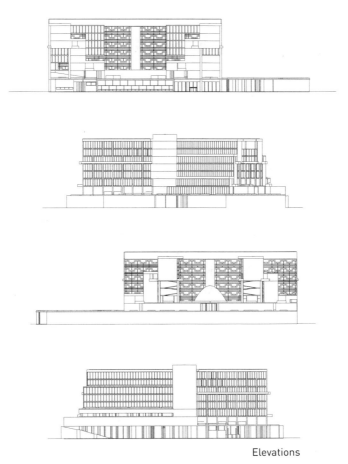

Elevations

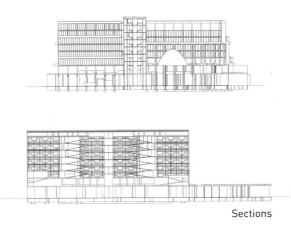

Sections

B-33
Musée à Croissance Illimitée

Design period: 1939
Location: None
Status: Unbuilt

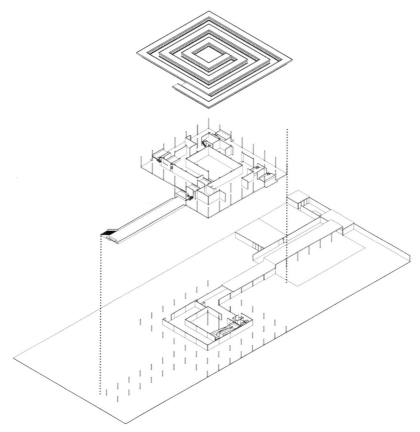

Axonometric drawing

It uses standard architectural elements like columns, beams, and floors. The design is a floating box supported by stilts. Visitors enter the main exhibition hall from the center of the building on the first floor, then gradually visit each of the exhibition halls along the spiral partition walls. The layout of the exhibition halls on the second floor are in the " 卍 " shape. The four beam heads under the roof façade are reserved for exhibition expansion, or unique façade effects.

Museum 237

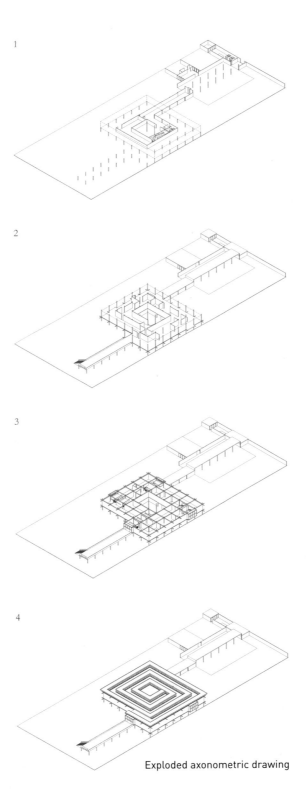

Exploded axonometric drawing

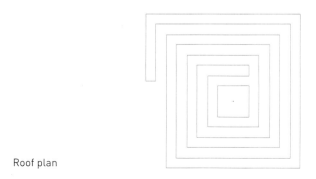

Roof plan

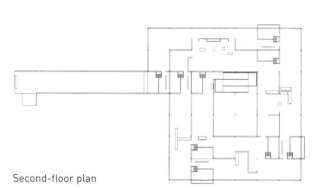

Second-floor plan

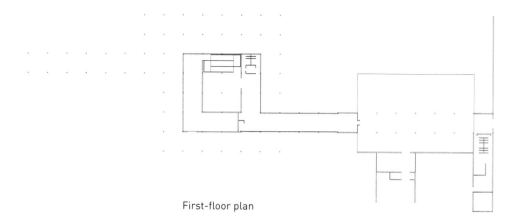

First-floor plan

Museum

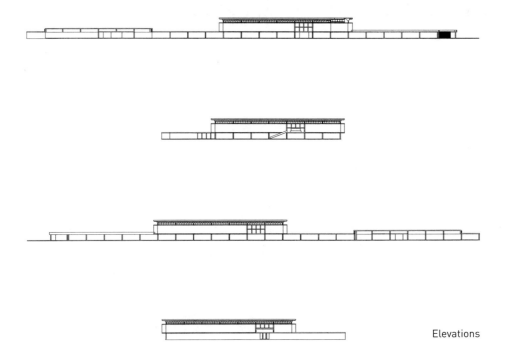

Elevations

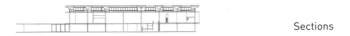

Sections

B-40
Musée et Lotissement Delaunay

Design period: 1946
Location: Delaunay's Lotissement
Status: Unbuilt

This plan hasn't been included in *Le Corbusier Complete Works*. It's a small, personal museum that was not built. The plan is a two-by-two square layout with a beam-column framework structure. The interior is a one-room space with two floors. The lighting aspect of the design results in the roof adopting high windows. There are two points worth mentioning: one is the middle column in the center of the plan that looks over the whole plan—its expression has been enlarged and presented in the works of later Japanese architects like Kazuo Shinohara. The other, is a protruding, exposed beam head on the building façade—the design Le Corbusier used in works like Musée à Croissance Illimitée (project 33) takes future museum extension into consideration, however, as a façade element of a single building, the beam-column structure is expressive.

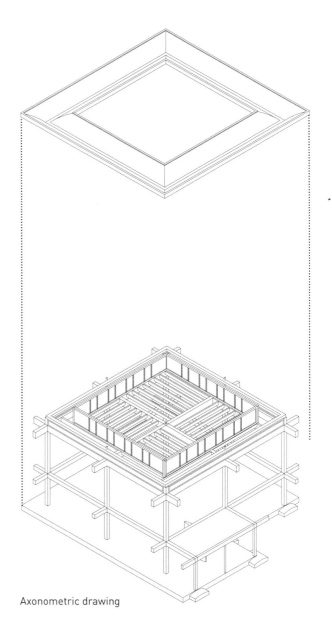

Axonometric drawing

Museum 241

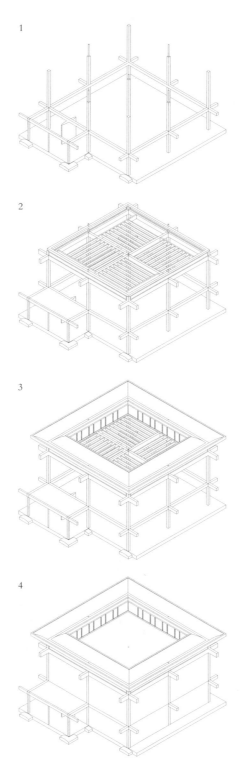

Exploded axonometric drawing

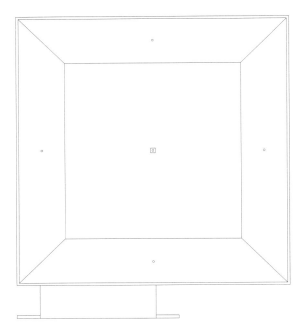

Roof plan

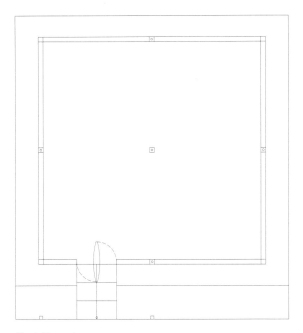

First-floor plan

Museum 243

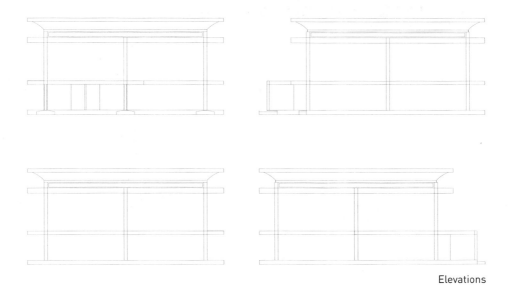

Elevations

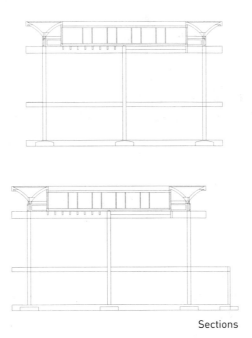

Sections

B-51
Musée de la Connaissance

Design period: 1952
Location: Chandigarh, India
Status: Unbuilt

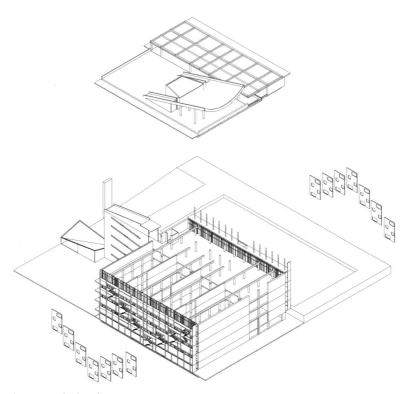

Axonometric drawing

In Le Corbusier's overall plan of Musée de la Connaissance, there is an unfinished museum plan in the administration buildings section. The museum's exhibition area is composed of four high halls—four sections that focus on economic, technological, social, and moral topics. In the plan, there is a movable partition wall to divide the four exhibition spaces. There is also a ramp transportation well on one side of the main space. The most creative place in the plan is a transportation corridor around the exterior of the exhibition space. From Le Corbusier's sketch, it is seen that there is a sunshade system for stronly lit areas. The concrete walls are arranged at a certain angle and the corridor has double-flight stairs connecting all the floors in a cascade style. The corridor is not only the sunshade system and transportation system, but also the corridor and balcony.

Museum   245

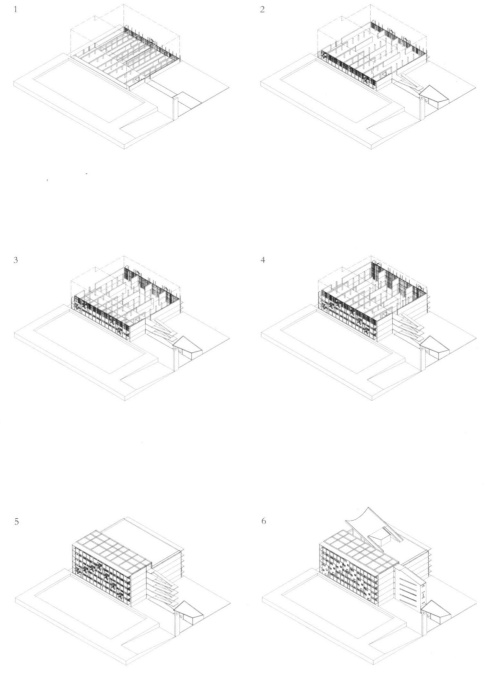

Exploded axonometric drawing

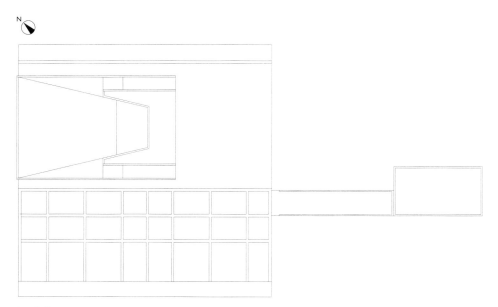

Roof plan

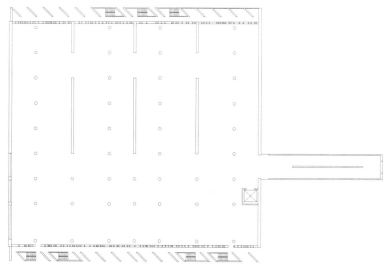

First-floor plan

Museum 247

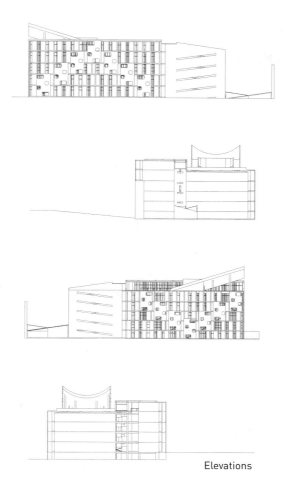

Elevations

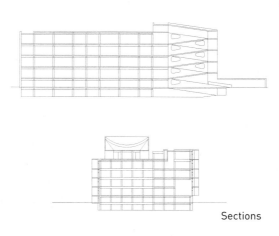

Sections

B-54
Musée, Ahmedabad

Conpletion: 1954–57
Location: Ahmedabad, India
Status: Built

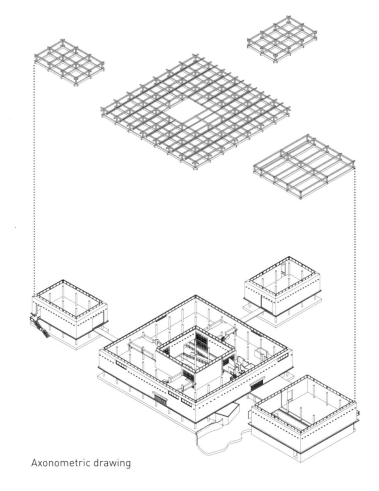

Axonometric drawing

The overall work is composed of a main exhibition hall and three small subsidiary halls. The interior of the main exhibition hall in the middle is in a square spiral layout. In the axonometric drawing, there is a 14-square-meter (45.9-square-foot) atrium in the middle, designed for heat insulation and cooling; visitors can enter the interior of the exhibition hall through the ramp here. There is an empty space between the roof and the interior exhibition hall used for laying wire lines and installing electronic devices. Around the external elevation there is a circle of flower beds. Apart from the natural insulating barrier, the flower beds' exposed concrete becomes one of the elements in the architecture's "magnificent symphony."

Museum <u>249</u>

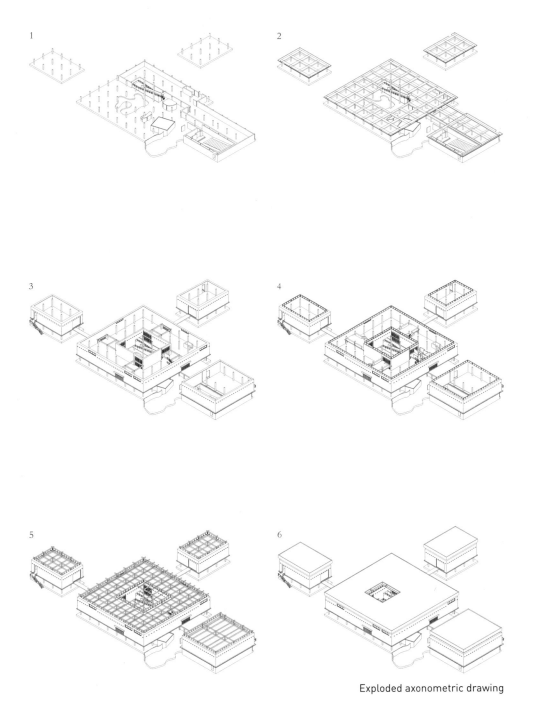

Exploded axonometric drawing

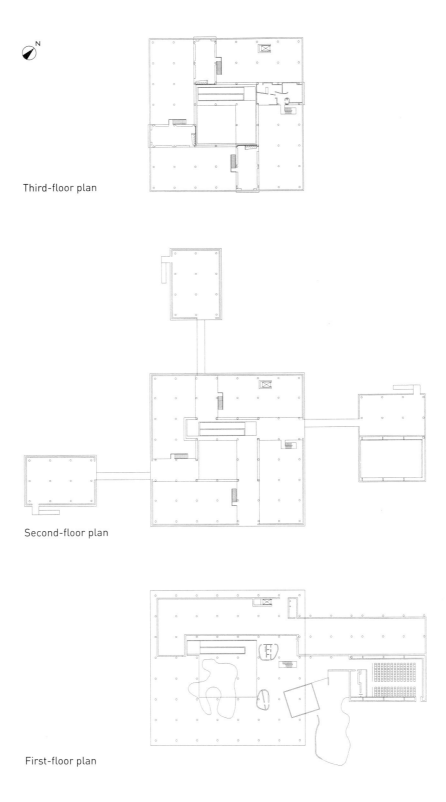

Third-floor plan

Second-floor plan

First-floor plan

Museum 251

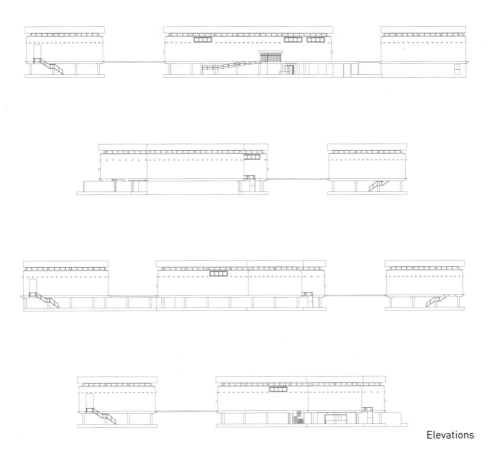

Elevations

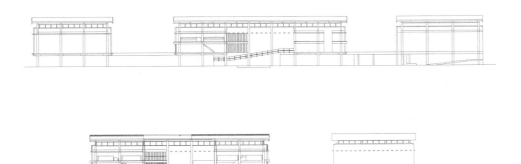

Sections

B-56
Musée National d'Art Occidental

Design period: 1957–59
Location: Tokyo, Japan
Status: Built

This project is located in Tokyo's Ueno Park. The Japanese government entrusted Le Corbusier to design a building for collecting Japanese items during his residence in Paris. Le Corbusier pointed out that the prototype for the plan is Musée à Croissance Illimitée, which he had been researching at that time. The architects on the construction site then were Maekawa Kunio and Sakakula Jyunzou, who used to work in Le Corbusier's firm. The exhibition hall of the work follows the shape of a "卍," and there is a pyramid-like skylight. Under the skylight, there is a high concrete column and a crossbeam, both full of spatial expressions; that's to say, it's the center of the whole building. In addition, the panels hanging on the external elevation of the building are precast concrete slabs inlaid with pebbles, representing exquisite Japanese craftsmanship.

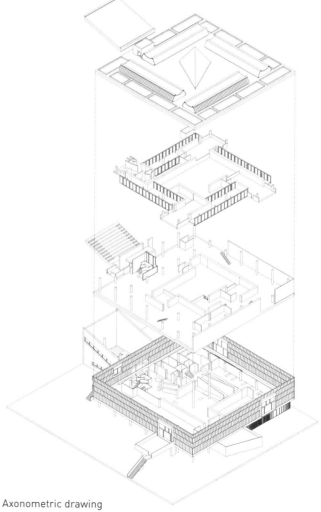

Axonometric drawing

Museum 253

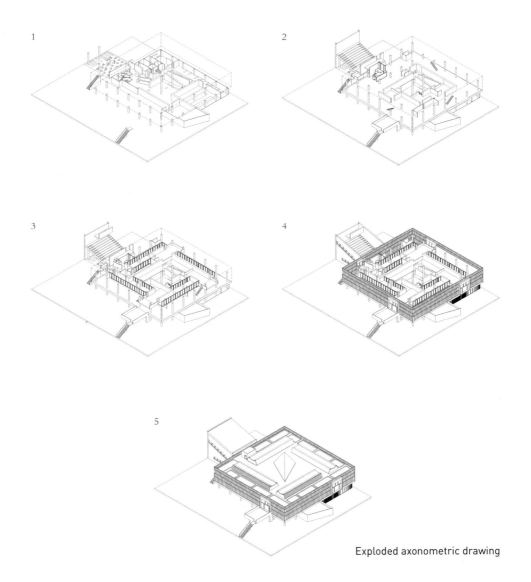

Exploded axonometric drawing

254

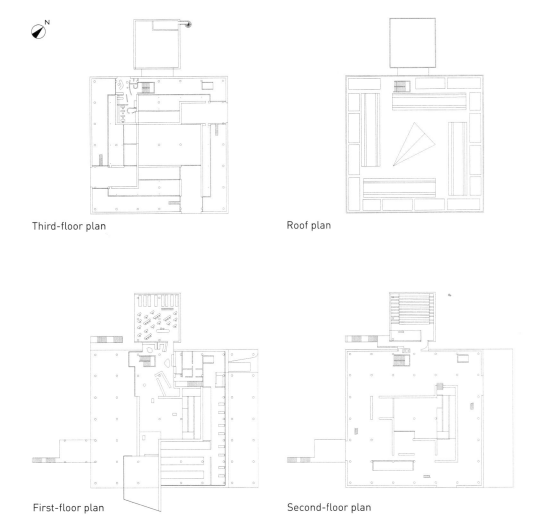

Third-floor plan

Roof plan

First-floor plan

Second-floor plan

Museum

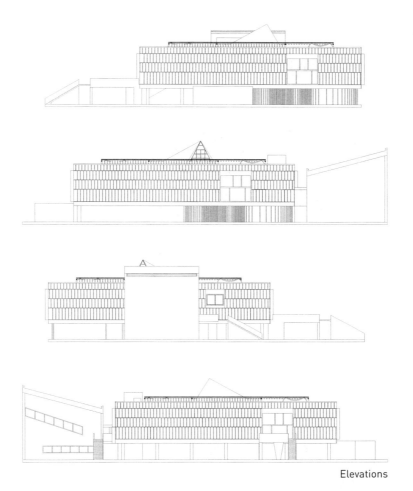

Elevations

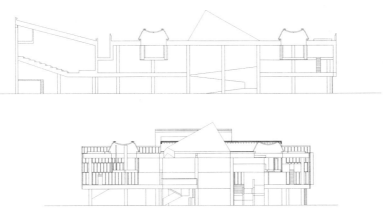

Sections

B-74
Musée, Chandigarh

Design period: 1964–68
Location: Chandigarh, India
Status: Built

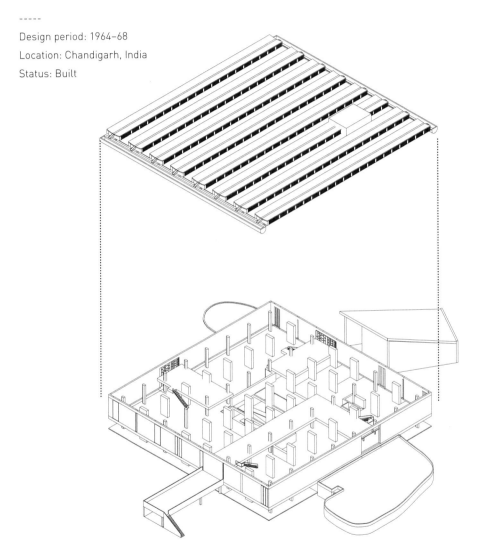

Axonometric drawing

As Le Corbusier said in *Le Corbusier Complete Works*, he has built two similar museums: one is Musée, Ahmedabad, India (project 54), and the other is Musée National d'Art Occidental, Tokyo (project 56). The design of Musée, Chandigarh, originates from the drawing of Musée à Croissance Illimitée (project 33). The difference of Musée, Chandigarh from the two finished museums is the roof design. Eight sunken high-window blocks are also the water grooves through which the water flows to the gutters, perpendicular to the water grooves on both sides.

Museum 257

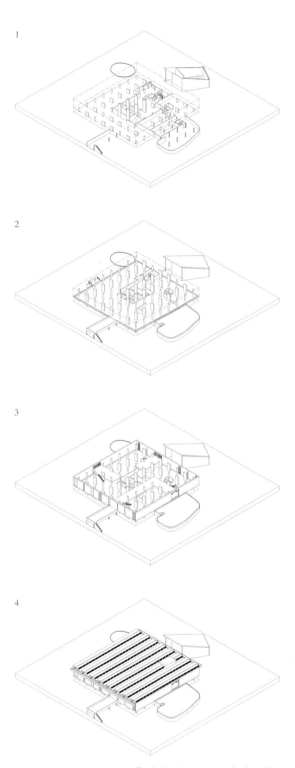

Exploded axonometric drawing

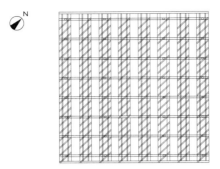

Roof plan

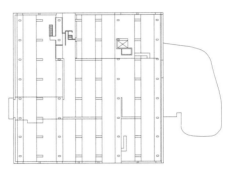

Second-floor plan

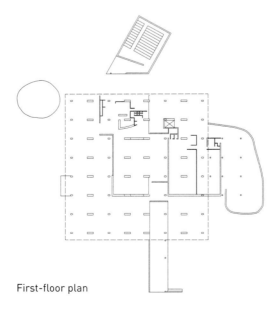

First-floor plan

Museum

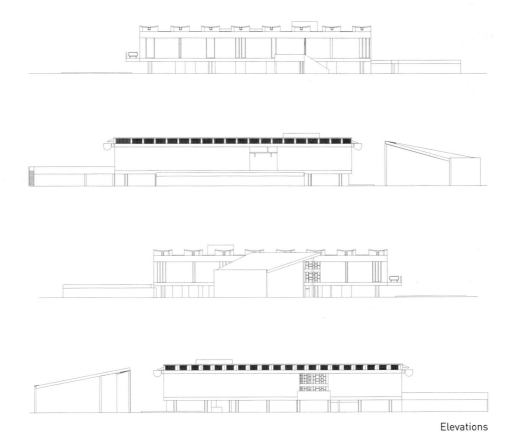

Elevations

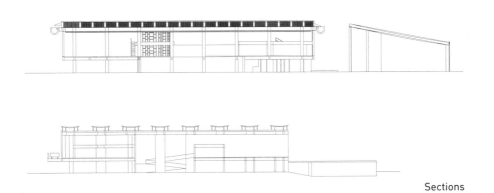

Sections

B-80
Musée du XXe Siècle

Design period: 1965
Location: Paris, France
Status: Unbuilt

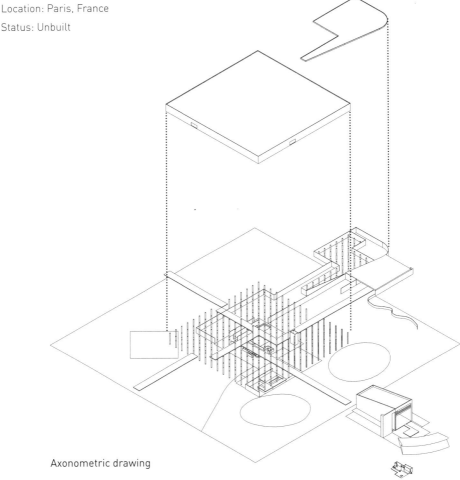

Axonometric drawing

This project is an unfinished plan, still in the preliminary design stage. The museum is supported by stilts at the bottom and the interior is a square spiral museum, similar to Musée à Croissance Illimitée (project 33). On the exterior of the square museum, Le Corbusier set up a subsidiary theater. There are some places without further design. In the preliminary conception sketches, the date June 29, 1965 has been indicated by Le Corbusier; it was the last planning sketch that Le Corbusier drew by himself. His museum projects, from Mundaneum, Musée Mondial (museum) (project 08) to this one, are based on Le Corbusier's decades-long research subject—Musée à Croissance Illimitée.

Museum 261

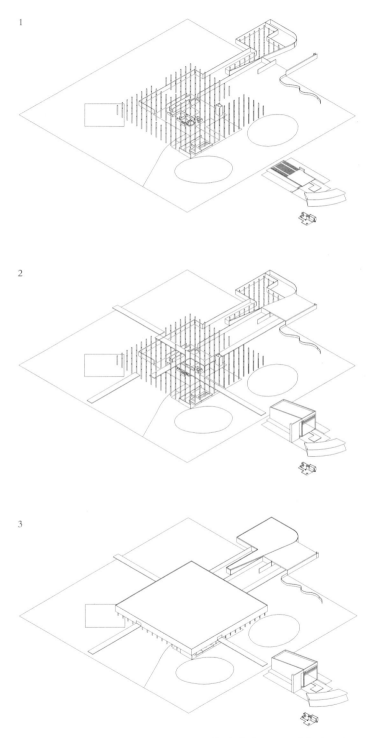

Exploded axonometric drawing

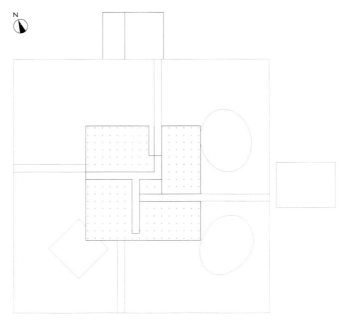

Third-floor plan

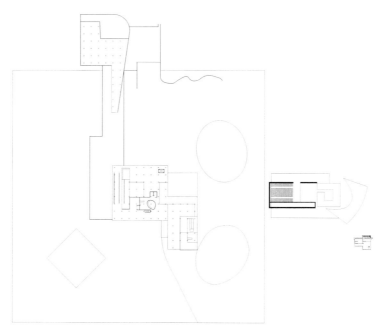

First-floor plan

Museum 263

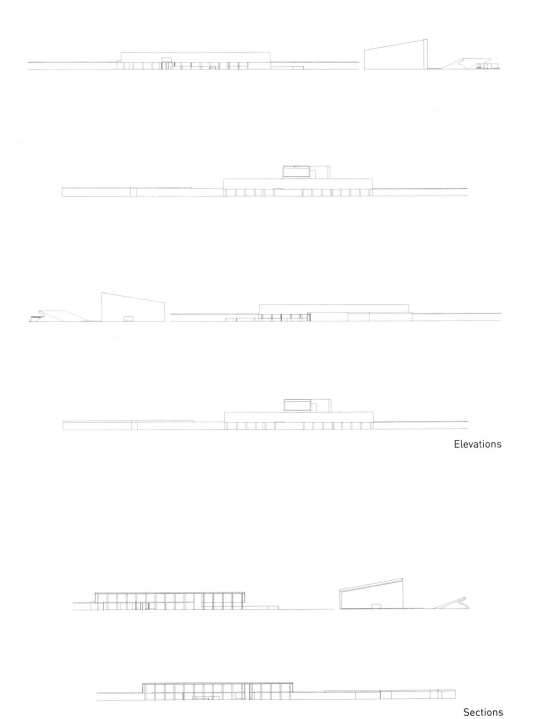

Elevations

Sections

EXHIBITION HALL

C-06
Pavillon Nestlé

Design period: 1928
Location: Paris, France
Status: Built

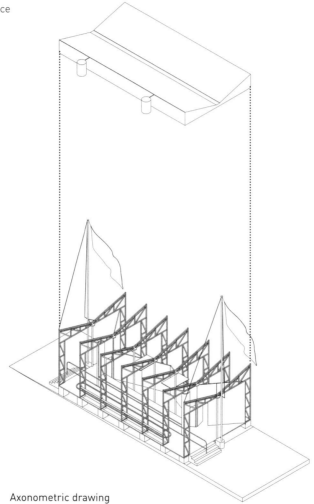

Axonometric drawing

This was a small, removable exhibition booth designed for Nestlé in 1928. The exhibition booth uses a metal framework, composed of seven metal trusses. A straight passageway is set on the side with a road. A marketing exhibition booth with a show window is set on the opposite side of the road. In addition, the architecture itself has a slight height difference. Le Corbusier designed a plan that shows consistent height within the basic components. People can get into and out of the exhibition booth by the stages on both sides of the path.

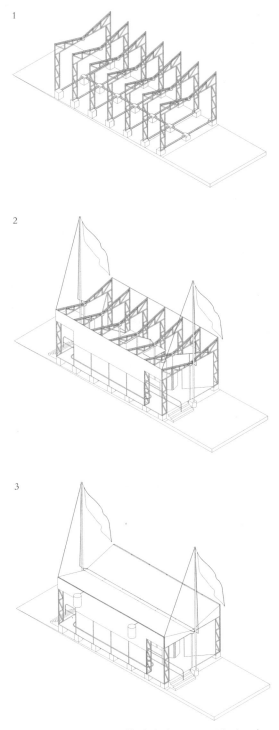

Exploded axonometric drawing

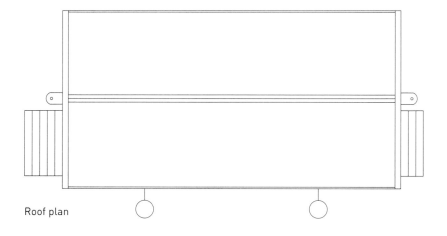
Roof plan

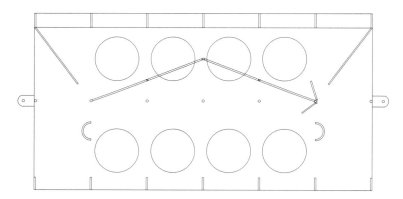
Second-floor plan

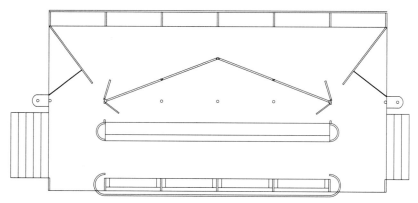
First-floor plan

Exhibition Hall

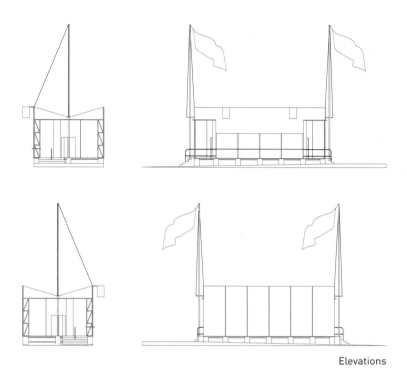

Elevations

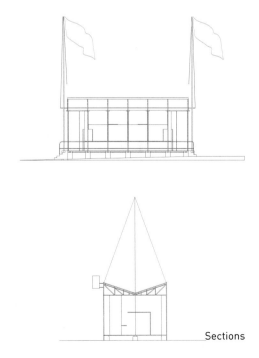

Sections

C-11
Pavillon d'Aviation S.T.A.R.

Design period: 1930
Location: Le Bourge, France
Status: Unbuilt

This plan isn't included in *Le Corbusier Complete Works*. Similar to the previous Pavillon Nestlé (page 264), the plan is a small metal framework booth. The roof trusses are supported by T-shaped and square structural columns. The plan is divided into two parts. In one part, is the office and restroom, and in the other, is the exhibition space. Le Corbusier designed a curved internal roof connected by several curved components and support columns on both sides. In addition, the subsidiary porch at the entrance is composed of flagpoles and flashings, like a sailing ship.

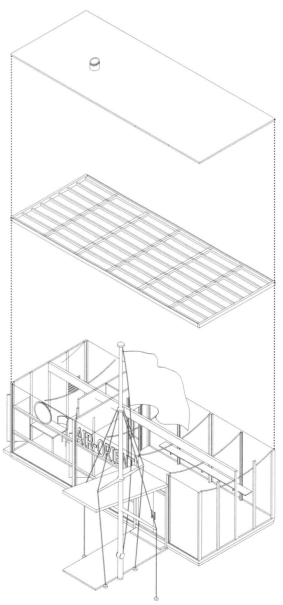

Axonometric drawing

Exhibition Hall 269

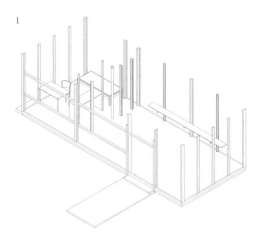

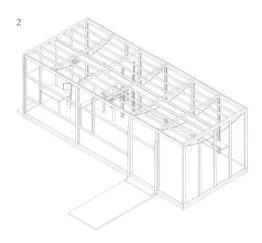

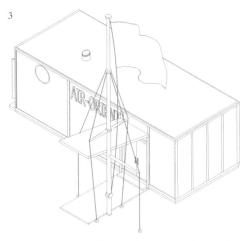

Exploded axonometric drawing

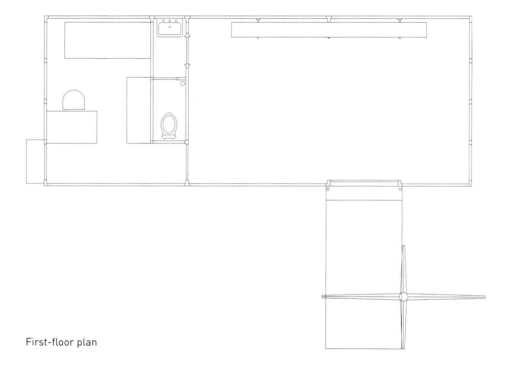

First-floor plan

Exhibition Hall **271**

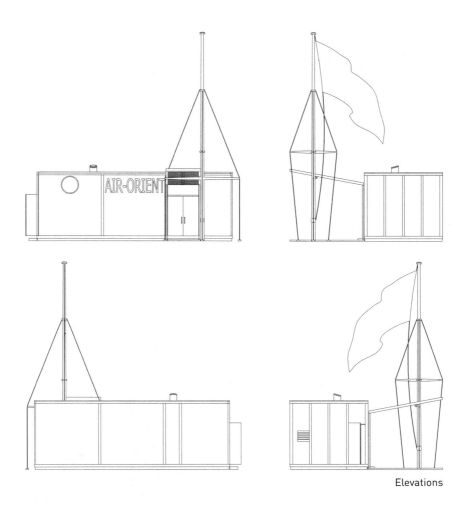

Elevations

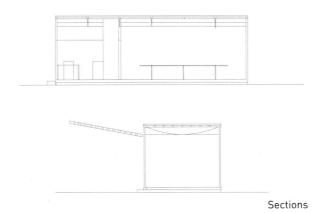

Sections

C-19
Centre d'Esthetique Contemporaine

Design period: 1935
Location: Paris, France
Status: Unbuilt

This plan is one from the the "Musée à Croissance Illimitée series." The whole building is supported by stilts. The layout of the interior exhibition space uses square spiral techniques. The roof is the metal truss structure. Le Corbusier said that this is an exhibition space without elevation, that uses special removable slabs made of asbestos cement. Visitors enter the interior of the exhibition space through the central hall; the square spiral wires are gradually spread out and circle around. The standard unit is 7 by 7 meters (23 by 23 feet). People can enter the empty space formed by roof trusses, and the light can be adjusted by the transparent and semi-transparent slabs.

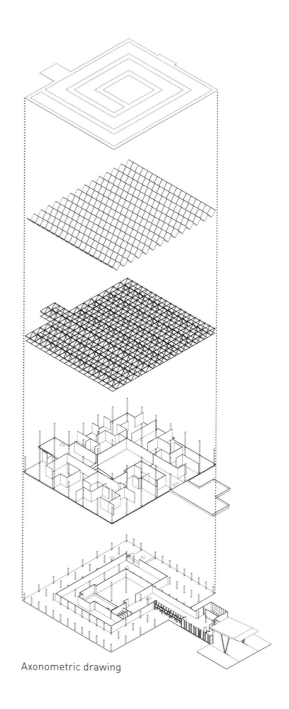

Axonometric drawing

Exhibition Hall 273

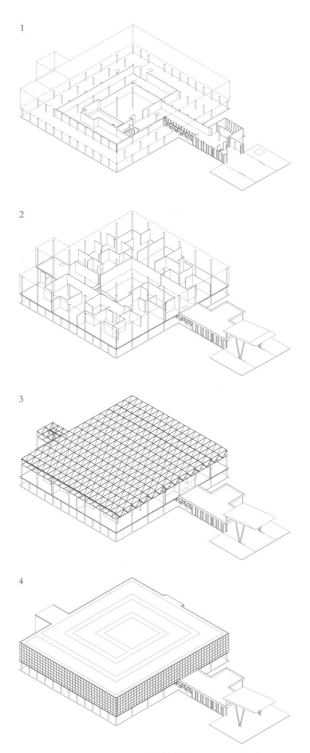

Exploded axonometric drawing

Roof plan

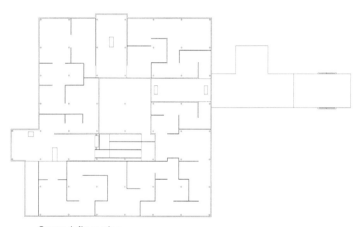

Second-floor plan

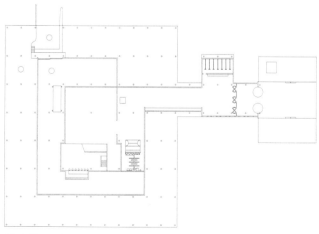

First-floor plan

Exhibition Hall 275

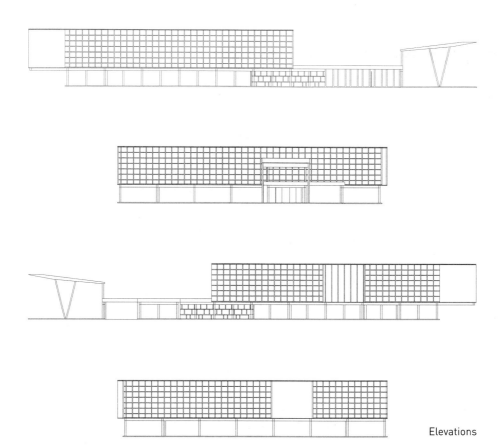

Elevations

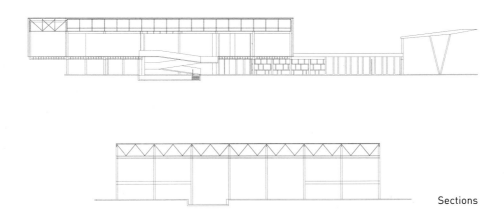

Sections

C-26
Pavillon des Temps Nouveaux

Design period: 1936
Location: Paris, France
Status: Built

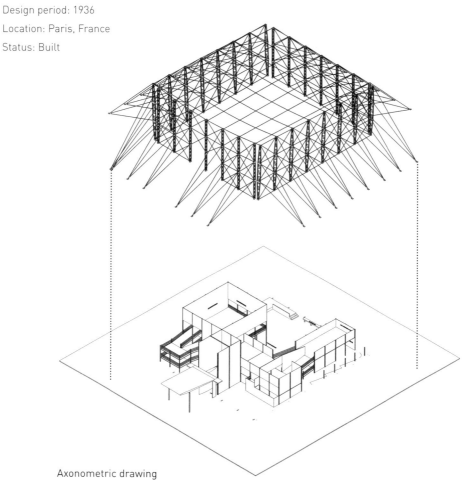

Axonometric drawing

After Le Corbusier's plan A, B, and C for the Paris Exposition Universelle were declined, plan D, Pavillon des Temps Nouveaux, finally came into being. The whole pavilion is composed of steel wires around the site, covered elevation, and canvases on the roof. In the interior, ramps and exhibition boards are used to organize the contents and routines, which are similar to nested boxes. From the section, we can see the structure clearly. The external tent serves as the container while the internal exhibition stage and ramps serve as the content. They form an obvious difference. The overall area of the pavilion is 15,000 square meters (3.7 acres). People enter the interior from the porch in the middle of the plan, then go upstairs to the second floor by the ramp on one side, and back downstairs from a ramp on another side. The whole pathway forms a loop for visitors, which represents the idea of Le Corbusier's architectural stroll.

Exhibition Hall

1

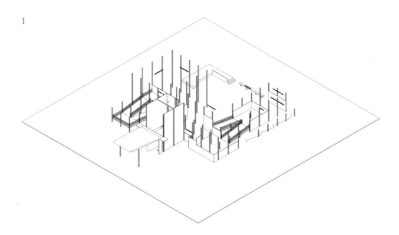

2

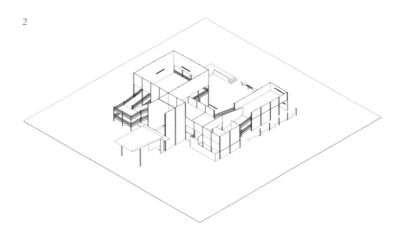

3

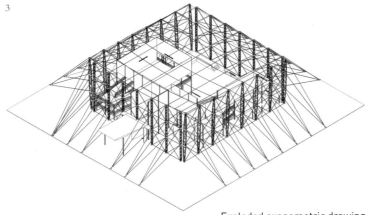

Exploded axonometric drawing

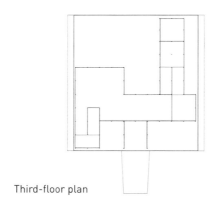
Third-floor plan

Second-floor plan

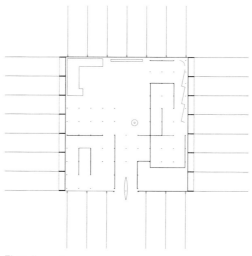
First-floor plan

Exhibition Hall

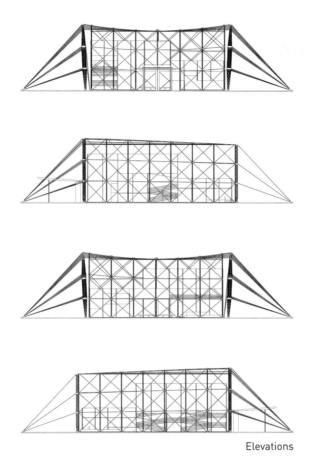

Elevations

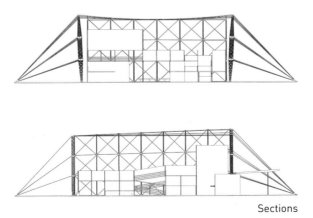

Sections

C-27
TN-Wagon Maison Pavillon

Design period: 1936
Location: Paris, France
Status: Unbuilt

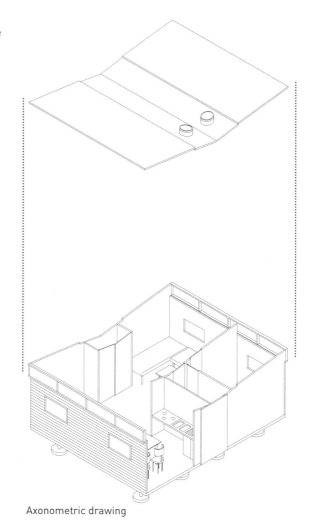

Axonometric drawing

This is an unbuilt residential pavilion plan that does not appear in *Le Corbusier Complete Works*. The whole building is a box framework supported by stilts. The plan is divided into three parts. The first part is a bedroom and office space; the second part is a restroom; and the third part is a kitchen and restaurant. The fundamental function of the house is shrunk into the little square plan; the roof applies the counter-slope. There are two purposes to this: the two raised sides of the roof can be used to set up the high windows and the sunken part can be used as drains to collect rain. The roof with a counter-slope is expressed more clearly in Le Corbusier's later works.

Exhibition Hall 281

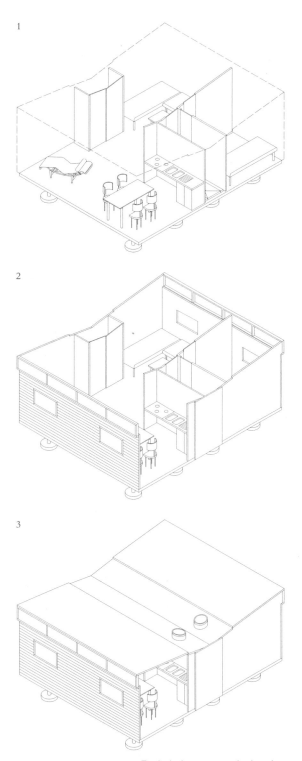

Exploded axonometric drawing

282

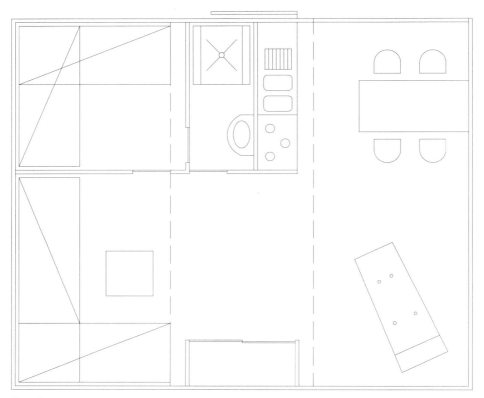

First-floor plan

Exhibition Hall 283

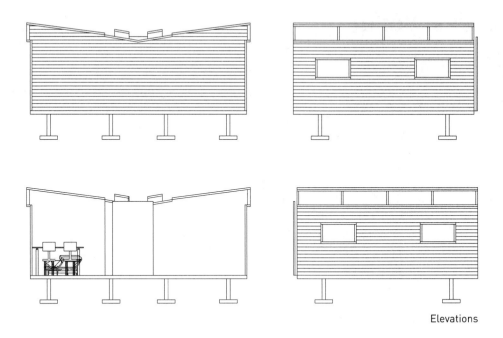

Elevations

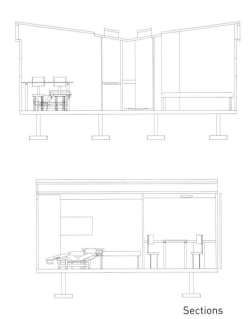

Sections

C-28
Pavillon Bat'a

Design period: 1937
Location: Paris, France
Status: Unbuilt

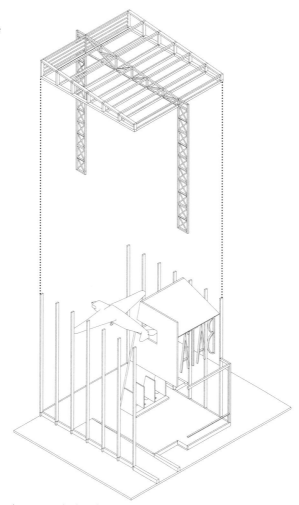

Axonometric drawing

This pavilion plan was never built. The construction plan uses I-steel to support the trusses of the roof, and features a glass roof and brown leather on the exterior wall. The interior uses standard boards to present the exhibition contents. In the center of the plan, there is a tilt partition in the room to create a dim atmosphere for movies. In the exhibition pathway, the entrance and exit are separate. In the exhibition area, besides the giant "BAT'A" neon signboard, are lightboxes and boots-display windows set at average eye-level. There is also an airplane overhead in the middle of the exhibition hall. The background of the roof is a world map.

Exhibition Hall 285

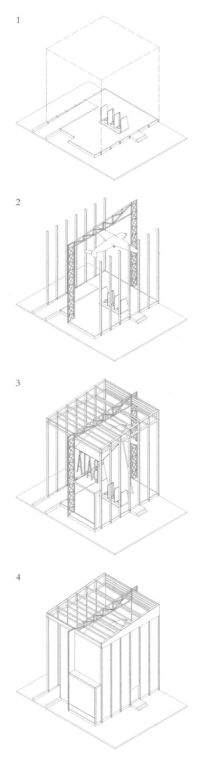

Exploded axonometric drawing

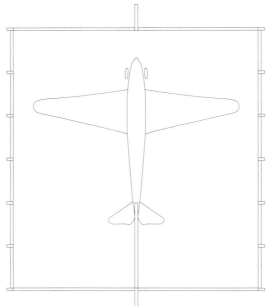

Second-floor plan

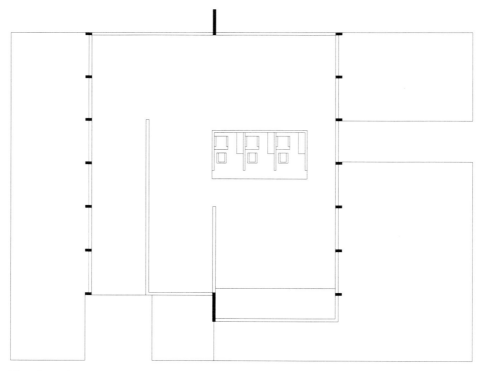

First-floor plan

Exhibition Hall 287

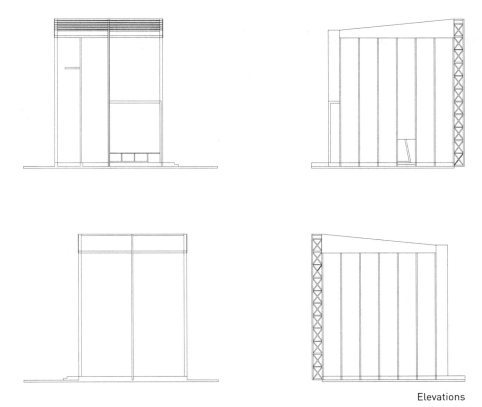

Elevations

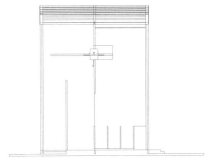
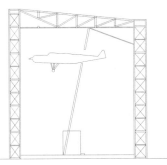

Sections

C-31
Pavillon de la France à l'Exposition de l'Eau

Design period: 1939
Location: Liege, Belgium
Status: Unbuilt

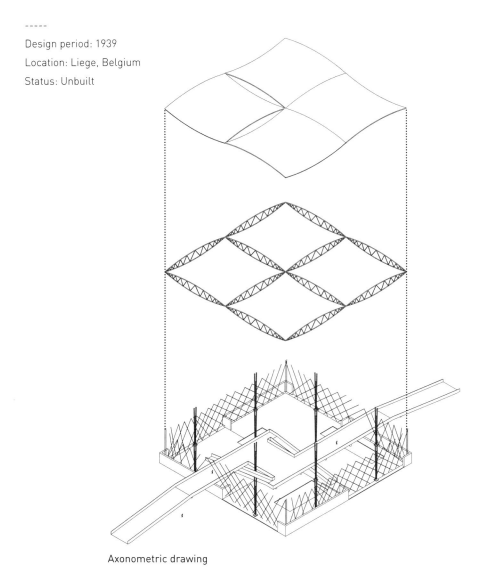

Axonometric drawing

Instead of simulating all the "true" built palaces in this project, Le Corbusier chose the initial exposition palace of the world: the Crystal Palace, London. In the plan, Le Corbusier also uses glass and steel as the main material. Twelve I-steel columns support four pieces of semi-flexible board on the roof, which is like a steel awning. The interior of the pavilion organizes the exhibition contents mainly through the walls and ramps. The wall layout is in the shape of a "卍" in the plan, which divides the whole area into four exhibition areas. There is a horizontally extending ramp throughout the square hall in the plan.

Exhibition Hall   289

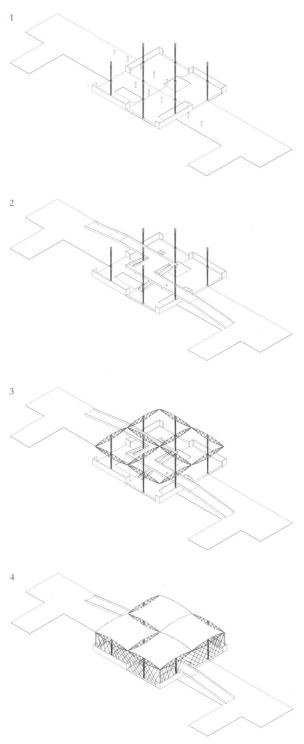

Exploded axonometric drawing

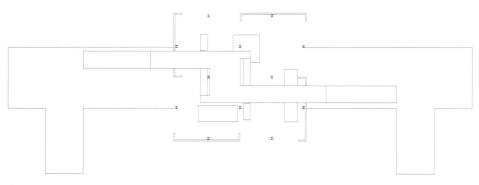

Second-floor plan

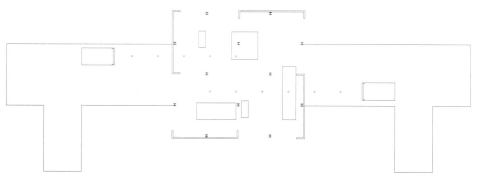

First-floor plan

Exhibition Hall 291

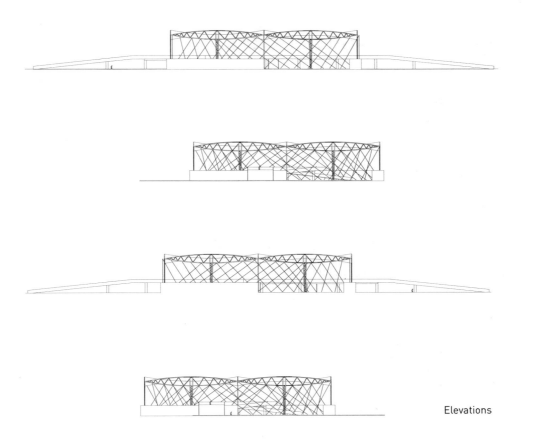

Elevations

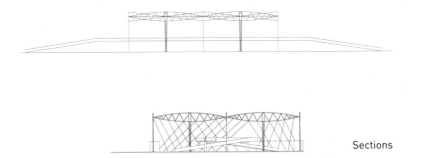

Sections

C-32
Ideal Home, Arundell Clarke

Design period: 1939
Location: London, United Kingdom
Status: Unbuilt

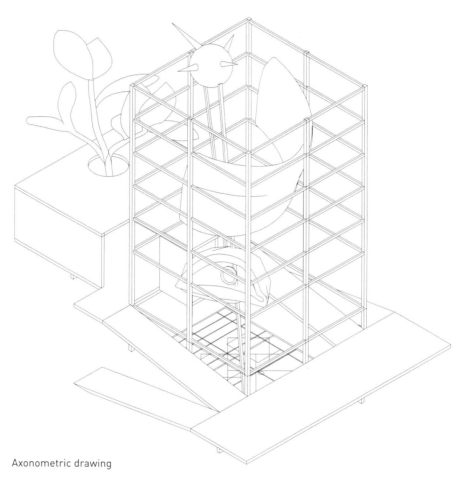

Axonometric drawing

This is an architectural plan of a pavilion designed to be an ideal home in London. In the work, Le Corbusier shows the ideas of future city planning and housing construction. The ideas contain stilts, frameworks, roof gardens, multiplied housing sections, as well as the most important subjects of exhibition light, space, and green areas. The pavilion itself is composed of scrap iron and papier-mâché. The interior has an "eye" and "ear" aiming at raising visitors' curiosity. The main exhibition hall at the bottom displays Le Corbusier's "La Ville Radiuse" planning ideas.

Exhibition Hall

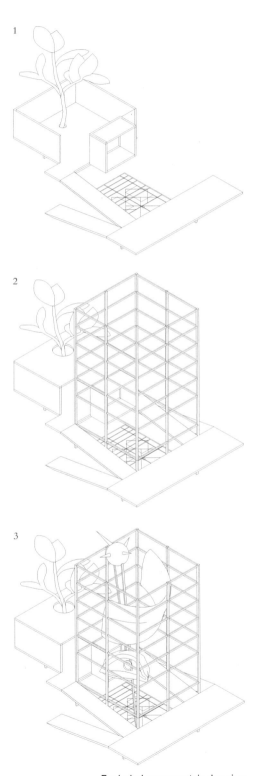

Exploded axonometric drawing

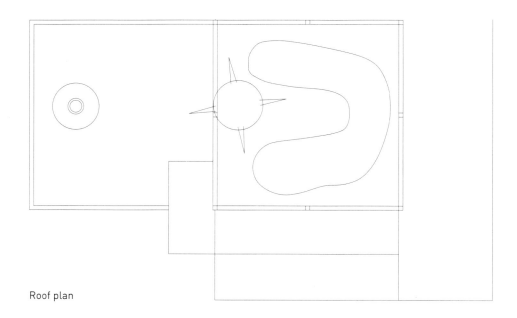

Roof plan

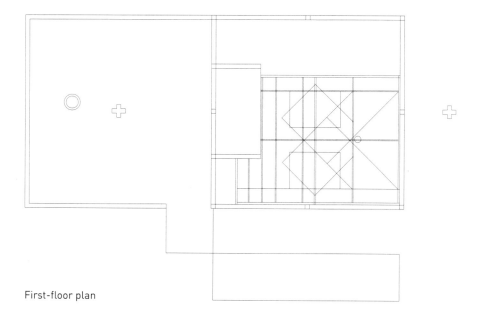

First-floor plan

Exhibition Hall 295

Elevations

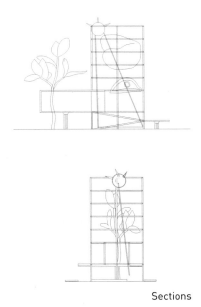

Sections

C-42
Musée Tent

Design period: 1950
Location: Ahmedabad, India
Status: Built

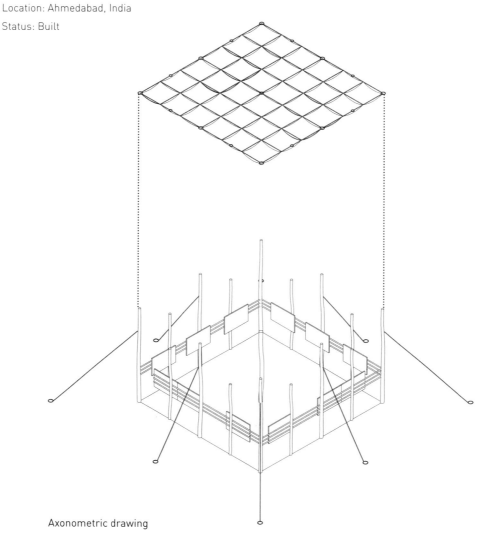

Axonometric drawing

This is the subsidiary architecture of Musée Tent, which is a simple tent that uses logs, with surrounding draglines supporting the roof and canvases. The structure uses rope-binding techniques and the whole construction is similar to the earlier plan of Pavillon des Temps Nouveaux in Paris (project 26). The column in the middle of the plan plays a role as the visual focus of the space.

Exhibition Hall

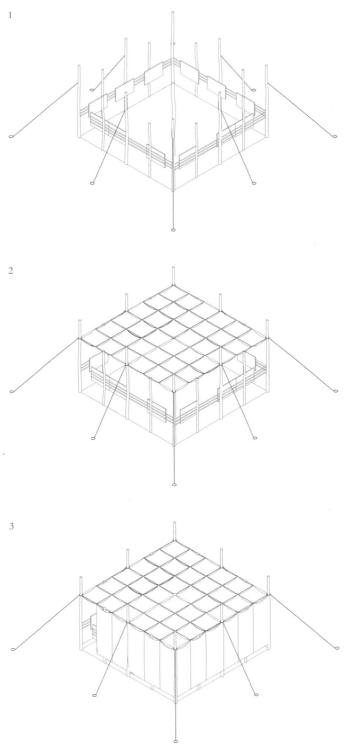

Exploded axonometric drawing

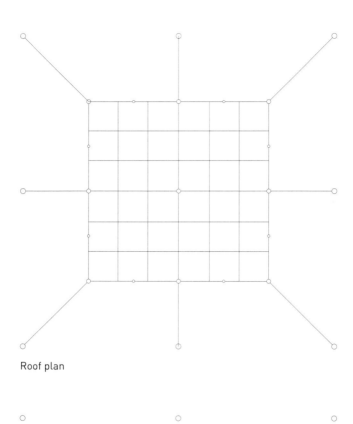

Roof plan

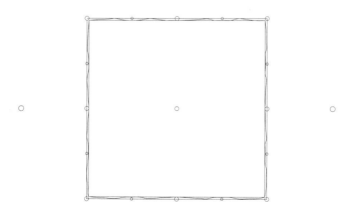

First-floor plan

Exhibition Hall 299

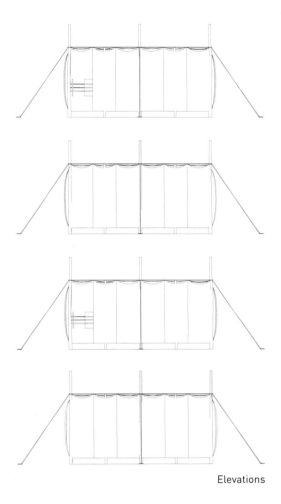

Elevations

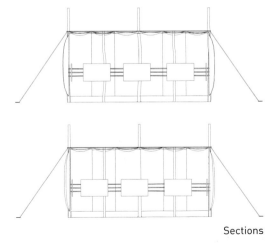

Sections

C-43
Porte Maillot

Design period: 1950
Location: Paris, France
Status: Unbuilt

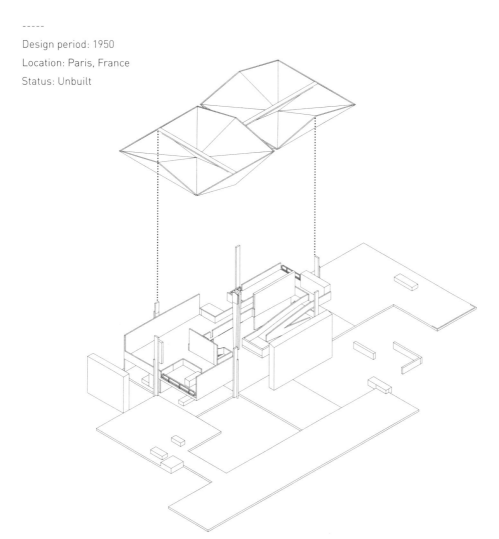

Axonometric drawing

This is the second version of the plan. The first version illustrates a light, wooden framework pavilion. The second version uses a metal framework. Seven structural steel columns support two parasol-shaped roofs. In the interior of the exhibition hall, partition walls, ramps, and stairs organize visitor pathways, and the pavilion extends to the external space. Inside, two metal framework umbrellas measuring 14 meters (45.9 feet) on the side shelter the pavilion. On the plan, the pavilion is composed of two squares of equal size. The whole structure appears many times in numerous exhibition plans; it is a popular prototype of Le Corbusier's pavilion, similar to the idea applied in the plan of Musée à Croissance Illimitée (project 33).

Exhibition Hall 301

1

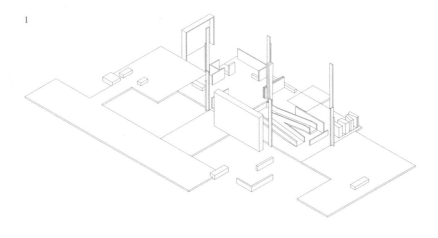

2

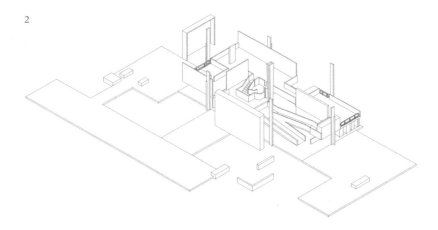

3

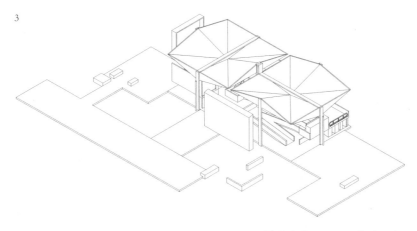

Exploded axonometric drawing

Second-floor plan

First-floor plan

Exhibition Hall 303

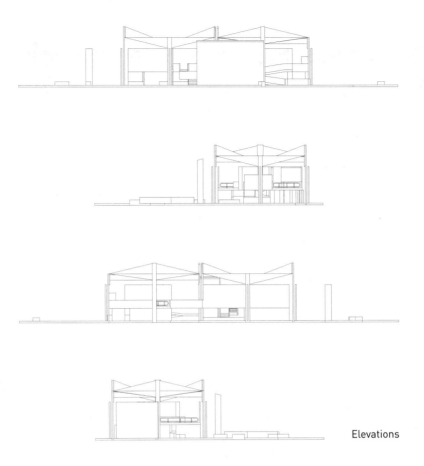

Elevations

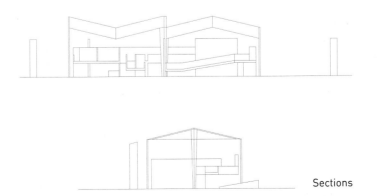

Sections

C-58
Pavillon Philips, Exposition Internationale de 1958

Design period: 1958
Location: Brussels, Belgium
Status: Built

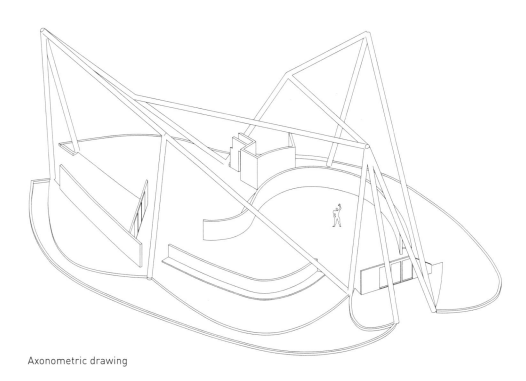

Axonometric drawing

This is a unique work in exhibition architecture. It adopts the "hyperbolic-parabolic" sail-like cable-tension structure. The construction starts by laying several hyperbolic steel concrete columns on the base. Then, based on the columns, cables are drawn taut to form steel messes. Finally, the prefabricated twisted concrete slabs are fixed into these steel messes. Le Corbusier refers to Pavillon Philips as "a display of electronic poems," identifying it as the new art form named "electronic show." Pictures, colors, languages, and music are mixed together.

Exhibition Hall

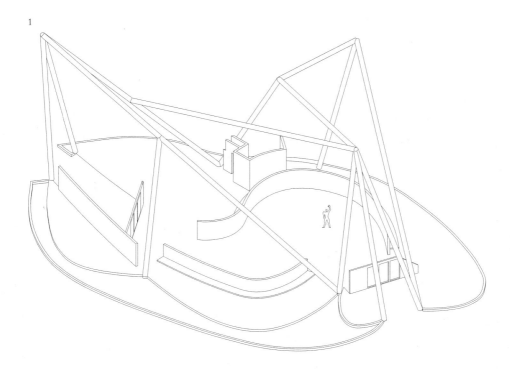

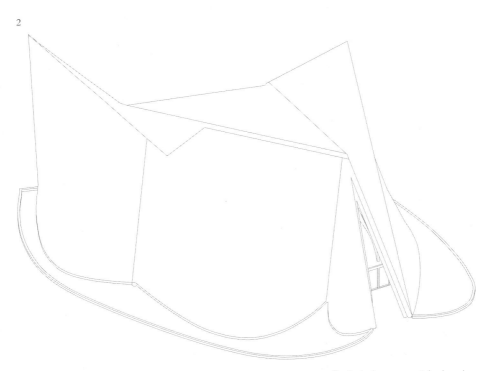

Exploded axonometric drawing

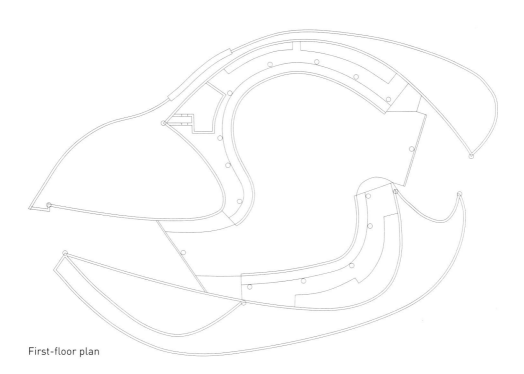

First-floor plan

Exhibition Hall   307

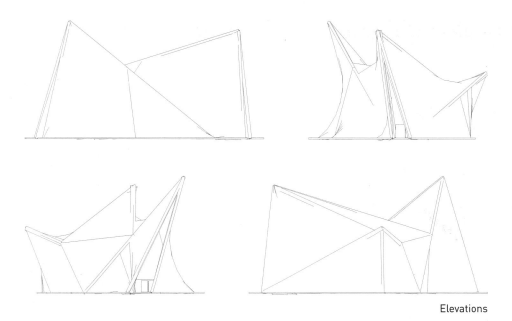

Elevations

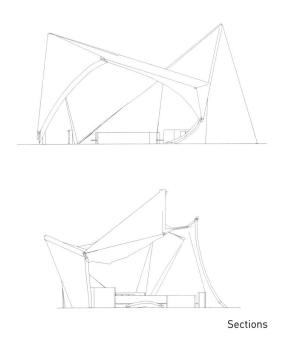

Sections

C-68
Pavillon d'Exposition, Stockholm

Design period: 1962
Location: Stockholm, Sweden
Status: Unbuilt

Axonometric drawing

Entrusted by a merchant, Le Corbusier designed a pavilion to display the works of three artists—Picasso, Matisse, and his. The base of the project is located in the sea. Facing the dock, the building connects to the land via a trestle bridge. The plan is mainly composed of two equal squares. On the exterior of the square, six steel columns support two pieces of umbrella-shaped roofs. The whole structure is similar to Porte Maillot (project 43). The first floor houses the artists' individual exhibition halls, while the second floor locates subsidiary functional areas, such as temporary exhibition halls, offices, storerooms, and restrooms.

Exhibition Hall 309

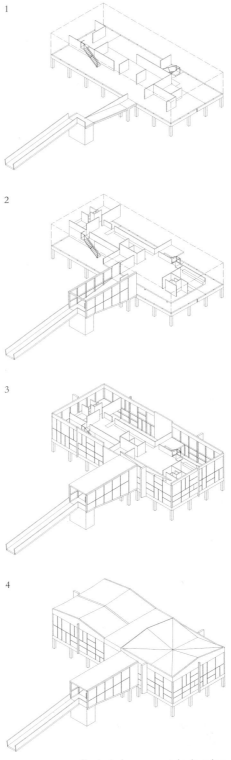

Exploded axonometric drawing

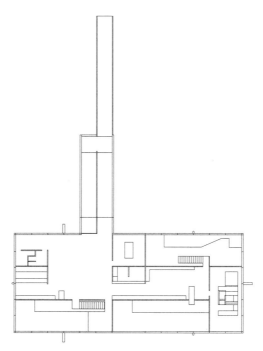

Second-floor plan

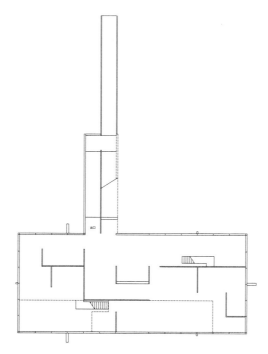

First-floor plan

Exhibition Hall 311

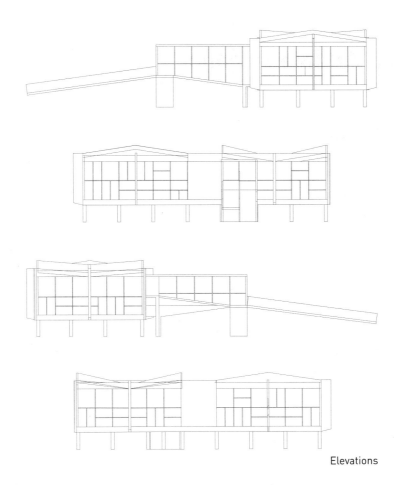

Elevations

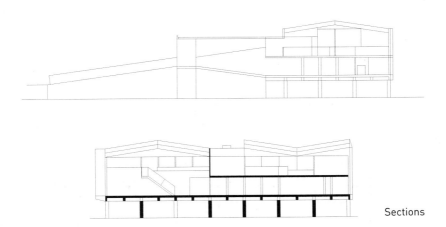

Sections

C-71
Centre d'Art International

Design period: 1963
Location: River Main, Germany
Status: Unbuilt

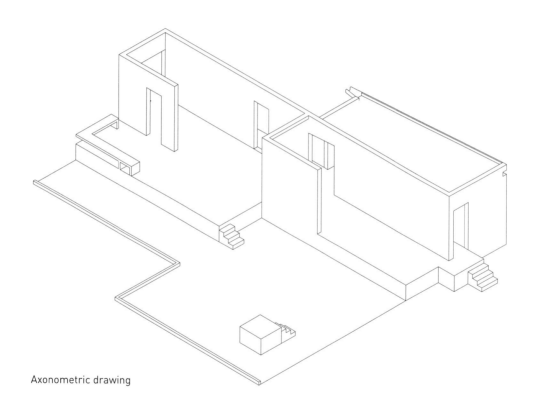

Axonometric drawing

The theater is set in a building that is a part of one of the plans that Le Corbusier designed for Centre d'Art International. And like Musée à Croissance Illimitée (project 33), it includes a "magic box," a "tour pavilion," a storeroom, and other such similar areas. In short, it is an exterior stage for all types of performances. It also includes a dressing room, main platform, auxiliary platform, and restroom facilities. The auditorium is located at the exterior of the main architectural plan, which doesn't include fixed audience seats. The theater doesn't have traditional wings for the actors to enter and exit the stage. Therefore, it is a genuine free theater. From the perspective of the axonometric drawing, only the dressing rooms behind the platform and restrooms have roofs. Other areas are exposed to the external environment.

Exhibition Hall

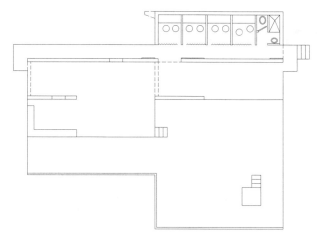

First-floor plan

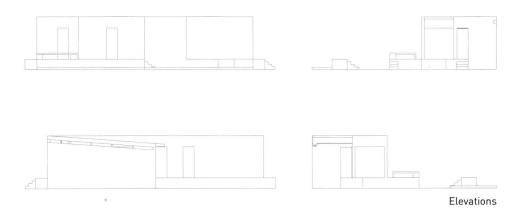

Elevations

Sections

C-72
Pavillon d'Exposition ZHLC, Zurich

Design period: 1963–67
Location: Zurich, Switzerland
Status: Built

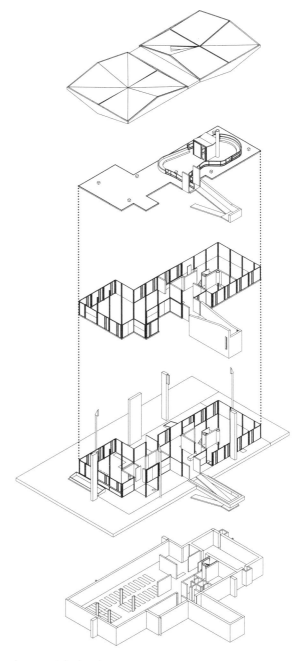

Another name for this project is "Human's home." A woman named Heidi Weber financed the project and the initial task was designing a building for organizing exhibitions and meetings. Since Porte Maillot (project 43), Le Corbusier had constantly used steel structural columns to support two-piece parasol-shaped roofs—that prototype is used in this construction. The building has a basement, two floors, and a roof terrace. The basement has an assembly area, meeting area, and storeroom. The first floor houses the main functional area, including restaurants, living rooms, and kitchens. The second floor mainly locates exhibition halls and libraries, and the top is a terrace for relaxing. There are stairs in the interior and ramps outside.

Axonometric drawing

Exhibition Hall 315

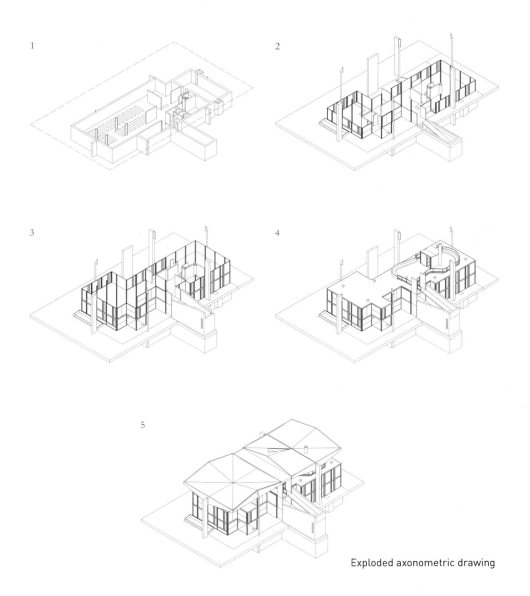

Exploded axonometric drawing

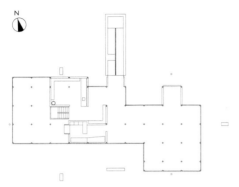

Second-floor plan

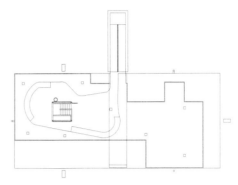

Third-floor plan

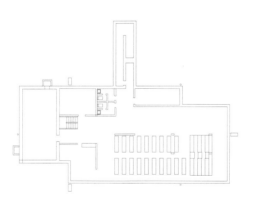

Basement floor plan

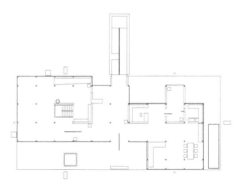

First-floor plan

Exhibition Hall 317

Elevations

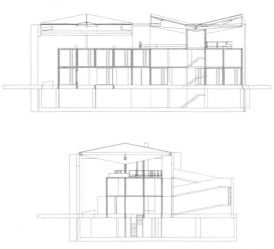

Sections

RELIGIOUS BUILDING

D-10
Église, Le Tremblay

Design period: 1929
Location: Tremblay, France
Status: UnfinishedUnbuilt

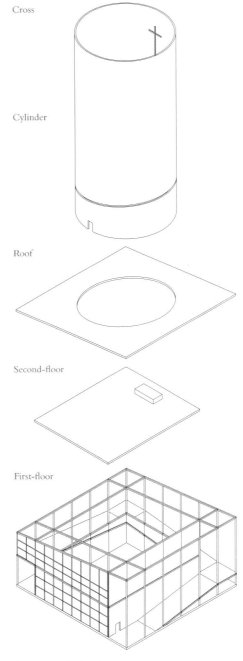

Axonometric drawing

There is little relevant information about this project, with only two design sketches on the Fondation Le Corbusier official website available for reference. From the perspective of the overall spatial construction, the project is composed of a column-shaped religious space and a square subsidiary space at the bottom; the column-shaped space is surrounded by ramps. It can be seen from the sketch that in front of the entrance of the religious space on the second floor, are the ramps which Le Corbusier designed to give a sense of ritual in religious worship. This is also true of both the ramp buffer and the cantilevered space formed between the first-floor entrance of ramps and middle column. Compared with Église Saint Pierre (project 64) in the later part of his career, his works in the period of white house design tended to be simplified and pure.

1
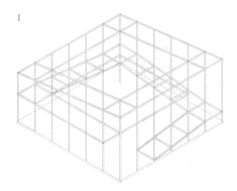

2
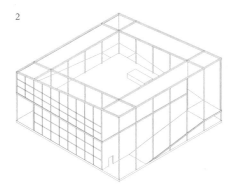

3
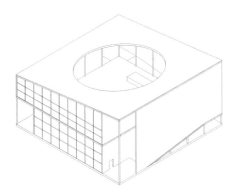

4
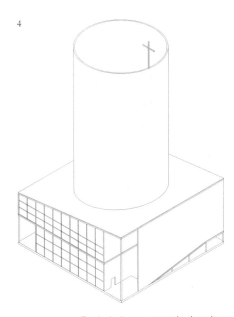

Exploded axonometric drawing

Roof plan

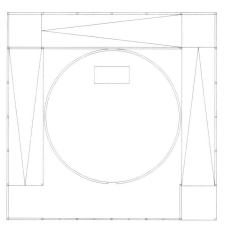
Second-floor plan

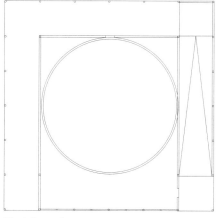
First-floor plan

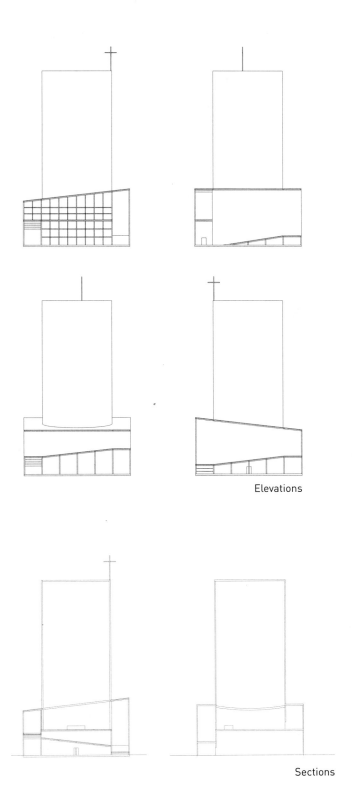

Elevations

Sections

D-41
Basilique, La Sainte-Baume

Design period: 1948
Location: Sainte-Baume, France
Status: Unbuilt

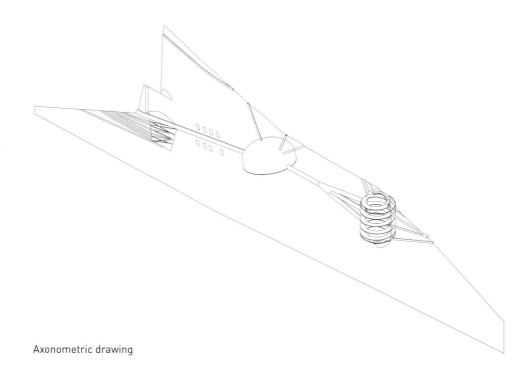

Axonometric drawing

This religious architecture is an unbuilt work that was planned for a plateau on La Sainte-Baume, France. The host is a land surveyor and priest. Le Corbusier was entrusted to construct an inherited wasteland into a place of religious piety. However, the rebuke of France's cardinal and archbishop abolished the plan. Le Corbusier's overall plan laid in maintaining the scenery at the site, so he intended for the middle of the mountain to be chiseled out to build La Sainte-Baume. Visitors would enter from one side of the cliff to get to the other side of the mountain, facing the sea directly. The rooms in the mountain are connected by horizontal ramps and spiral ramps. Lighting relies on the natural light from the end of the shaft, as well as artificial lights.

Religious Building 323

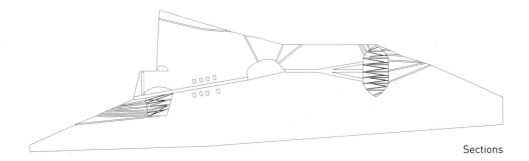

Sections

D-44
Chapelle Notre Dame du Haut

Design period: 1950–54
Location: Vosges Mountains, France
Status: Built

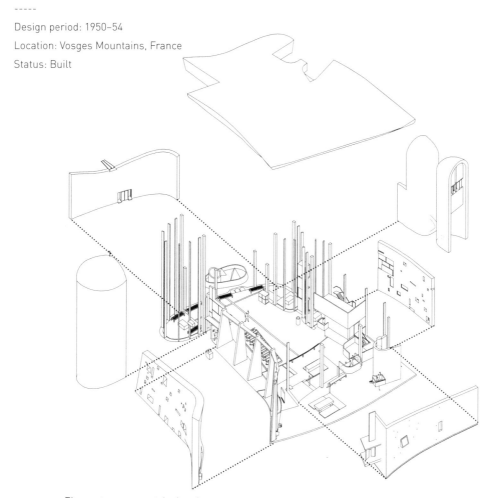

Elements axonometric drawing

One of Le Corbusier's great representative works, Chapelle Notre Dame du Haut is located in Massif des Vosges and is composed of characteristic forms. Adopting a more sculptural form technique, it reflects the vague contours of painting works. It can be seen from the plan that it is mainly composed of a middle hall—with the capacity to hold 200 people—and three altars, with lighting towers at the top. The building walls are constructed by concrete airbrush, and the structural columns in the wall support the gigantic roof. The concrete "light wall" on the south is actually a window set as the wall instead of making holes in the wall. Openings' shapes and locations on internal and external surfaces are different; from the indoor perspective, they look like light launchers. The walls aren't connected directly, but are separated from each other. The gaps are used for either entrances or lighting.

Religious Building 325

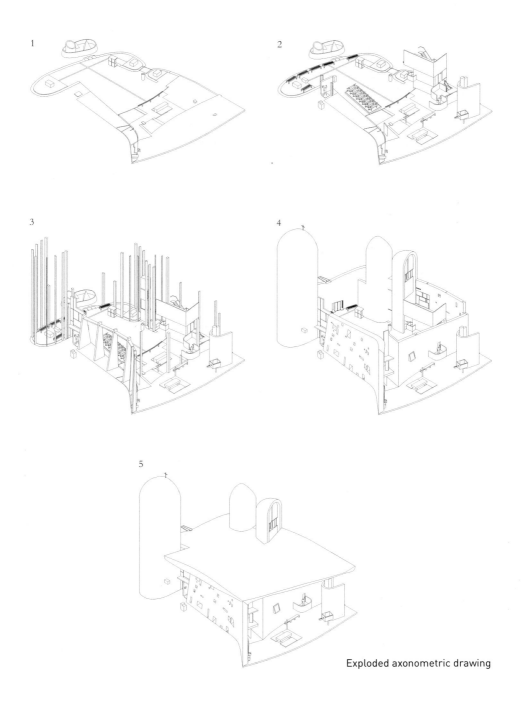

Exploded axonometric drawing

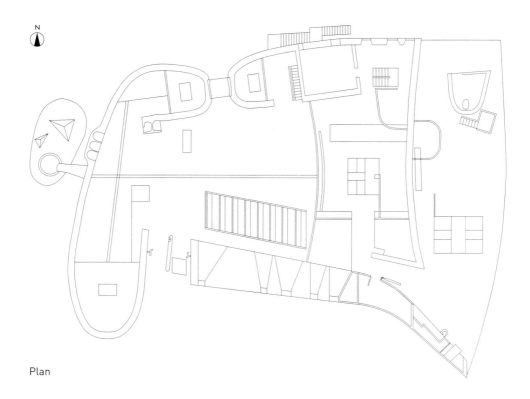

Plan

Religious Building

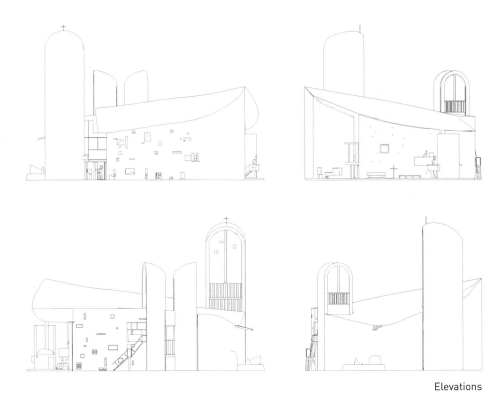

Elevations

Sections

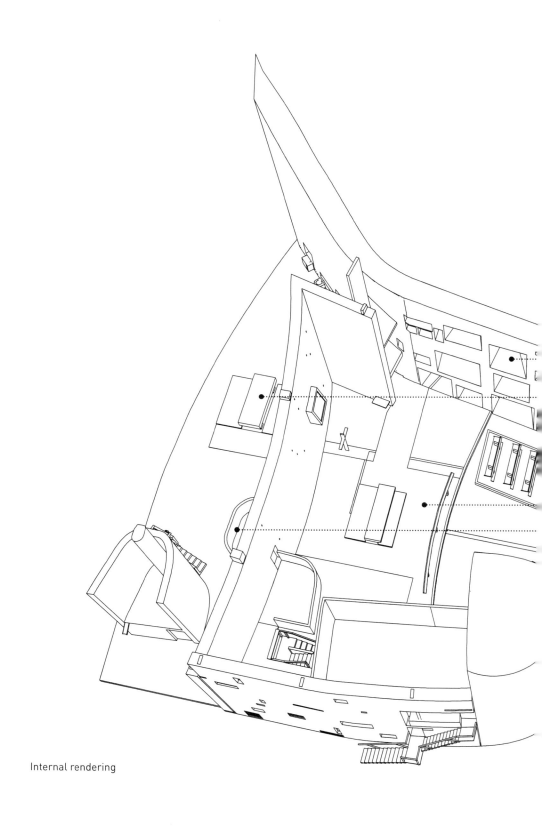

Internal rendering

Religious Building 329

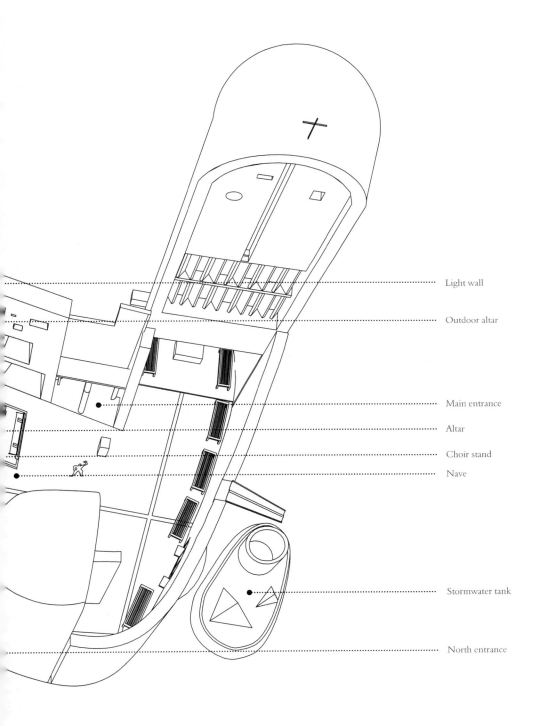

- Light wall
- Outdoor altar
- Main entrance
- Altar
- Choir stand
- Nave
- Stormwater tank
- North entrance

D-47
Chapelle Funeraire Delgado-Chalbaud

Design period: 1951
Location: Venezuela
Status: Unbuilt

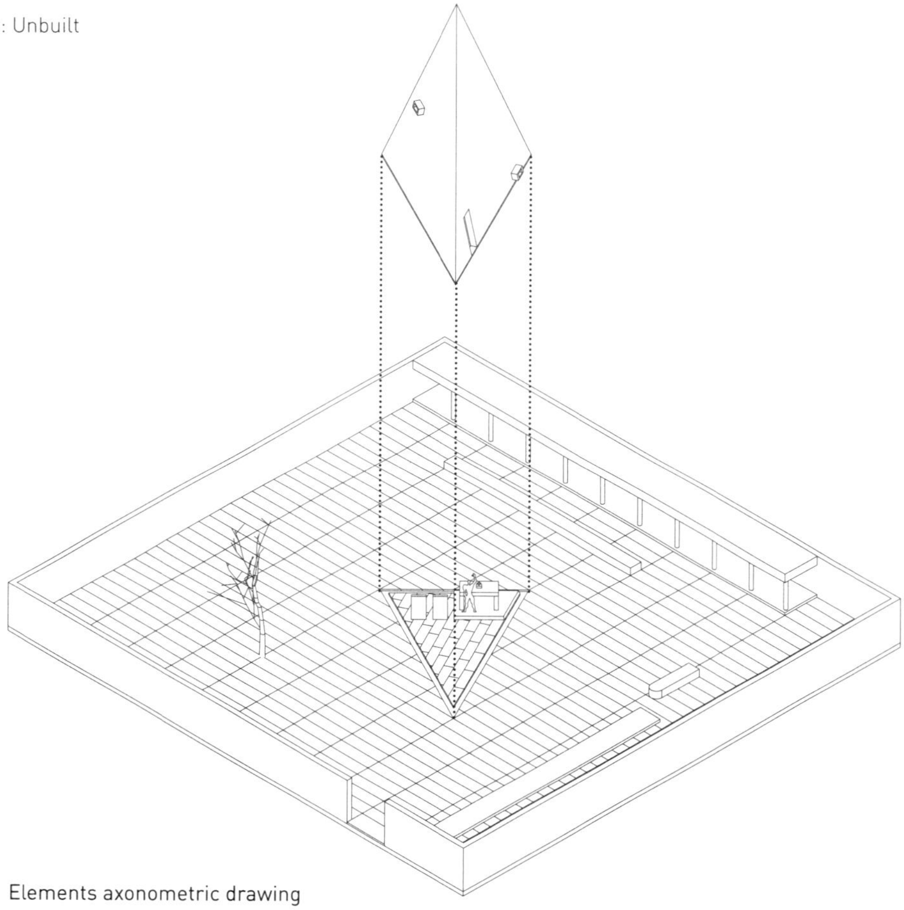

Elements axonometric drawing

The entire construction is simple. At the center of a square courtyard, stands a pyramid-like altar, and a semi-open pavilion is set at one side of the interior courtyard. There is also a half-underground cubicle for laying coffins. On the altar wall are two square windows that are perpendicular to the wall. The plan has similarities with works in the later period, such as Haute Cour (project 50) and Couvent Sainte-Marie de la Tourette (project 57); all the works show a centralized layout. It's known from the plan design that the height of the courtyard wall and altar entrance is about 2.26 meters (7.4 feet). Le Corbusier uses the modular approach in the control of ratio and scale.

Religious Building 331

1

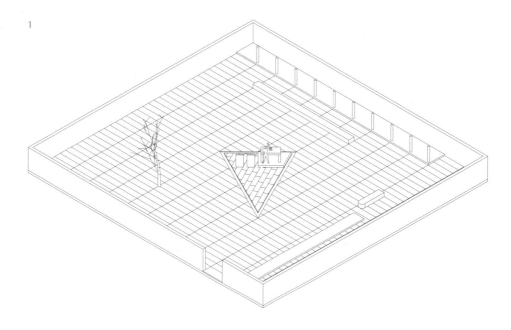

2

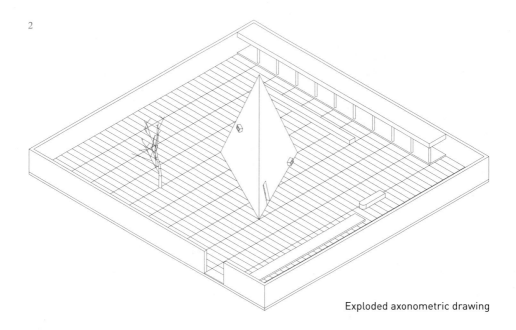

Exploded axonometric drawing

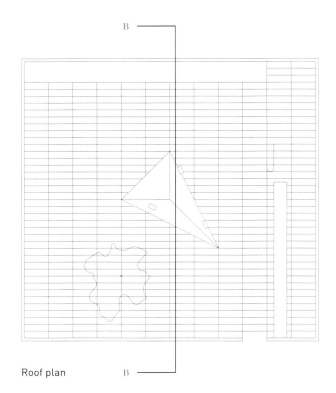

Roof plan

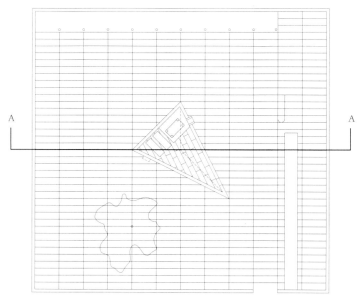

First-floor plan

Religious Building 333

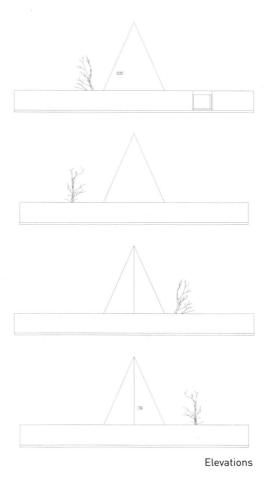

Elevations

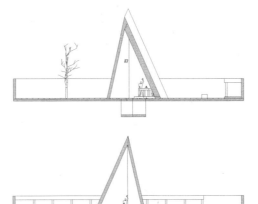

Sections

D-57
Couvent Sainte-Marie de la Tourette

Design period: 1957–60
Location: Eveux-sur-l'Arbresle, France
Status: Built

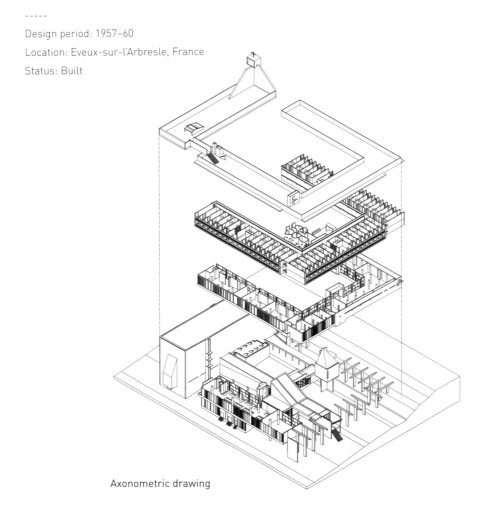

Axonometric drawing

This design is a brilliant pastiche in Le Corbusier's later practice. Located in Eveux-sur-l'Arbresle near Lyon, Couvent Sainte-Marie de la Tourette includes a church, a monks' dormitory, a study room, and a library. The base itself has height differences leaning from the eastern entrance of the plateau to the western restaurant and assembly hall. The top two floors are monk dormitories arranged in a U-shape; they are supported by stilts standing on the slope. On the north of the convent, there is a single church with a rectangular shape. An internal courtyard is enclosed by the convent and the church. In the square courtyard, Le Corbusier designed a cross-shaped traffic corridor. There is also a vertical tube stairway and a prayer room in the shape of a pyramid. The whole courtyard looks like a stage of geometry, with cylinder, cuboid, and pyramid-type shapes. All of this has been enclosed by the external contour.

Religious Building 335

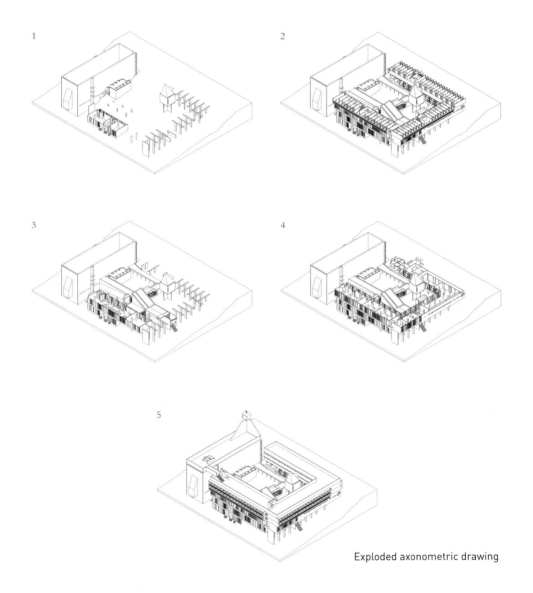

Exploded axonometric drawing

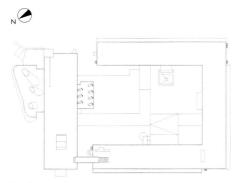

Roof plan

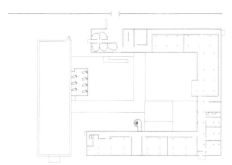

First-floor plan

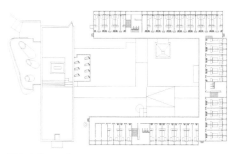

Third-floor plan

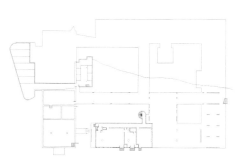

Second basement floor plan

Basement floor plan

Religious Building

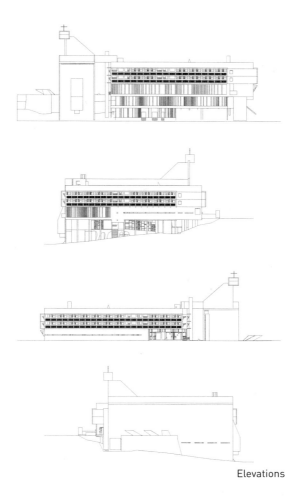

Elevations

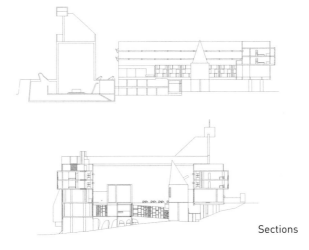

Sections

D-64
Église Saint Pierre

Design period: 1960–69
Location: Firminy, France
Status: Built

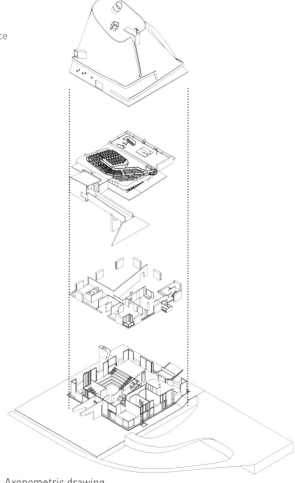

Axonometric drawing

This is Le Corbusier's third characteristic religious building after Chapelle Notre Dame du Haut (project 44) and Chapelle Funeraire Delgado-Chalbaud (project 47). The main body of the church is composed of a ruled camber shell and a square base. The lower floors mainly belong to function rooms, such as the assembly hall, reception, and a classroom. The upper shell encloses seats, altars, and such. On the shell, Le Corbusier designed a light symphony—natural light and shadows gradually change throughout the day, giving the altar space a sense of "sacred." In addition, there is a drainage pipe on the external surface of the shell. Water flows from the top and trickles along the concrete grooves. Through the design of vertical and horizontal drains, Le Corbusier consciously borrows architectural language to express the relationship between architecture and nature.

Religious Building 339

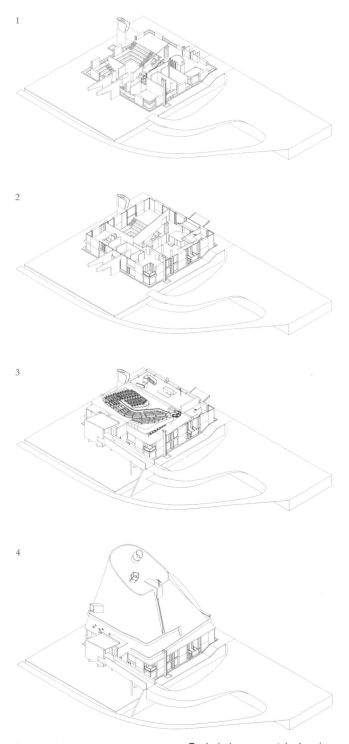

Exploded axonometric drawing

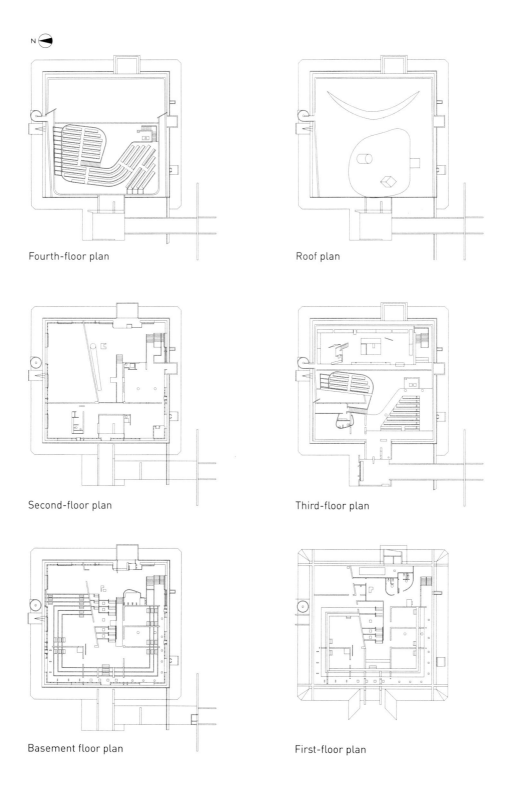

Fourth-floor plan

Roof plan

Second-floor plan

Third-floor plan

Basement floor plan

First-floor plan

Religious Building 341

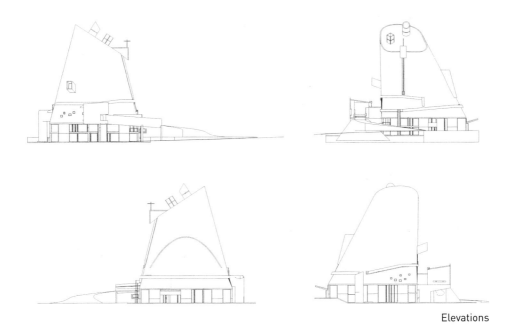

Elevations

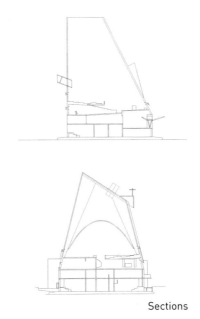

Sections

D-67
Église, Bologna

Design period: 1962
Location: Bologna, Italy
Status: Unbuilt

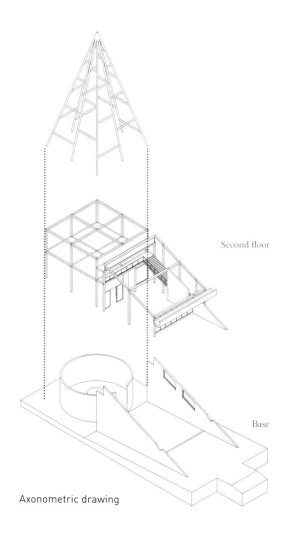

Second floor

Base

Axonometric drawing

This is an unfinished work designed in 1962. The plan is a rectangle. The main body of architecture is contained on the second floor. On the upper part of the altar is a pyramid. The ground itself has a height difference, and the entrance is set on the higher side; visitors can go directly to the second floor via stairs. It can be seen from the three design sketches that Le Corbusier maintained the natural height difference of the ground, reflecting topographical elements in the interior space through ramps. Also notable, is the recurvate drain he designed on the roof of the entrance façade, which he also used in Palais de l'Assemblée (project 48).

Religious Building 343

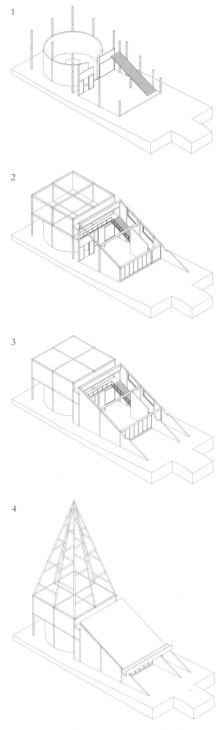

Exploded axonometric drawing

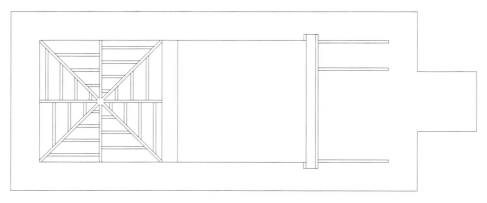

Roof plan

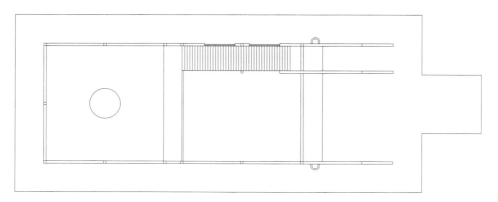

Second-floor plan

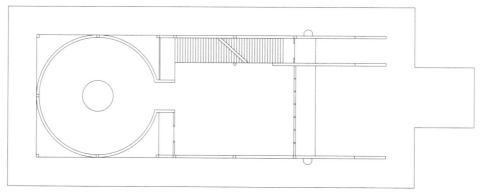

First-floor plan

Religious Building 345

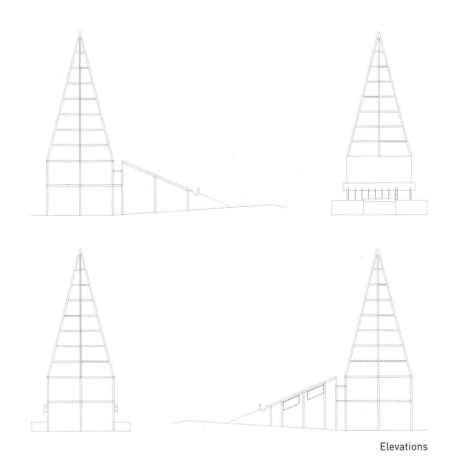

Elevations

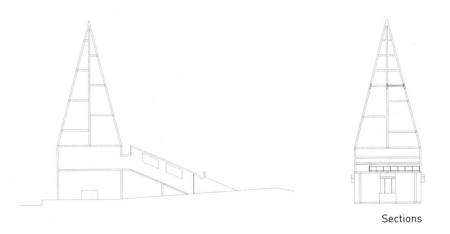

Sections

D-78
Église, Venice

Design period: 1964–65
Location: Venice, Italy
Status: Unbuilt

This church was intended as part of the large hospital that Le Corbusier designed. It was to be in a single building located on the north of the overall project, but it was never built. In the design, there is an altar on the first floor. The section plan shows that above the altar, there is a lightwell for lighting the whole building. The bottom of the modification is in the shape of a wedge. The main worship space on the first floor is surrounded by water. Le Corbusier borrows the square shell of the building and embraces water in the architecture to echo the fame of Venice as the "water city."

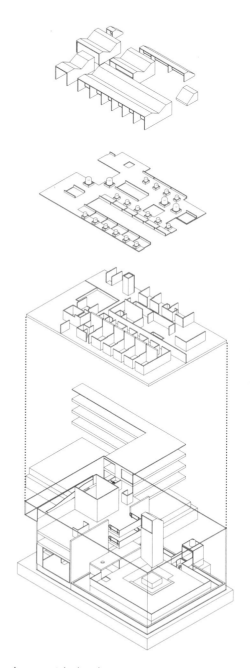

Axonometric drawing

Religious Building 347

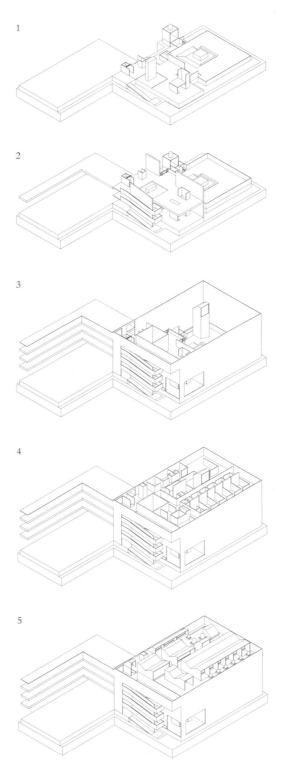

Exploded axonometric drawing

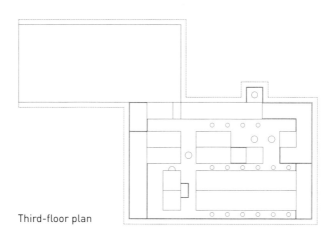
Third-floor plan

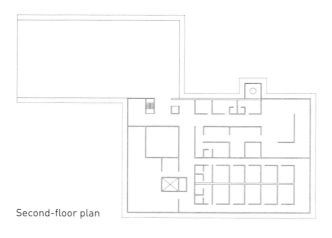
Second-floor plan

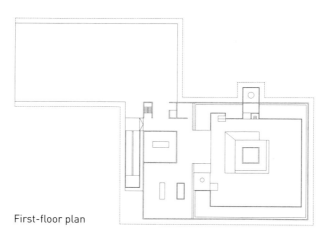
First-floor plan

Religious Building   349

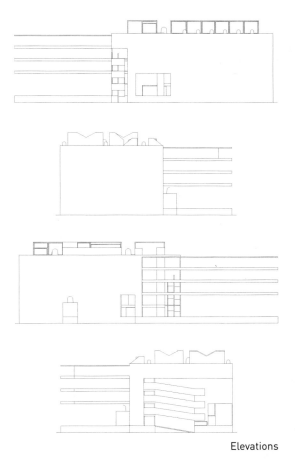

Elevations

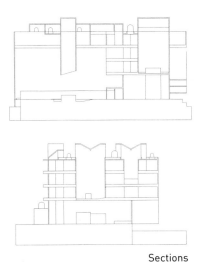

Sections

SCHOOL

E-01
Ateliers d'Artistes

Design period: 1910
Location: None
Status: Unbuilt

The project was designed in 1910. It is the first work discussed in *Le Corbusier Complete Works, Volume 1*. The plane is in a centripetal layout, with a large classroom in the middle and workshops for stone carving, wood carving, murals, and so on. The workshops are surrounded by a small courtyard for outdoor work. Four tall towers stand at the four corners of the plan, with a pyramid roof in the middle. From the plane construction or the block construction, the building reflects traces of an ancient Byzantine church. In addition, the small workshop units in a central layout reflect the standard theme brought about by industrial technology in the twentieth century.

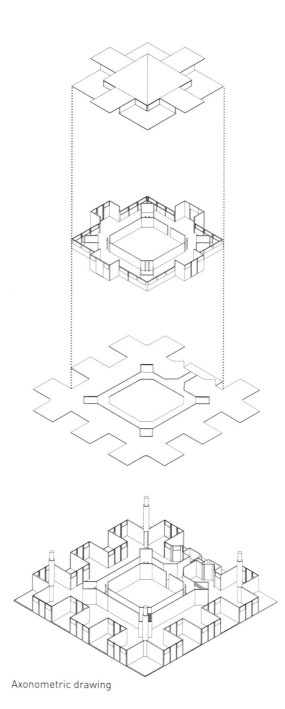

Axonometric drawing

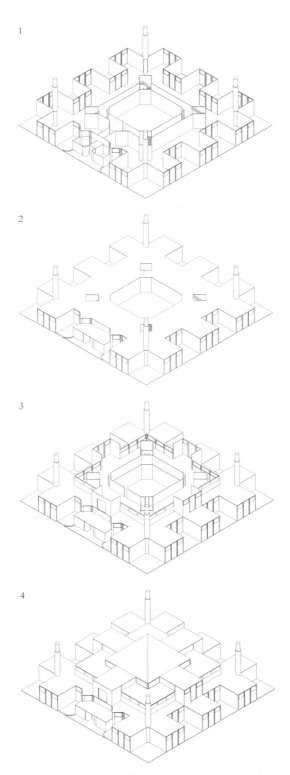

Exploded axonometric drawing

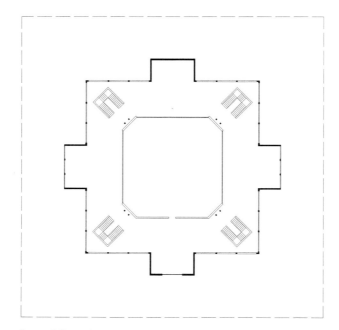

Second-floor plan

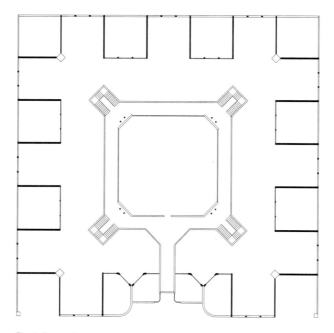

First-floor plan

School 353

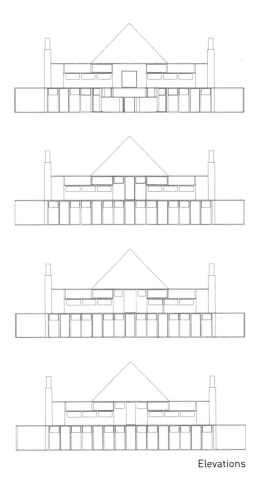
Elevations

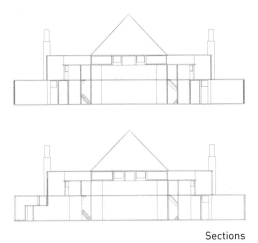
Sections

E-12
Pavillon Suisse, Cité Internationale Universitaire

Design period: 1930–32
Location: Paris, France
Status: Built

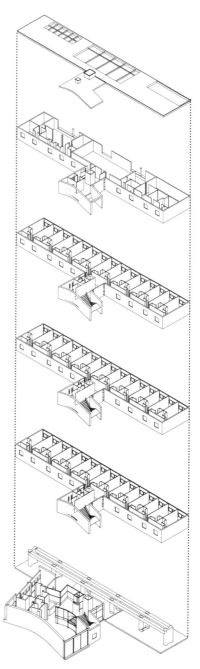

Axonometric drawing

The building has five floors built above the ground, which compose a library at the bottom followed by a four-story dormitory. The building's bottom is elevated and six groups of huge oval concrete columns support the whole upper building. The elevated space at the bottom is the embodiment of Le Corbusier's idea to solve the traffic problems in big cities. On the ground floor, irregular modular surfaces are used in the library and stairs outside the rectangular, slab-type building to obtain a more spacious feeling.

School 355

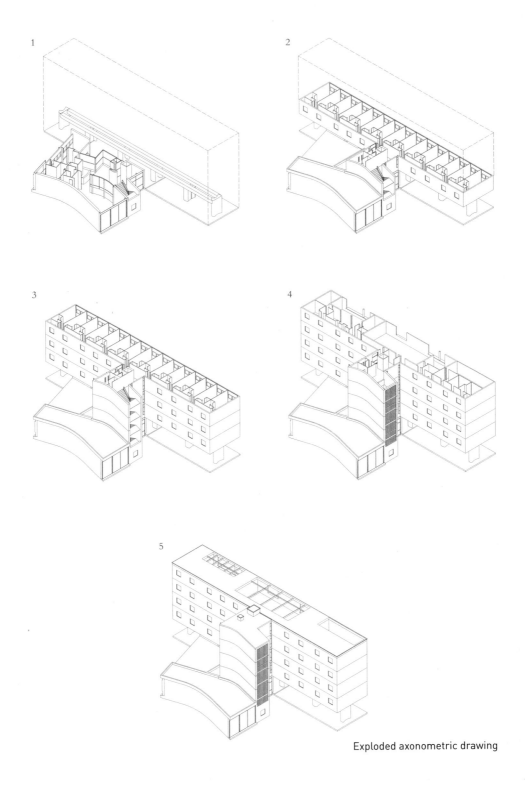

Exploded axonometric drawing

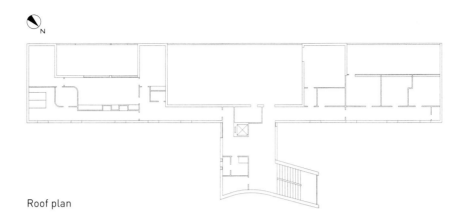

Roof plan

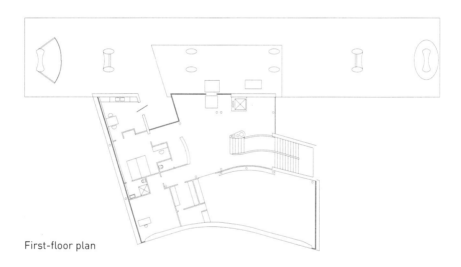

First-floor plan

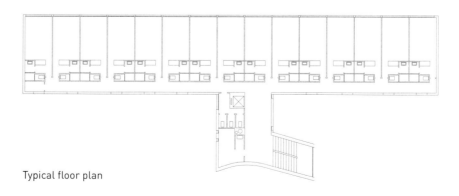

Typical floor plan

School 357

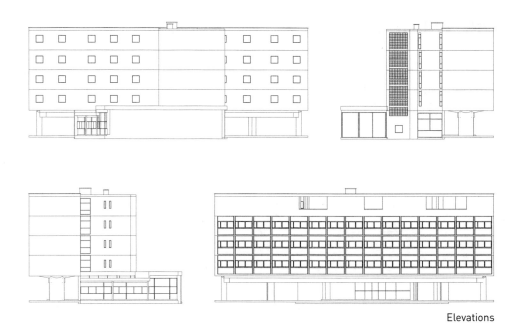

Elevations

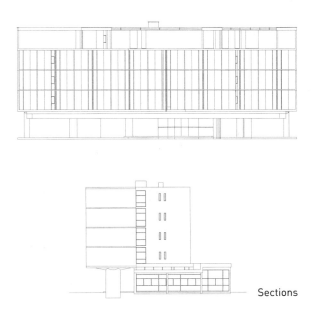

Sections

E-36
École Volante

Design period: 1940
Location: None
Status: Unbuilt

This is an efficient and cheap construction scheme provided by Le Corbusier for war refugees. It is not only a school, but also has a canteen, assembly hall, and other facilities. The overall construction is simple, using folding steel-plate roof trusses and wooden boards to complete the construction. The roof framework is supported by a row of columns in the center of the rectangular plane. These columns are formed by two components inclined toward each other. The triangle design strongly ensures the stability of the structure. The interior space is inspired by the Citroën residence proposed by Le Corbusier.

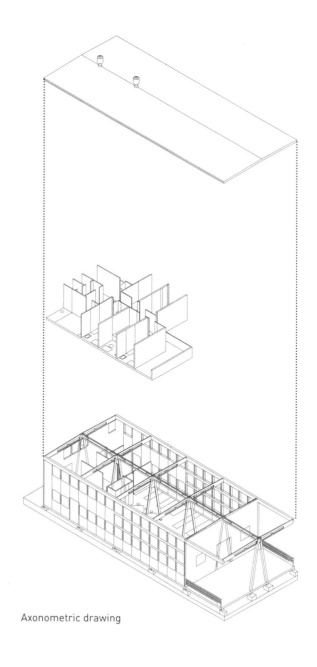

Axonometric drawing

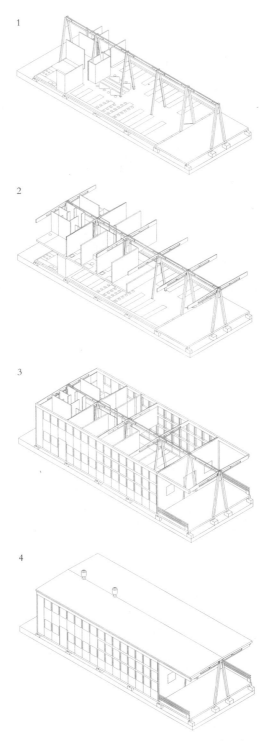

Exploded axonometric drawing

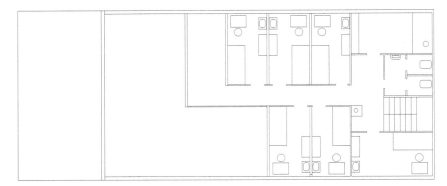

Second-floor plan

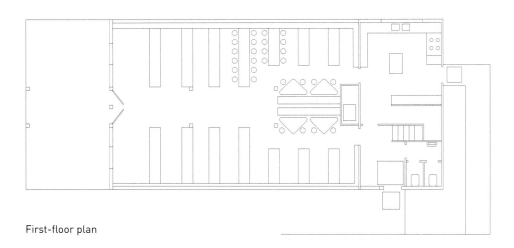

First-floor plan

School 361

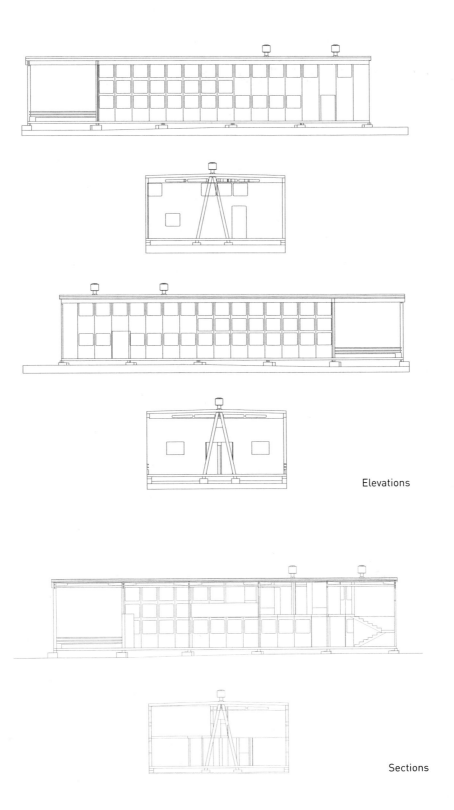

Elevations

Sections

E-60
Maison du Brésil, Cité International Universitaire

Design period: 1958
Location: Paris, France
Status: Built

Similar to Pavillon Suisse, Cité Internationale Universitaire (project 12), this building is composed of a slab-type main building used as a students' dormitory, and has a podium supported by overhead columns. The east side of the building is equipped with a sunshade system. On the ground floor, there are public spaces such as an entrance, office, public kitchen, and auditorium. These functions are arranged in the subsidiary area running through the front and rear sides of the main building. The curved plane around the huge concrete support column of the main building increases the diversity of the space.

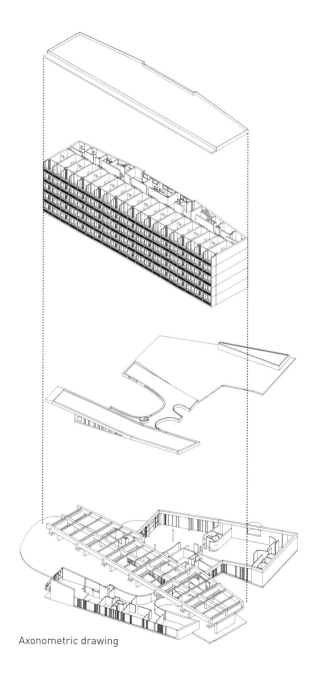

Axonometric drawing

School 363

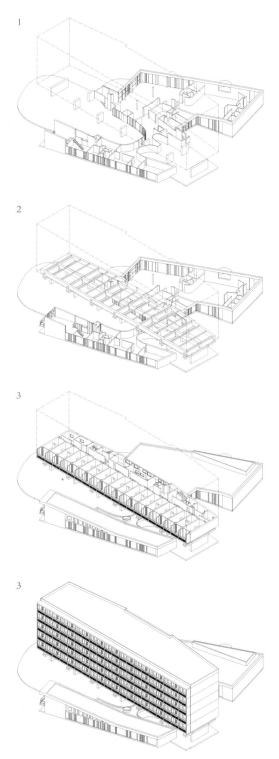

Exploded axonometric drawing

First-floor plan

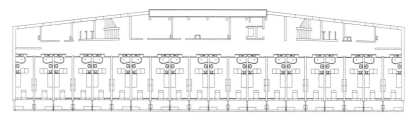

Typical floor plan

School 365

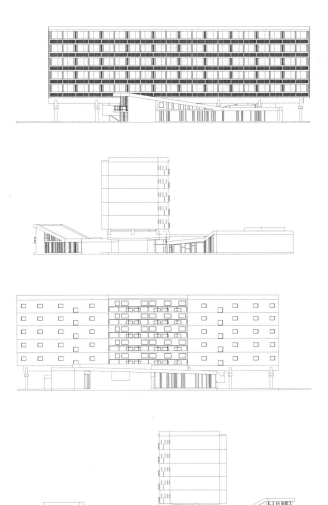

Elevations

Section

E-66
Carpenter Center for Visual Arts, Harvard University

Design period: 1961–64
Location: Massachusetts, United States
Status: Built

This is Le Corbusier's first work in the United States, on a small plot on the campus of Harvard University. In this building, Le Corbusier realized a core concept: visitors can pass through the building via a ramp that runs throughout the building; at the same time, the internal and external space can be connected. The building plane is set closely around the ramp. The two blocks separated by the ramp are independent and meet on the third floor. One of the blocks is supported by the concrete walls at the bottom, forming an open, elevated space at the bottom.

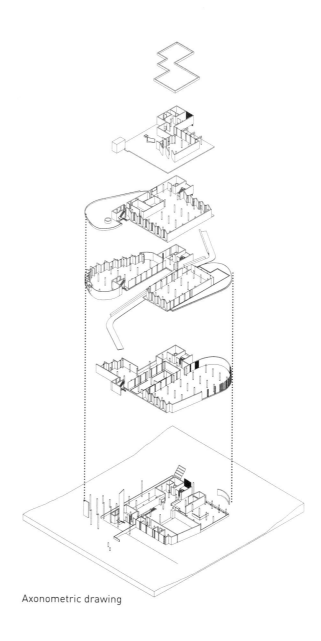

Axonometric drawing

School 367

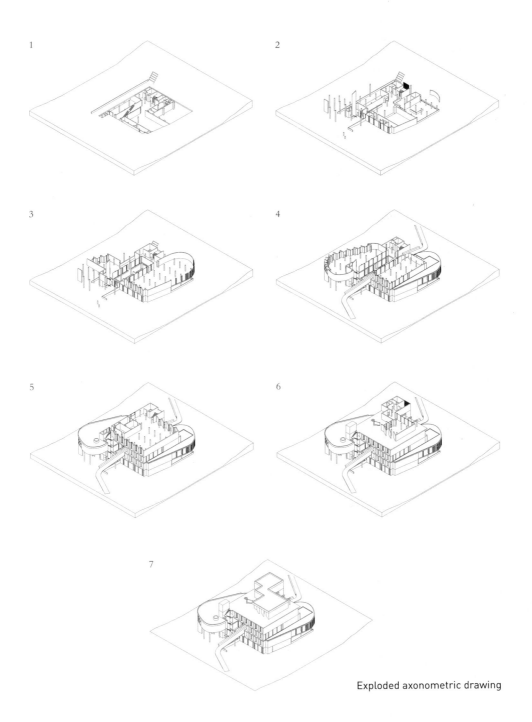

Exploded axonometric drawing

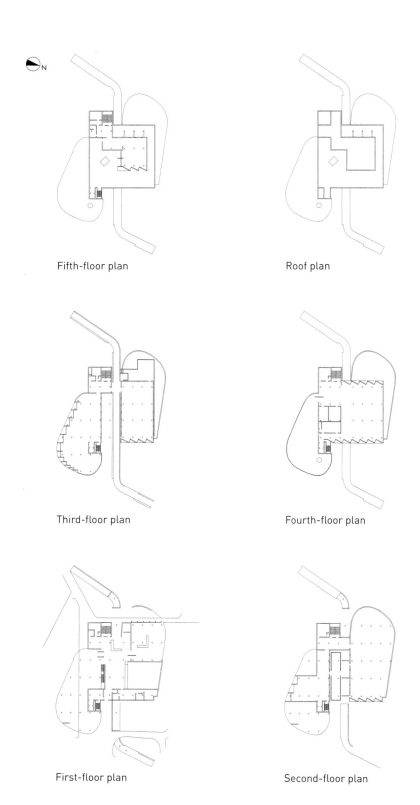

School 369

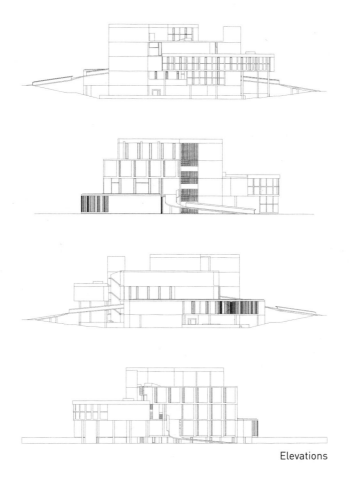

Elevations

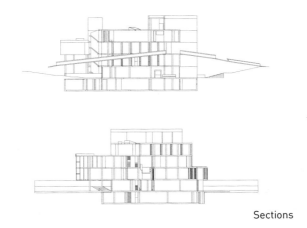

Sections

E-73
École d'Art et d'Architecture

Design period: 1964–69
Location: Chandigarh, India
Status: Built

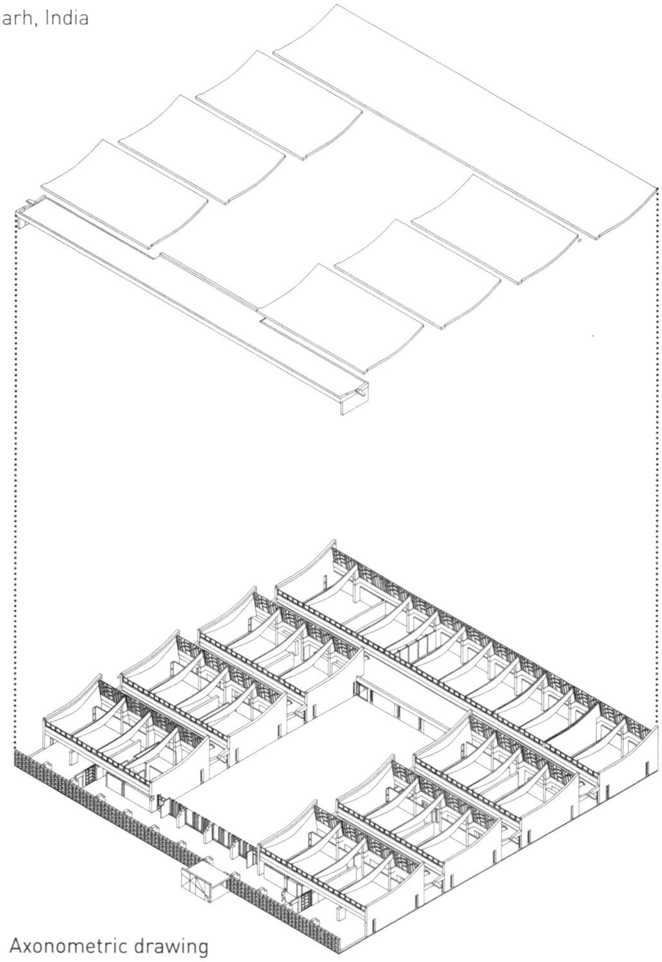

Axonometric drawing

This project was located near the government square in Chandigarh. Le Corbusier used local red bricks as the main material to set-off the concrete complex in the government square. In terms of plane structure, the inner courtyard is the center, and classrooms and studios are organized around it. These classrooms and studios are connected in the form of standard units. Their continuity can be seen from the side elevation. In order to solve the problem of lighting from the north, Le Corbusier adopted an inclined-arc roof, so the south of the roof is very low and the north-facing windows are larger. The design concept of the pre-stressed arches in groups on the section originated from the "My Home" scheme proposed by Le Corbusier in 1929.

School 371

1

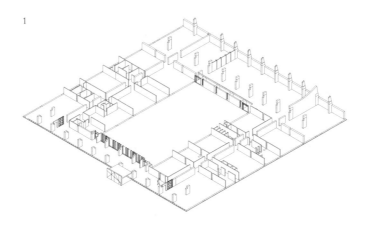

2

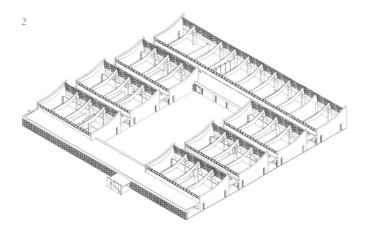

3

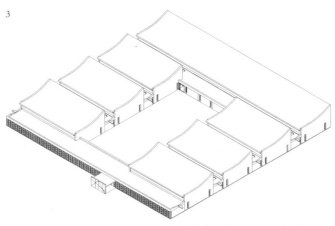

Exploded axonometric drawing

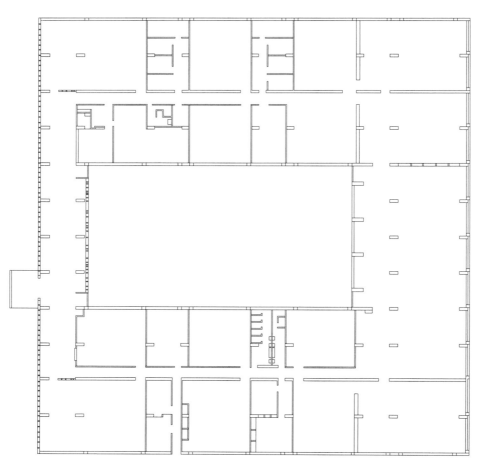

First-floor plan

School 373

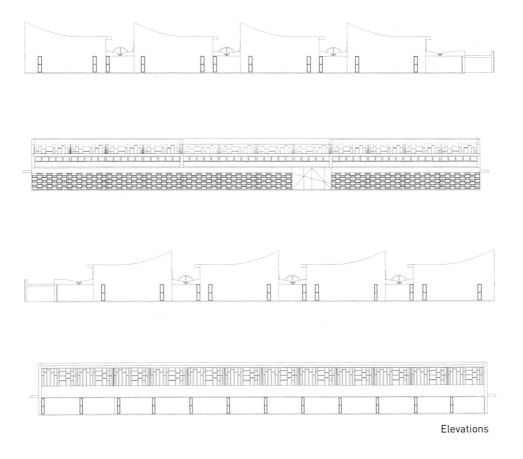

Elevations

Section

SPORTS FACILITY

F-21
Plan d'une Piscine a Vagues, Domaine de Badjarah

Design period: 1935
Location: Algiers, Algeria
Status: Unbuilt

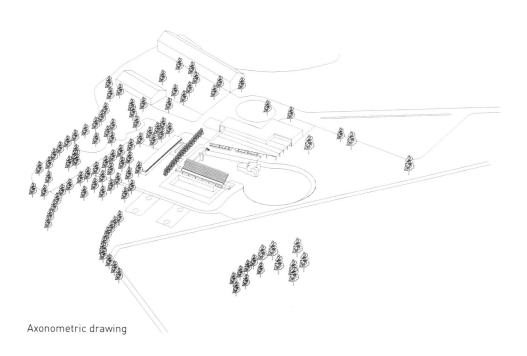

Axonometric drawing

The project is located in a small valley in Algiers, a known holiday destination. Le Corbusier designed a swimming pool, a restaurant, and a coffee shop, but they were unfortunately not built. In the general layout, the curved pool is a children's paddling pool. These pools can be used for different functions. The stand in the section is Y-shaped, with one side facing the standard pool and the other side providing shelter for the deep-water area. The Y-shaped section in this unbuilt project can provide a reference for the modern architects in their city practice, such as solving the problem of maximizing the uses of a space in a limited environment.

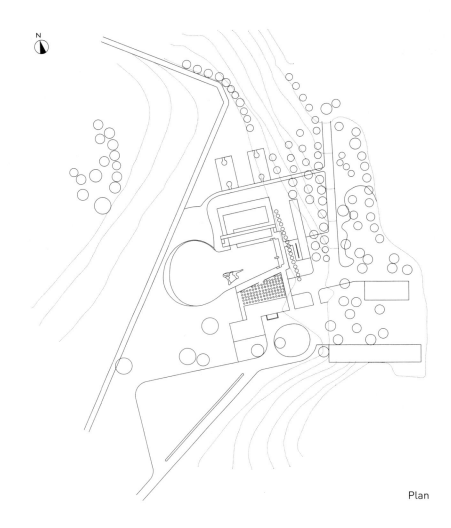

Plan

Elevation

Section

F-24
Stade de 100.000 Places

Design period: 1936–37
Location: Paris, France
Status: Unbuilt

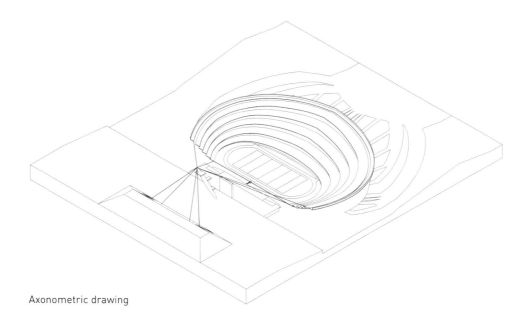

Axonometric drawing

This was meant to be a comprehensive stadium based in Paris, able to accommodate 100.000 people. In addition to the circular stand, there is also a pyramid platform for large-scale performances, a mast supporting the ceiling, a movie screen, and a stage. The circular stand surrounds the Olympic track. Using the cable structure, Le Corbusier uses a flexible roof to solve the shelter problem of the stadium.

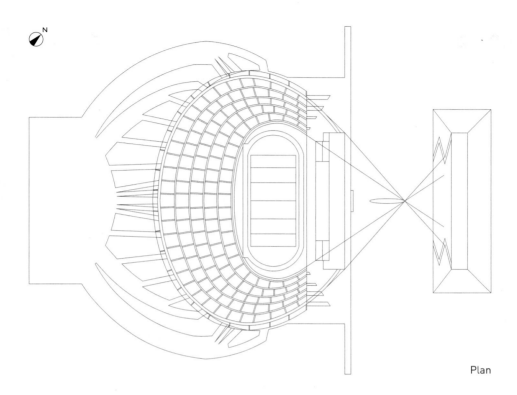

Plan

Elevation

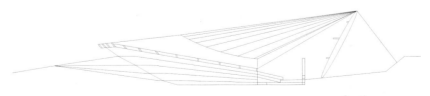

Section

F-35
Aménagement Station de Sport d'Hiver et d'Été

Design period: 1939
Location: Vars, France
Status: Unbuilt

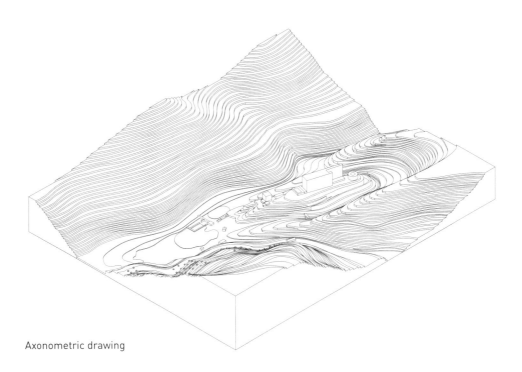

Axonometric drawing

Located in Vars, the work was designed in 1939 to provide for leisure activities. The project design includes a business center, a swimming pool, a skating rink, and a hotel. The independent box hotels are located on the hill of one side of the base. It is clear from the general layout that these independent hotels are arranged in a parallel formation along the contour line of the base.

Sports Facility

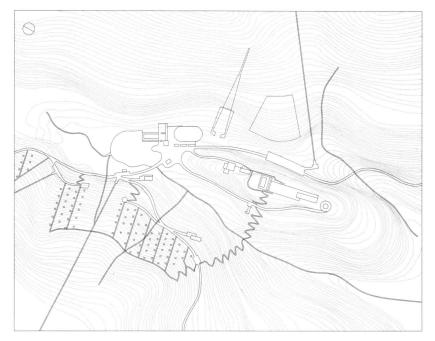

Site plan

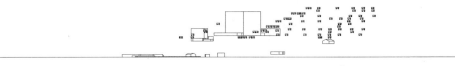

Elevation

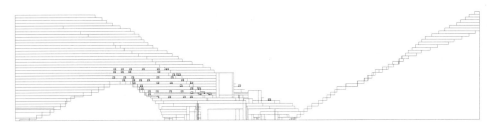

Section

F-63
Maison de la Culture

Design period: 1960–65
Location: Firminy, France
Status: Built

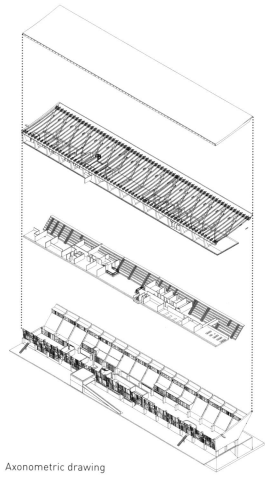

Axonometric drawing

The plane of the building is in the shape of a slender rectangle, with a length of 112 meters (367.5 feet). One side faces the road and the other side faces the stadium, and there is a height difference between the two sides. The building is overhanging on the side facing the stadium. The building's bottom is elevated and the stairs are located inside. The roof is supported by 132 parabolic steel cables. Both ends are fixed by welded steel supports and the roof cladding is fixed by steel cables. These roof slabs are light-weight, porous concrete slabs, and holes for fixing the cables can be seen in the elevation. Le Corbusier takes the height difference of the plot into consideration and deliberately incorporates the steps to negotiate the relationship between Maison de la Culture and other facilities, like the stadium (project 79), in the overall project.

Sports Facility

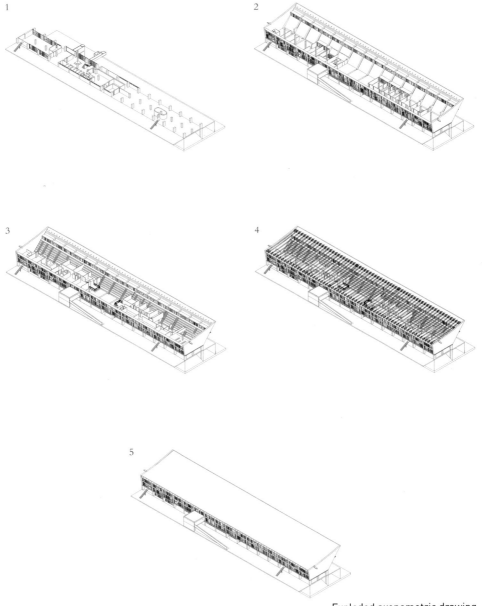

Exploded axonometric drawing

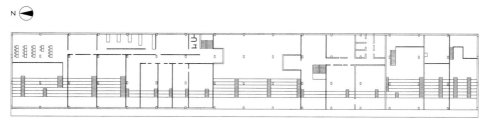

Third-floor plan

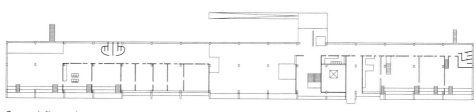

Second-floor plan

First-floor plan

Sports Facility

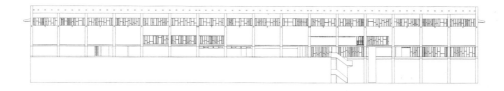

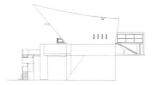

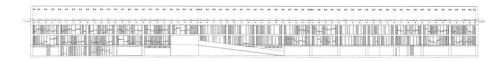

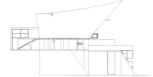

Elevations

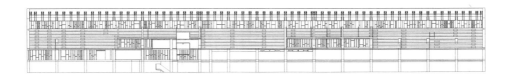

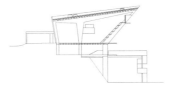

Sections

F-79
Stade, Firminy

Design period: 1965–69
Location: Firminy, France
Status: Built

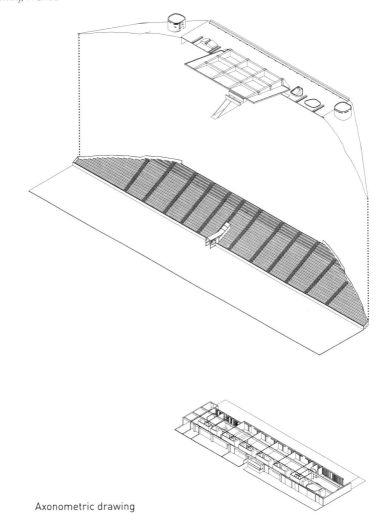

Axonometric drawing

The stadium is located opposite Maison de la Culture (project 63) and the two encircle a circular runway. The first floor of the stadium is dedicated to an athletes' dressing room, a lounge, an office, and other subsidiary rooms. The second floor holds stands for spectators. An entrance is set in the middle of the side facing the runway and an inclined canopy roof truss is set on the upper part of the stand. The sloping composition of the stand and canopy of the stadium contrast with the overhanging Maison de la Culture on the opposite side.

Sports Facility 385

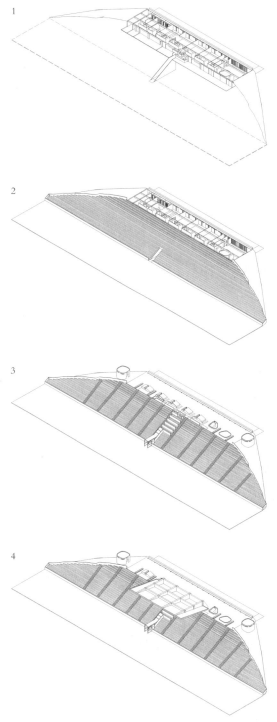

Exploded axonometric drawing

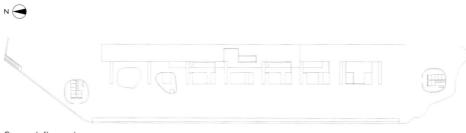

Second-floor plan

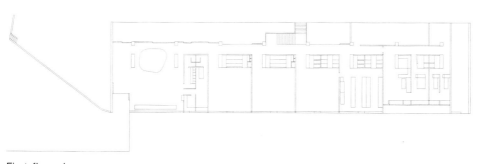

First-floor plan

Sports Facility

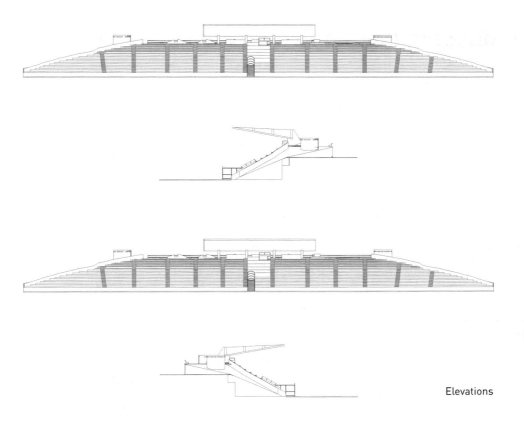

Elevations

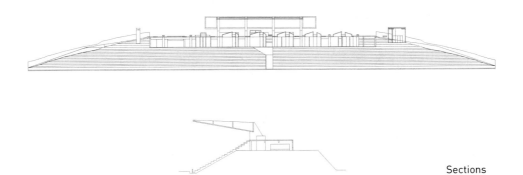

Sections

PUBLIC BUILDING (WATER CONSERVANCY)

G-03
Château d'Eau

Design period: 1917
Location: Podensac, France
Status: Built

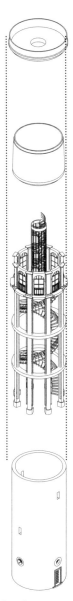

This is a finished water construction not included in *Le Corbusier Complete Works*. Its plan is circular, with eight pillars dividing it into eight equal parts. At the center of Château d'Eau stands a viewing platform, which can be reached along the spiral staircase along the inner wall of the building's exterior walls. Windows and balustrades are arranged in the octagonal compartment of the viewing platform and at the very center of this floor is a small spiral staircase that leads to the roof of Château d'Eau. In such an octagonal compact plan, only spiral staircases with circular flat surfaces can be accommodated; its roof has a small canopy. As a prototype of water construction, Château d'Eau's design was gradually used as a vertical traffic tower in Le Corbusier's later works, such as the spiral staircase cylinder in the corner of the inner courtyard of Couvent Sainte-Marie de la Tourette (project 57), similiar to how he applied the prototype of the industrial tower to the assembly hall of Palais de l'Assemblée (project 48).

Axonometric drawing

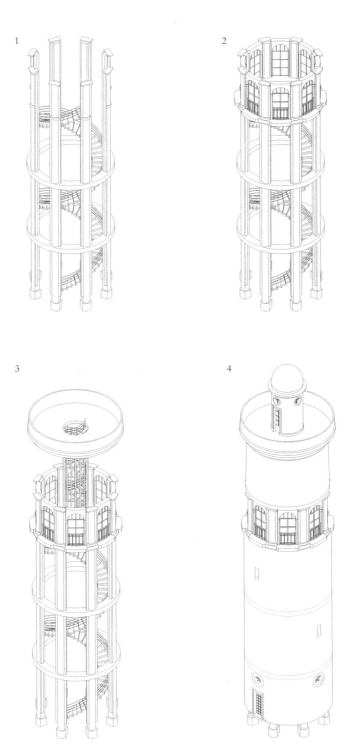

Exploded axonometric drawing

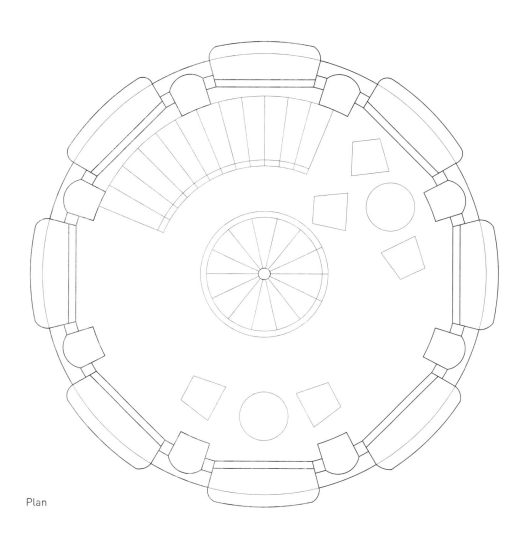

Plan

Public Building (Water Conservancy)   391

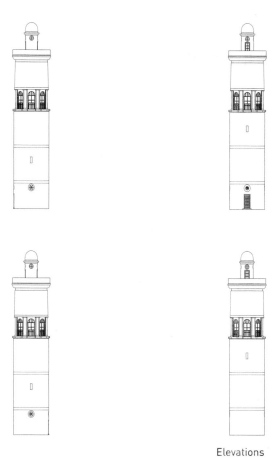

Elevations

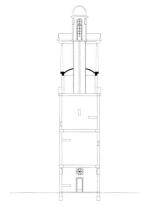 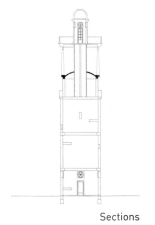

Sections

G-61
Bâtiments de l'Écluse

Design period: 1959–62
Location: Between Rhone River and Rhine River, Kembs-Niffer, France
Status: Built

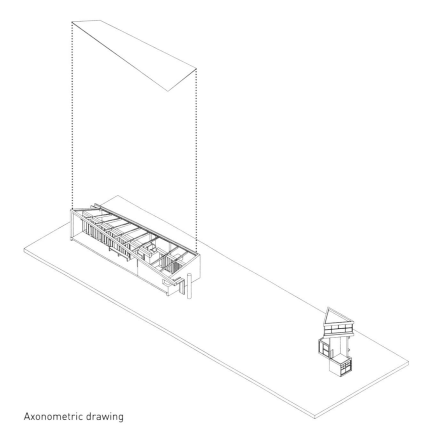

Axonometric drawing

Bâtiments de l'Écluse is composed of a control tower for the lock keeper, a machine room, and a checkpoint, and the base is at the junction between the Rhône River and the main channel of the Rhine River. The control tower supports the platform of the roof through a T-shaped concrete construction and the double running stairs are put aside and disconnected from the platform. The ground level of the checkpoint is used for offices of shipping scheduling and inspection, and below it are a garage, staff room, and boiler room. The plan is square and the roof is in the form of a broken line rising diagonally, with rainwater flowing out from two low corners—designed to imitate a waterfall. Drainage is the basic problem in all construction and Le Corbusier accepts it as a factor of building, like what he does in Église Saint Pierre (project 64).

Public Building (Water Conservancy) 393

1

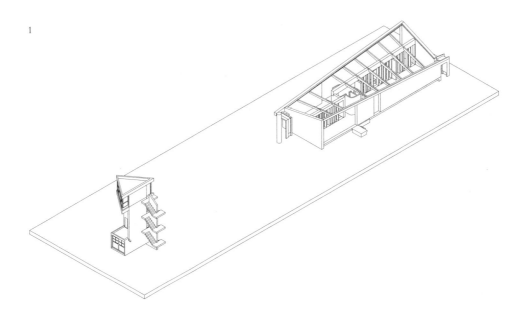

2

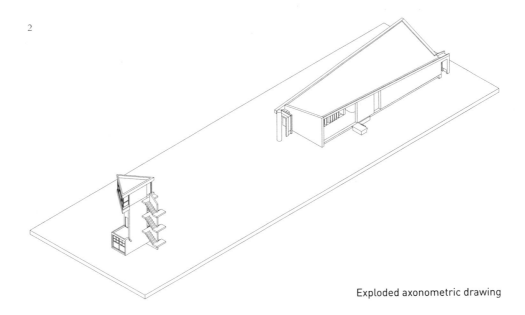

Exploded axonometric drawing

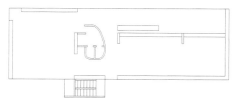

First-floor plan

Public Building (Water Conservancy) 395

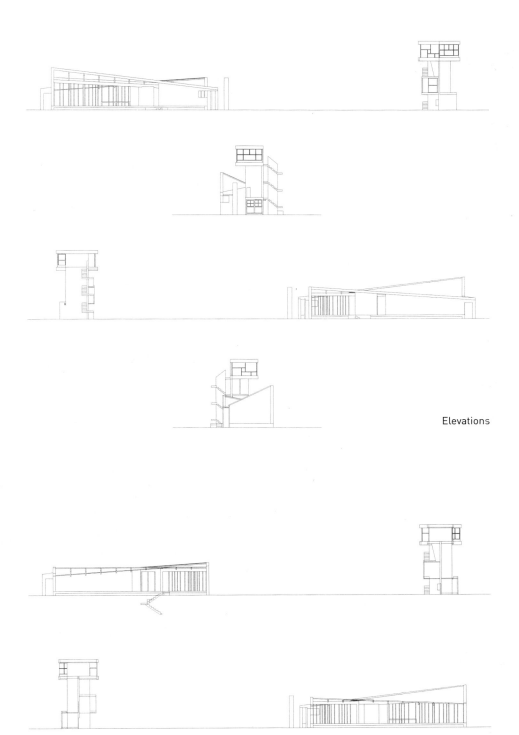

Elevations

Sections

H-04
Gratte-Ciel Cartésien

Design period: 1922
Location: None
Status: Unbuilt

Gratte-Ciel Cartésien was designed at Salon d'Automne, an art exhibition held in France in 1922, when Le Corbusier put forward a plan of "a contemporary city for 3,000 people." In 1935, when Le Corbusier first came to America, he said to an American journalist: "These skyscrapers are so small and densely arranged." From "a contemporary city for 3,000 people" to "a radiant city," the theme of the urban planning in this project is sun, green space, and air, which inspire smaller covering areas and a larger building density. Gratte-Ciel Cartésien's Y-shape solves the lighting problem in the north that results from the cross-shaped plan of Le Corbusier's city architecture planning. The ground floor is reserved for pedestrians, and 5 meters (17.2 feet) above that are motorways, expressways, and bus stops. The middle contains standard offices and at the top stands the roof garden.

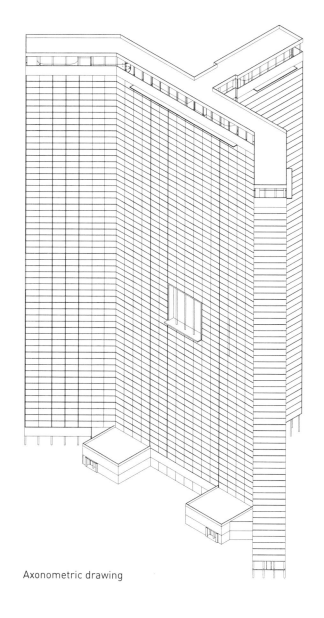

Axonometric drawing

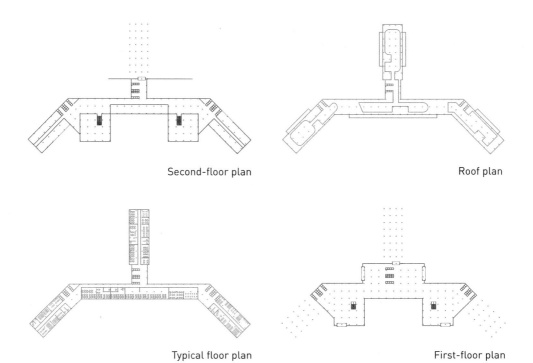

Second-floor plan

Roof plan

Typical floor plan

First-floor plan

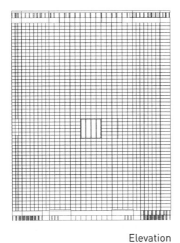

Elevation

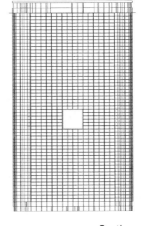

Section

H-18
Réorganisation Agraire, Ferme et Village Radieux

Design period: 1934–38
Location: None
Status: Unbuilt

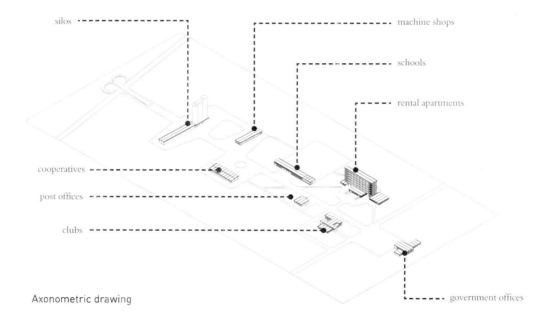

Axonometric drawing

After designing the theoretical model of "La Ville Radiuse," Le Corbusier expressed his theory of "a radiant farm" through his ideas of cooperative farms in the countryside of the new era. In addition to some traditional facilities, such as government offices, schools, and post offices, the building complex embodies the new agencies of collective living—silos for production control, clubs for various activities, rental apartments for new family life, cooperatives for necessities of life, and machine shops for assembling and constructing metal components. On the whole, this is a planning theory with a utopian vision that promotes a rural collective life and public services. Architecturally, Le Corbusier used flat arches to unify all farm facilities. The project adopted a flat-arch thin-shell cast by a detachable mold and has its upper floor covered with a soil layer for planting grass and shrubs.

Complex 399

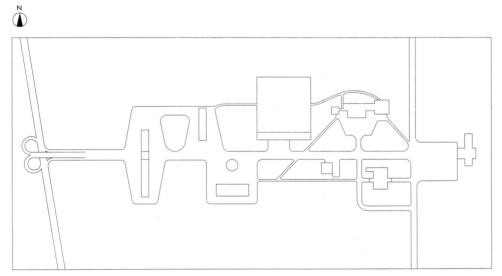

Site plan

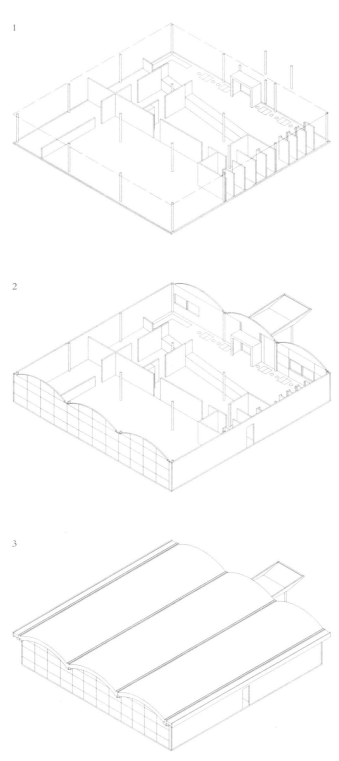

Post office – exploded axonometric drawing

Complex 401

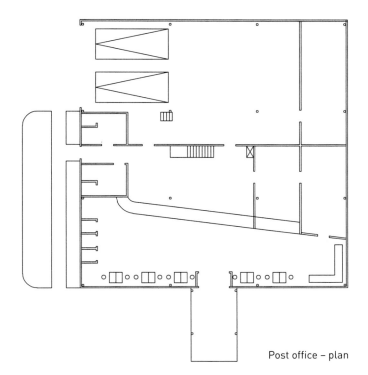

Post office – plan

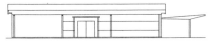

Post office – elevations

Post office – sections

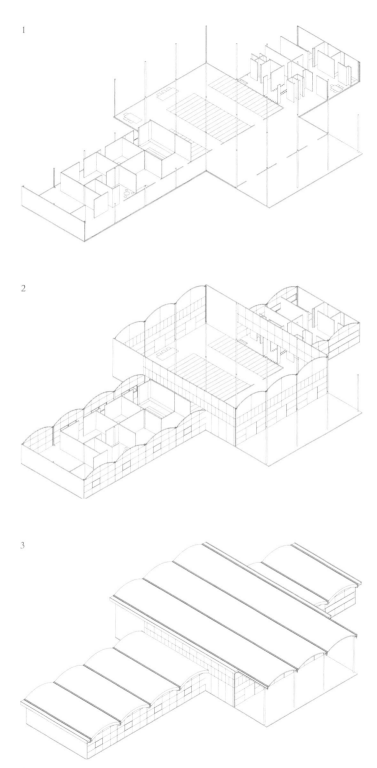

Government office – exploded axonometric drawing

Complex 403

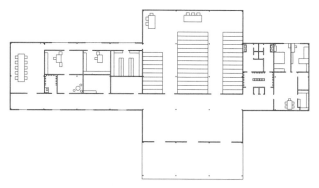
Government office – plan

Government office – elevations

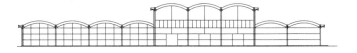

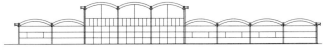
Government office – sections

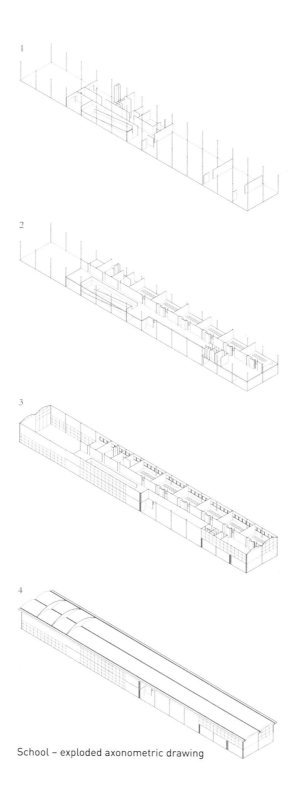

School – exploded axonometric drawing

Complex 405

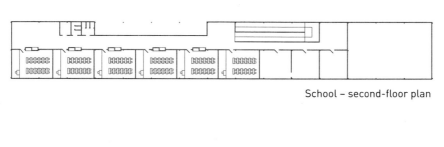

School – second-floor plan

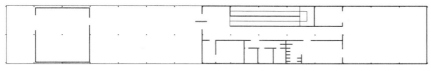

School – first-floor plan

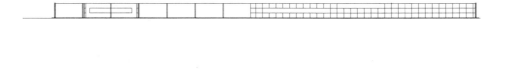

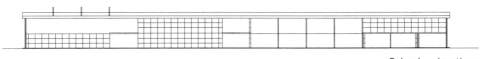

School – elevations

School – sections

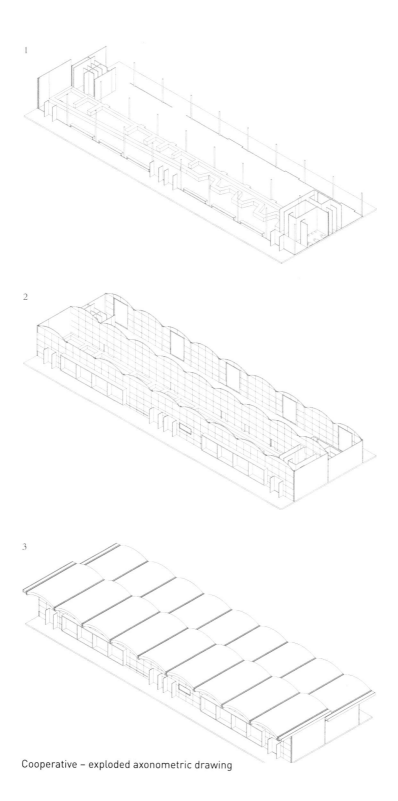

Cooperative – exploded axonometric drawing

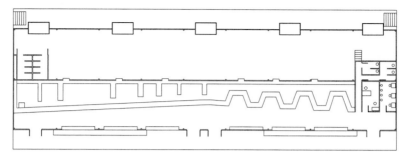

Cooperative – plan

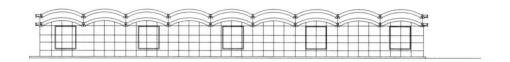

Cooperative – elevations

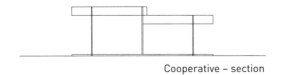

Cooperative – section

1

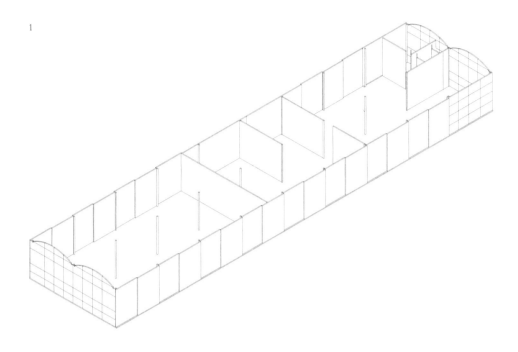

2

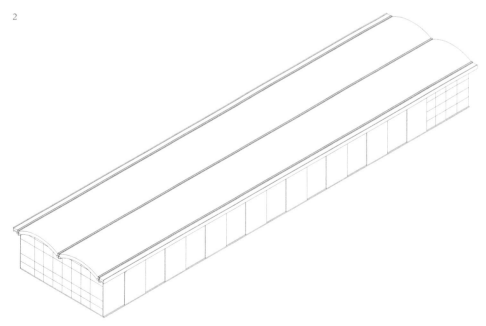

Machine shop – exploded axonometric drawing

Complex   409

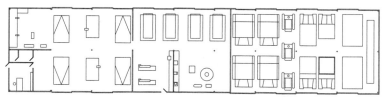

Machine shop – plan

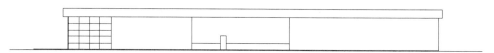

Machine shop – elevation

Machine shop – section

410

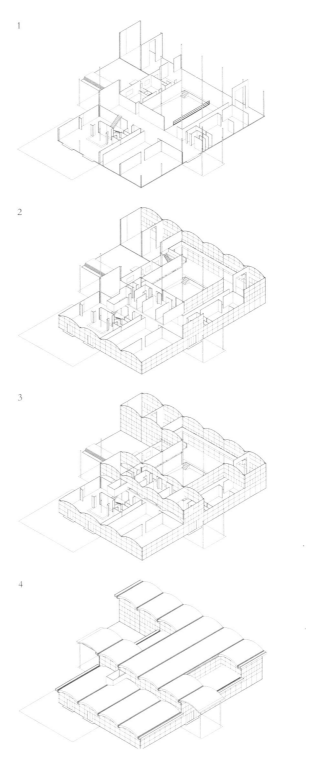

Club – exploded axonometric drawing

Complex 411

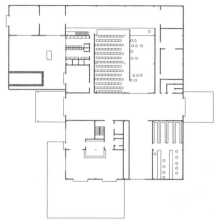

Club – first-floor plan

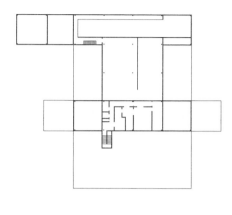

Club – second-floor plan

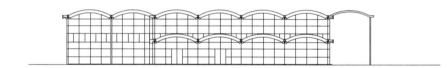

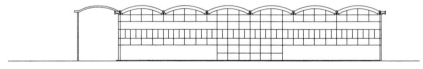

Club – elevations

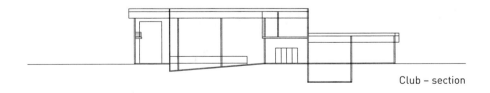

Club – section

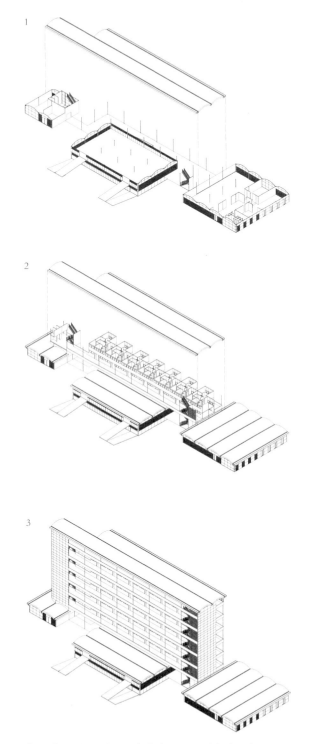

Rental apartment – exploded axonometric drawing

Complex 413

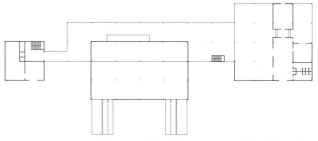
Rental apartment – first-floor plan

Rental apartment – typical floor plan (upper floor)

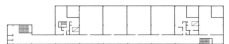
Rental apartment – typical floor plan (lower floor)

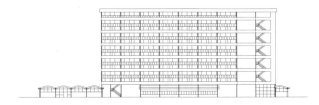
Rental apartment – elevations

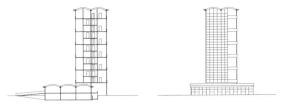
Rental apartment – sections

H-22
Lotissement Durand, Oued Ouchaia

Design period: 1935
Location: Algiers, Algeria
Status: Unbuilt

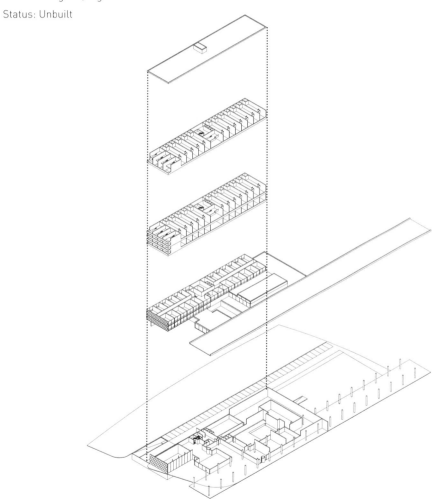

Axonometric drawing

The location was close to an elevated expressway and the work considers blocks in its planning. The lower floor has garages and machine shops; the first floor has standing bars, hotel entrances, shops, and shopping malls for the public and passengers; the second and third floor has passenger hotels; and the upper floor has apartments for officials.

Complex 415

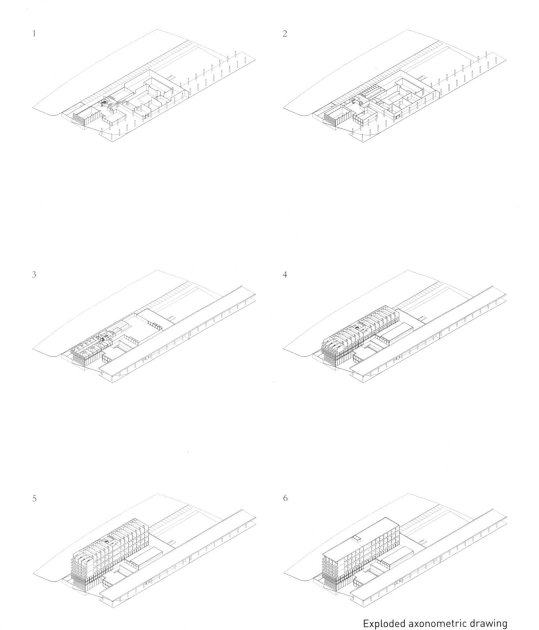

Exploded axonometric drawing

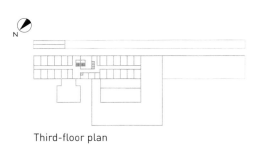

Third-floor plan

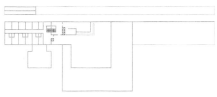

Second-floor plan

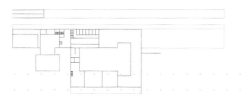

Mezzanine floor plan

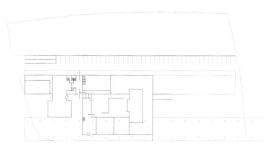

First-floor plan

Typical floor plan (upper floor)

Typical floor plan (lower floor)

Complex **417**

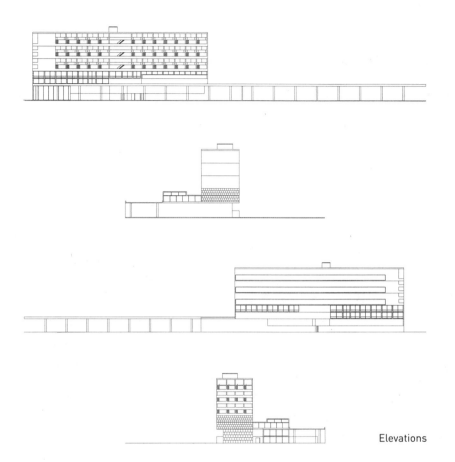

Elevations

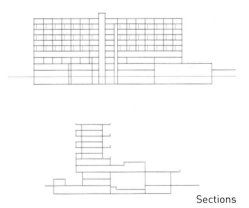

Sections

H-30
Gratte-Ciel, Quartier de la Marine, Cité des Affaires

Design period: 1938–42
Location: Algiers, Algeria
Status: Unbuilt

The building was designed to be 150 meters (492 feet) high with two floors of basement garages. The entrance to the hotel is at the top of Gratte-Ciel on the second basement floor. The entrance hall, a pedestrian entrance ramp, and a vehicle port are arranged on the first elevated floor. On the whole, the lowest floor of Gratte-Ciel is used to streamline the movement of pedestrians and vehicles, with administrative buildings at the center, and hotel rooms on the top floor. The plan is shaped like a shuttle, with narrow ends and a wide middle. In the middle are multiple elevators. In the surrounding area are open offices or partitioned hotel rooms, with glass-decorated walls. The façades of the building are shaded by a concave balcony.

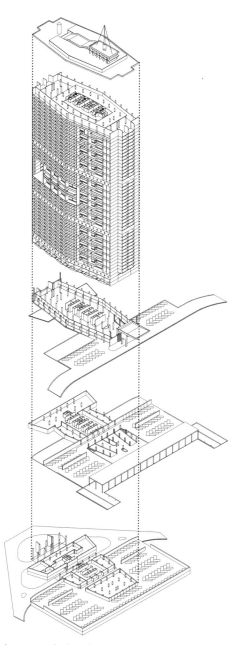

Axonometric drawing

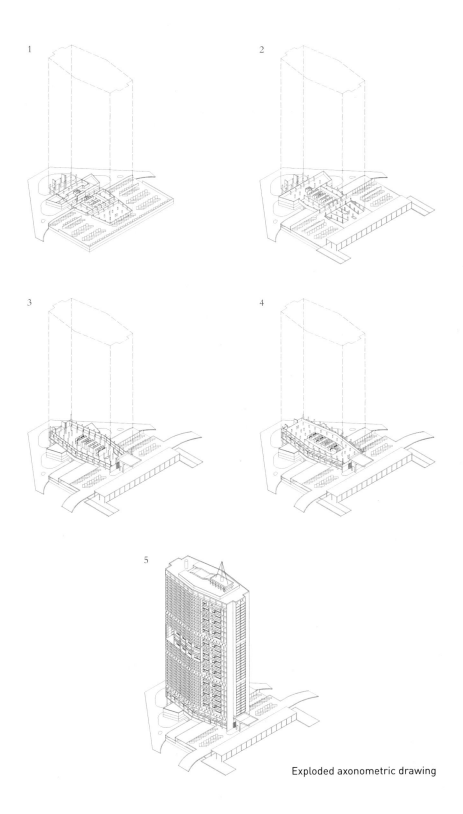

Exploded axonometric drawing

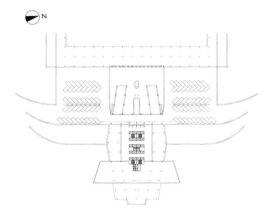

First-floor plan

Elevated first-floor plan

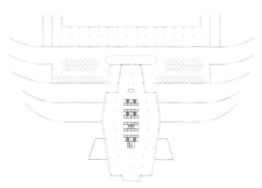

Second basement floor plan

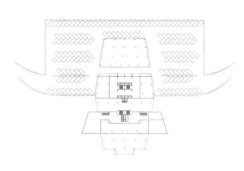

Basement floor plan

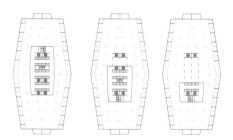

Typical floor plan

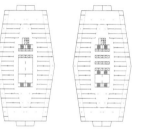

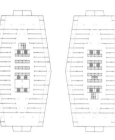

Complex 421

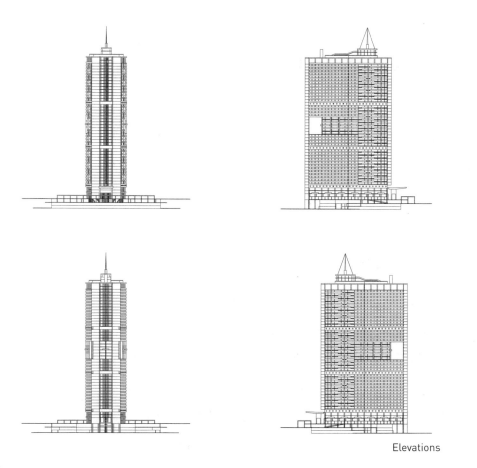

Elevations

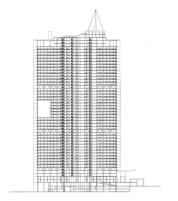 

Sections

H-37
Unité d'Habitation

Design period: 1945
Location: Marseille, France
Status: Built

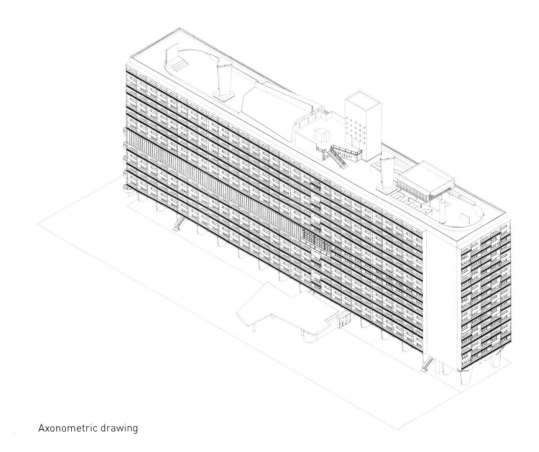

Axonometric drawing

This was one of Le Corbusier's later representative works in standard collective housing that provides multiple housing types according to the number of people in each family. In addition to the housing functions, Unité d'Habitation is arranged with a "road" to bring supplies in and includes many service facilities found in urban areas, such as food stores, bars, restaurants, kindergartens, a children's playground on the roof, indoor and outdoor sports venues, a 300-meter (984-foot) running track, and an area for sunbathing. The whole building is elevated on thick concrete pillars and the standard floors of the apartments are shown as the interlocking spring layer.

Complex 423

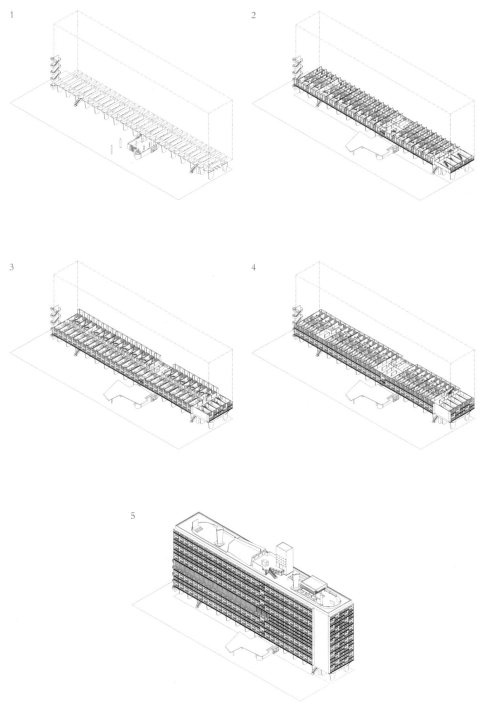

Exploded axonometric drawing

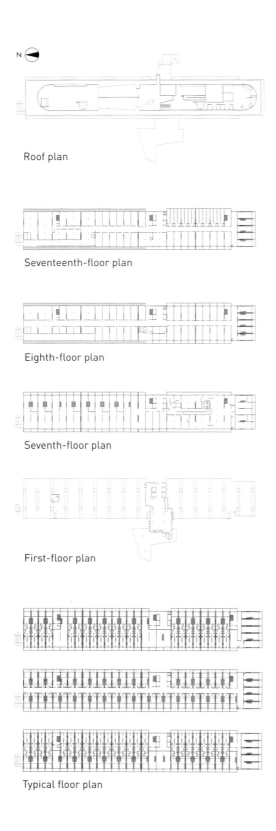

Roof plan

Seventeenth-floor plan

Eighth-floor plan

Seventh-floor plan

First-floor plan

Typical floor plan

Complex 425

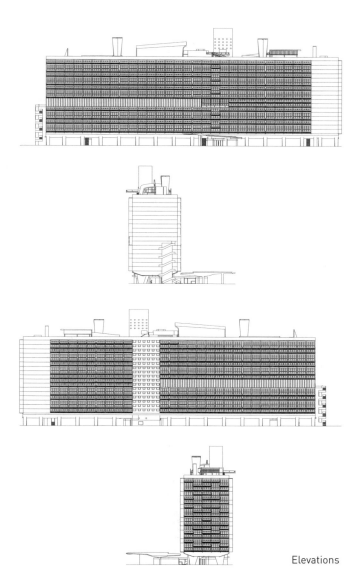

Elevations

Section

H-65
Gare d'Orsay

Design period: 1961
Location: Paris, France
Status: Unbuilt

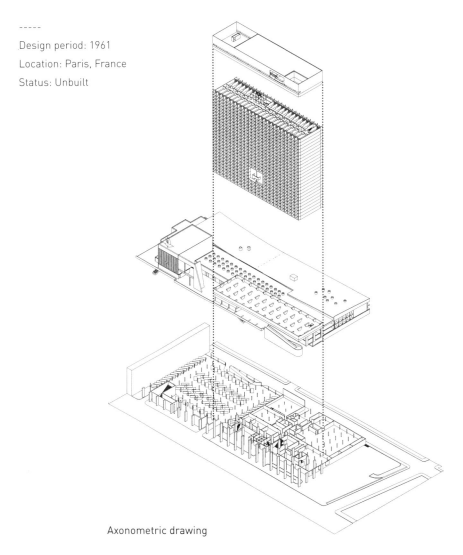

Axonometric drawing

Close to the Seine, the block performs as a multipurpose cultural center for meetings, exhibitions, music performances, and as a theater. The plan of the building is arranged to accommodate hotels, conferences, and cultural areas, and it is shaped as a high-rise hotel with subsidiary annexes. The first floor is for entrances and public facilities; the one side near the street is spaciously designed, and other rooms are for hotel service facilities, such as a food warehouse, laundry room, and pantry. On the third floor, are lobbies, bars and restaurants, a conference room, and art galleries. The hotel level has a standard design—corridors with guest rooms on each side. In the middle of the backstreet-side are elevators and stairs, and every guestroom has a balcony.

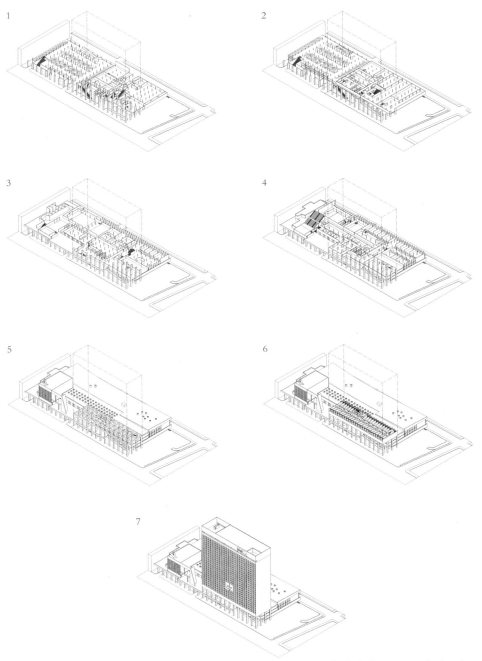

Exploded axonometric drawing

Fourth-floor plan

Roof plan

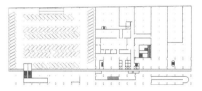
Second-floor plan

Third-floor plan

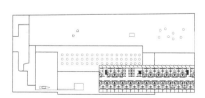
Typical floor plan

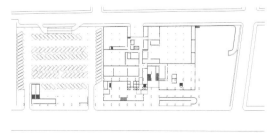
First-floor plan

Complex 429

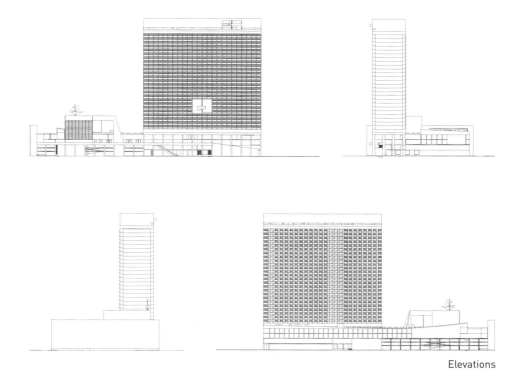

Elevations

Sections

I-02
Cinéma "La Scala"

Design period: 1916
Location: La Chaux-de-Fonds, Switzerland
Status: Built

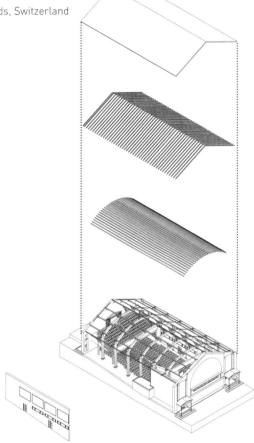

Axonometric drawing

This was an early work created before Le Corbusier's "white house" (La Maison Blanche) located in La Chaux-de-Fonds. The base is a finished theater building, but is not included in *Le Corbusier Complete Works*. Compared with Le Corbusier's other works, this is a project that retains classicism. It can be seen from the elevation of the two "mountain walls" in the theater that the roof is constructed in a gable-shaped two-slope style, with the elevation retaining axial symmetry, and a small porch setting at both sides of the entrance. The main body of the theater supports the roof with an arched beam frame—with the supporting column covered, and then purlin-laid. The inner space is divided into two floors, with one floor for stage and seats. Across from the stage is a semi-overhanging stand, and people can reach it by a straight staircase on the inner side of the first floor or two sets of stairs at the outer entrance.

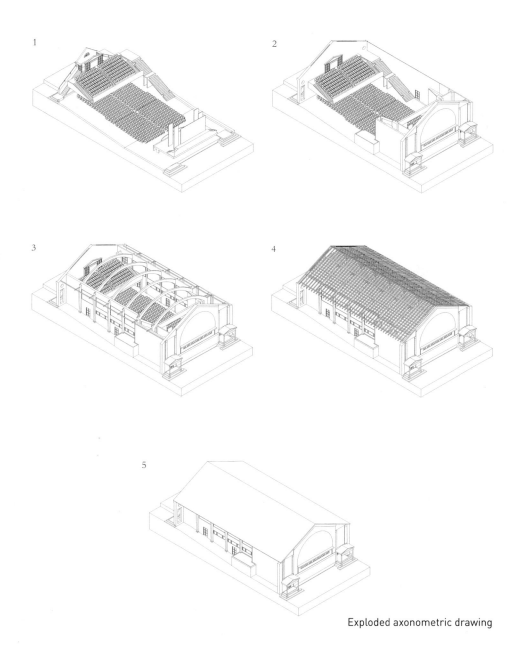

Exploded axonometric drawing

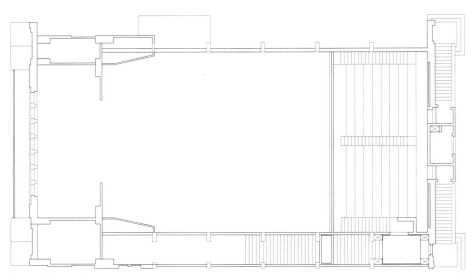

Second-floor plan

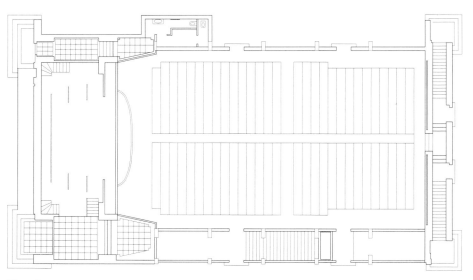

First-floor plan

Commercial Building 433

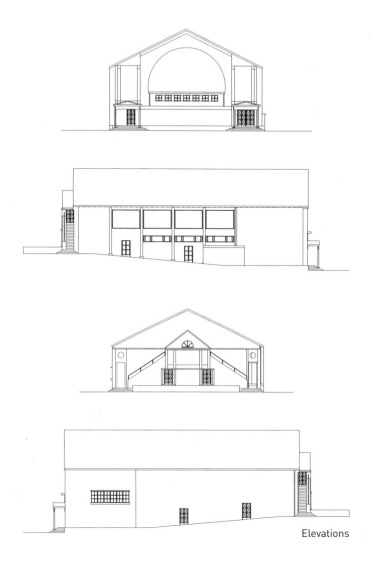

Elevations

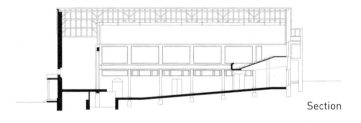

Section

I-13
Cinéma à Montparnasse

Design period: 1931
Location: Paris, France
Status: Unbuilt

This is an unfinished theater plan; the main feature lies in its departure from the traditional concept of a "flat" floor. It can be seen from the section that the four evenly distributed pillars run across the five sections, supporting the floor and roof. In order to satisfy the demands for step-style seats in theaters, the floor is inclined and connected by "ladders" or staircases. The "five points of the new building" of the frame structure include a free plan and elevation. It is through the plan that Le Corbusier showed free section.

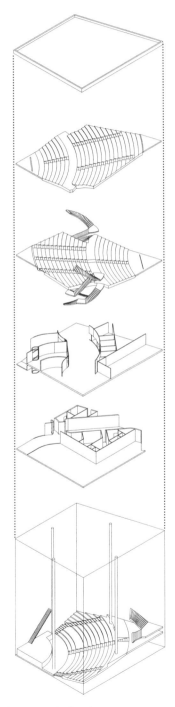

Axonometric drawing

Commercial Building 435

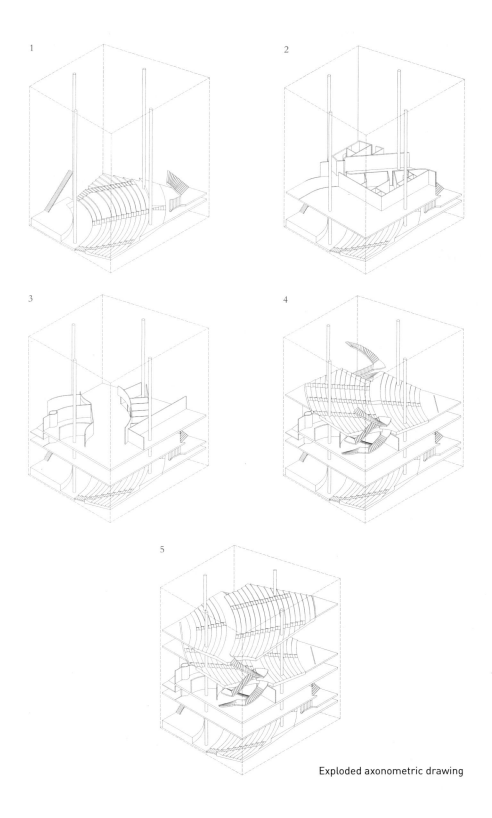

Exploded axonometric drawing

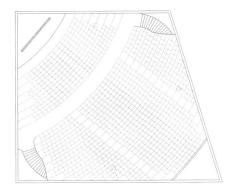

Fifth-floor plan

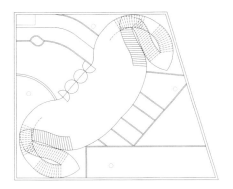

Third-floor plan

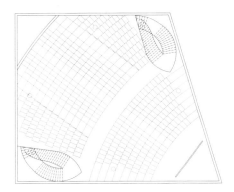

Fourth-floor plan

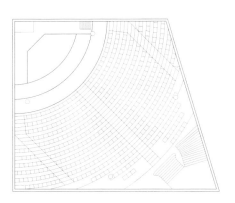

First-floor plan

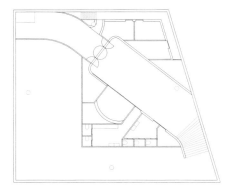

Second-floor plan

Commercial Building 437

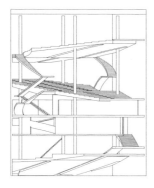
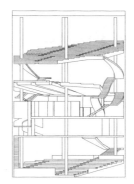
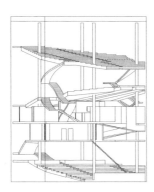
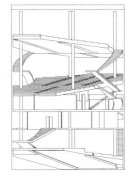

Elevations

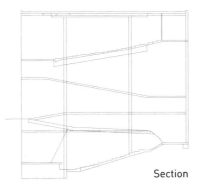

Section

I-25
Boutique Bat'a

Design period: 1936
Location: None
Status: Unbuilt

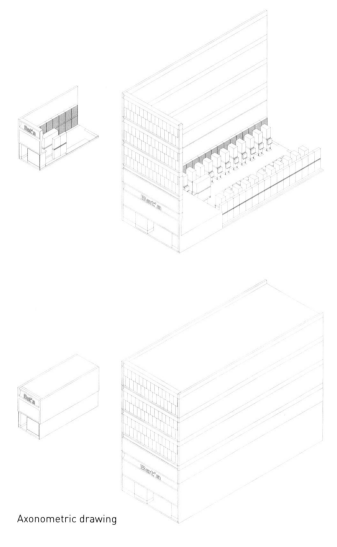

Axonometric drawing

This is a design proposal that is a standard for urban stores. Le Corbusier designed the corresponding standard plans after ensuring "standard" shelves, cabinets, seats, and other components; also considered was how large the store would be—whether in a single or double layer; how many showcases it would accommodate; and the location of the store. The light box is set in the section to attract people. This seems to be the standard style that Le Corbusier created for business buildings.

Commercial Building 439

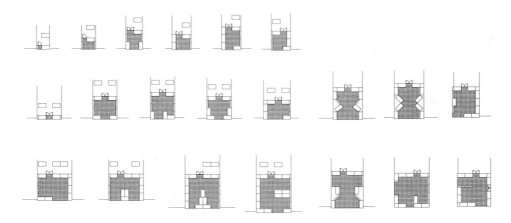
Plan

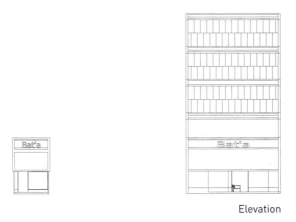
Elevation

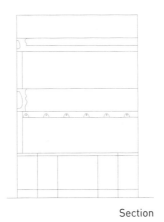
Section

I-59
City Center, Chandigarh

Design period: 1958-69
Location: Chandigarh, India
Status: Unbuilt

This is a standard building system Le Corbusier designed for Chandigarh. If the "domino" system proposed in the 1910s is the most basic standard building pattern for all buildings, then this plan for a center business area is a standard designed for some new towns in Chandigarh. It is able to provide multiple functions for offices, businesses, restaurants, and facilities, and the plan can be adjusted to meet future changing demands. The difference between this plan and the "domino" system lies in the varied elevation design. Considering the climate in India, Le Corbusier designed a sunshade system by withdrawing the used space from elevation to spare the veranda. From the elevation, the concrete grille baffles are stored in the standard bay. The basic principle of the building system is the standard frame structure system of beams and columns.

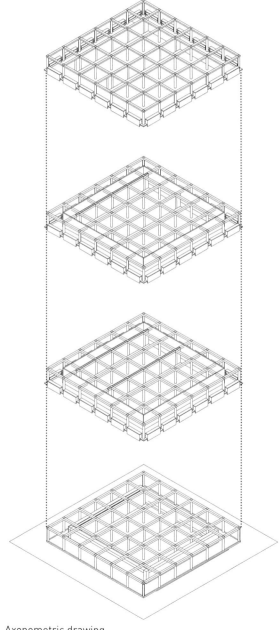

Axonometric drawing

Commercial Building 441

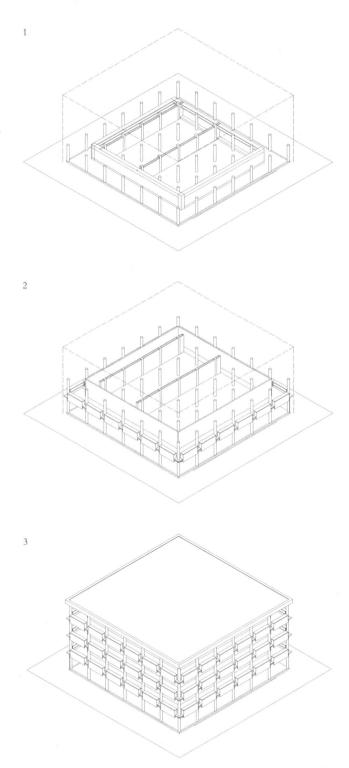

1

2

3

Exploded axonometric drawing

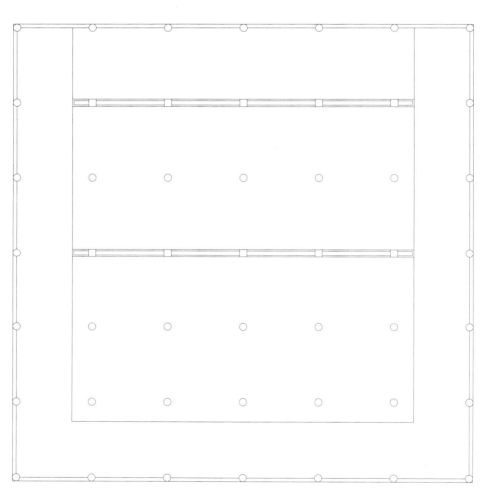

Plan

Commercial Building   443

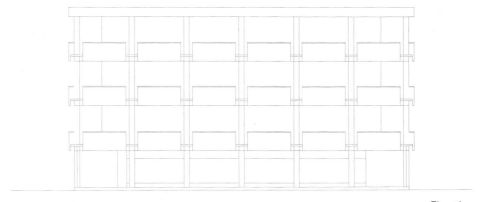

Elevation

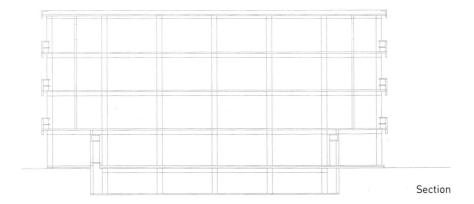

Section

I-70
The Club House

Design period: 1963–65
Location: Chandigarh, India
Status: Built

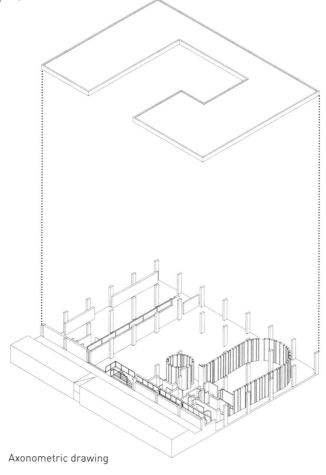

Axonometric drawing

The block is located near the square complex of the government of Chandigarh, and near the Club House. In order to maintain a wide view of the government square facing the Himalayas, the club is constructed 3 meters (9.8 feet) below the road surface, beyond the sight of pedestrians. In addition, the simple structure blends with the surrounding environment. The square club has one floor with a U-shaped space surrounding an open courtyard. In addition to the open teahouse in the center, there are a hall, kitchen, staff office, storage room, and other functional rooms. The frame structure makes the whole building open, particularly the side toward the Club House.

Commercial Building 445

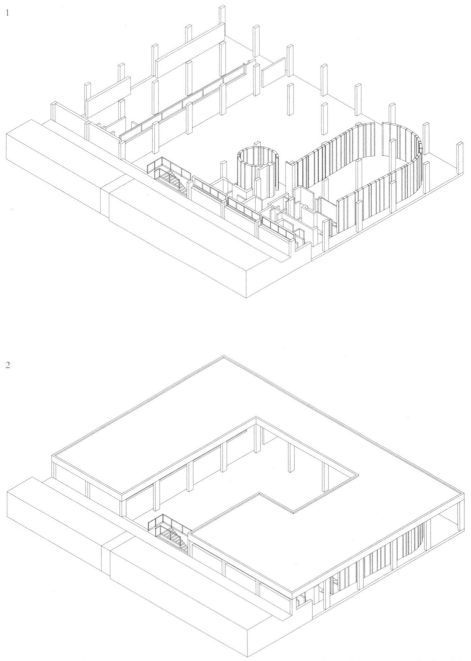

Exploded axonometric drawing

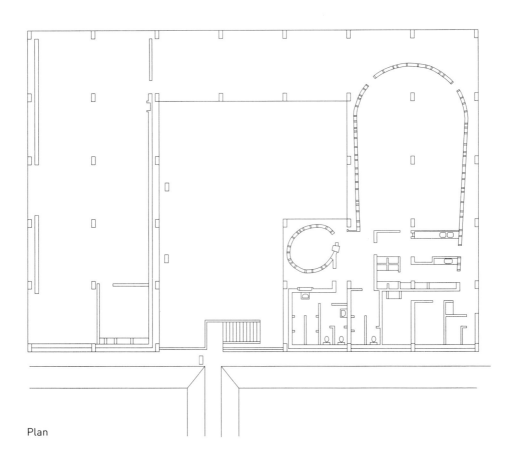

Plan

Commercial Building 447

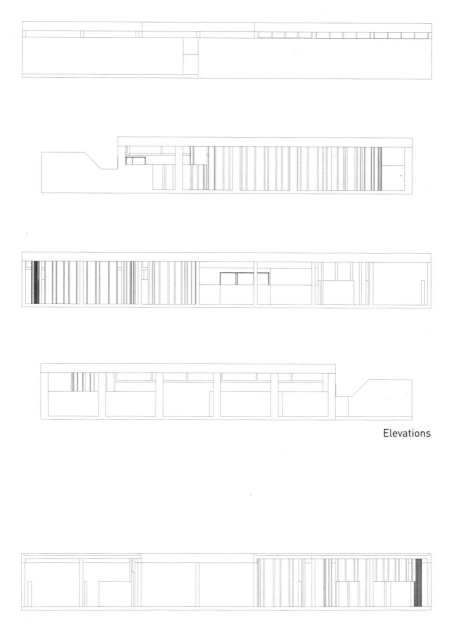

Elevations

Sections

J-29
Monument Paul Vaillant-Couturier

Design period: 1937–38
Location: Paris, France
Status: Unbuilt

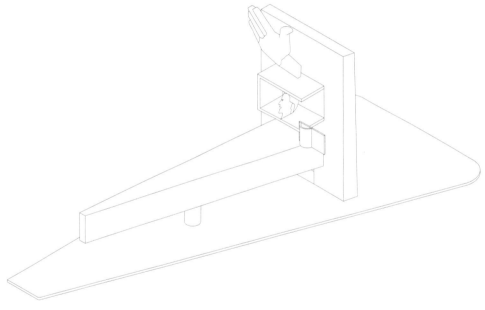

Axonometric drawing

Vaillant-Couturier (1892–1937) was a member of the Communist Party and a Parisian journalist; he was also the editor of *L'Humanité*. The monument that Le Corbusier designed for him was to be located in the intersection of two roads in Paris. It can be seen from the floor plan that its block is almost ladder-shaped and the plan of the monument shrinks according to the shape of the block, parallel to the boundaries of the block. The monument mainly consists of three geometrical blocks: one vertical thick wall, one nearly tetrahedron in a triangular plane, and one cylindrical supporting pillar. The wall includes sculptured designs of hands, portraits, and books.

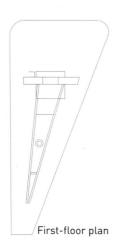
First-floor plan

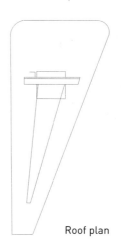
Roof plan

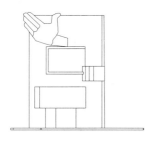
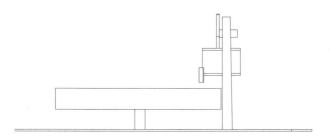
Elevations

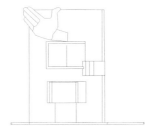
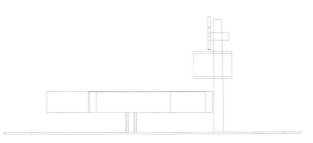
Sections

J-45
Main Ouverte, Chandigarh

Design period: 1951–57
Location: Chandigarh, India
Status: Built

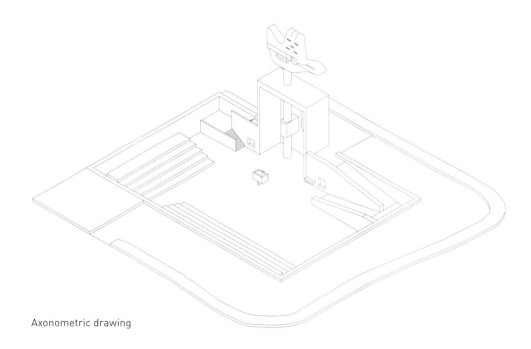

Axonometric drawing

This is the most famous work of Le Corbusier's monuments. It is located in the new town in Chandigarh, facing the Himalayas. Supported by wooden frames, the main body can rotate around the vertical axis and its "hand" itself is riveted by forged iron. The "open hand" is arranged on the outdoor sinking square called "the pit of meditation" and visitors can reach the bottom through stairs and ramps on both sides. In the middle of the square is a lecture forum surrounded by outdoor seats.

Monument 451

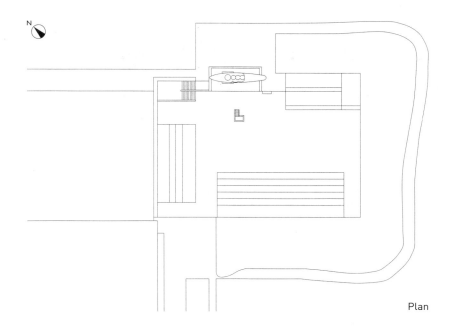

Plan

Elevations

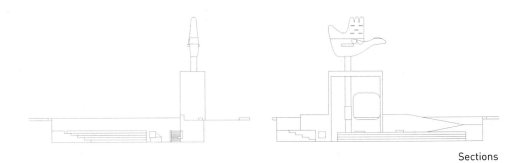

Sections

J-46
Monument des Martyrs, Chandigarh

Design period: 1951–57
Location: Chandigarh, India
Status: Built

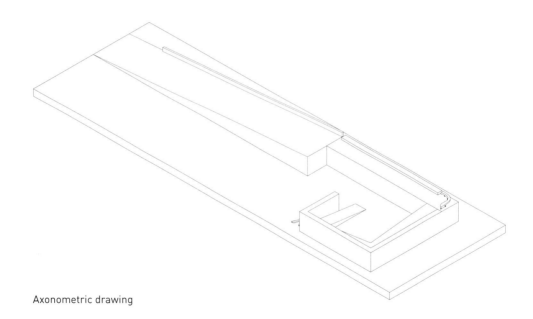

Axonometric drawing

Monument des Martyrs is located in the square of the Chandigarh government and is close to Tour d'Ombres (project 52). The main body of the monument is ramp-shaped. One side of the long ramp reaches the platform level, and then the circulation leads back down multiple ramps to the ground. Monument des Martyrs is included in *Le Corbusier Complete Works, Volume 8*, but there is still no detailed introduction on it.

Monument   453

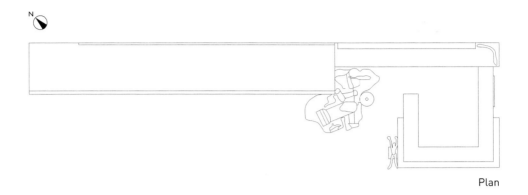

Plan

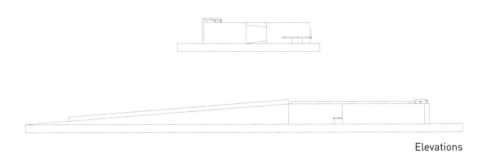

Elevations

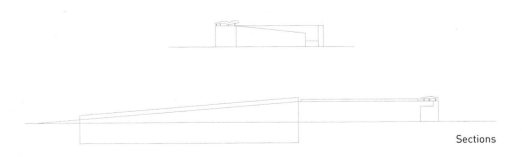

Sections

J-52
Tour d'Ombres

Design period: 1952
Location: Chandigarh, India
Status: Built

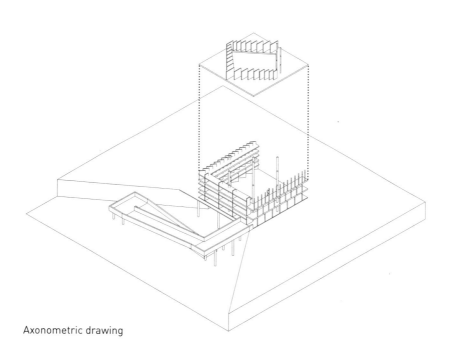

Axonometric drawing

The Tour d'Ombres shows Le Corbusier's precise shading against the sun. It faces south and north as it looks to the symmetry of the government square in Chandigarh. The north of the building remains totally open, with the left three sides arranged with sunshades. Seen on the plan, nine pillars are arranged along squares at the same distance and they are inclined at an angle to the square frame of the outer ring of the building. Seen on the section, the building is divided into four levels, and the three floors at the bottom are a circle of sunshade grilles set on the periphery of the building; the interior is a high-rise space and the plane of the top floor is inclined toward the other three floors, reflecting the arrangement of the pillars. In addition to the frame structure of the main body, the south of the building has an auxiliary ramp leading to the sunken ground floor.

Monument 455

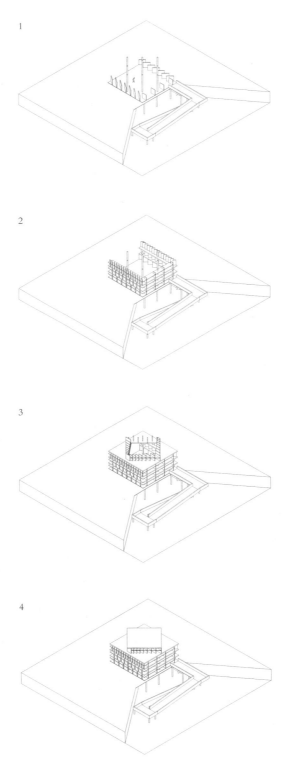

Exploded axonometric drawing

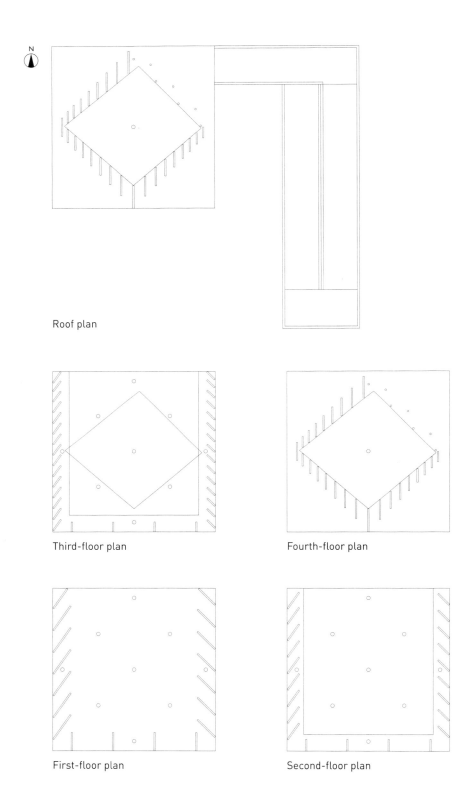

Monument   457

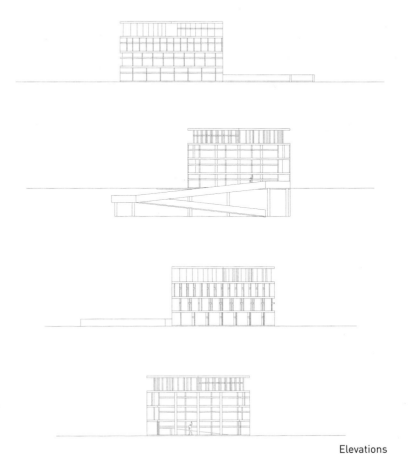

Elevations

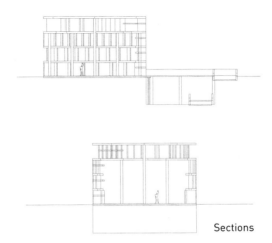

Sections

J-55
Tombe de Le Corbusier

Design period: 1955
Location: Cap Martin, France
Status: Built

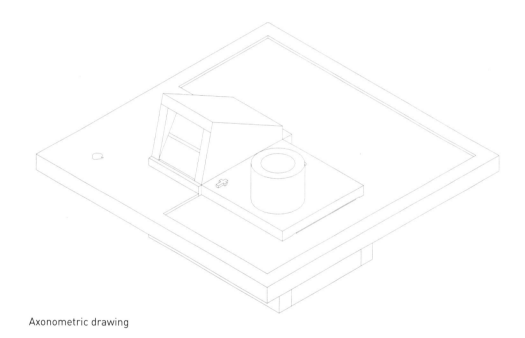

Axonometric drawing

Le Corbusier designed Tombe de Le Corbusier for his wife and himself before his wife passed away in 1957. The surface is a large square, subdivided into geometric figures. The cylinder on the right side, with a cross beside it, was designed in memory of his wife, while the opening and inclined pentahedron on the left side, with a shell brand, are in his own honor. Tombe de Le Corbusier expresses Le Corbusier's love with pure geometry; Mediterranean plants are planted in the square block nearby.

Monument 459

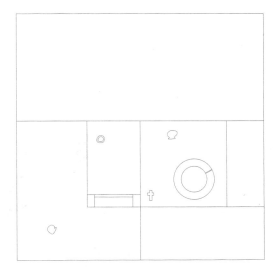
Plan

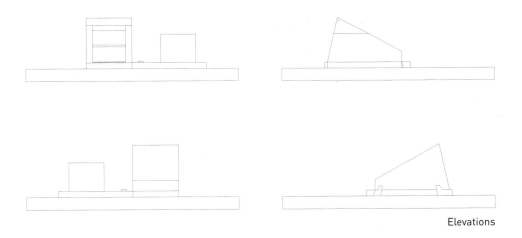
Elevations

Section

K-77
Hôpital, Venice

Design period: 1964–65
Location: Venice, Italy
Status: Built

The block is located in the city of rivers, Venice. Le Corbusier demonstrated his many skills in the design of this large-scale hospital to be on par with Venice's strong, splendid history. He decided that the building would not be designed tall, but rather, as a low-rise "horizontal Hôpital;" another choice he made was to maintain the height of the building at 13.66 meters (44.8 feet), which is the average height of urban buildings in Venice. The building consists of three levels: the first floor focuses on auxiliary service facilities and public entrances; the second floor is concentrated on medical necessities/facilities, such as procedures, recovery, and special treatment; and the third floor is the in-patient area, mainly hospital ward rooms. It can be seen from the plan of the third level that the hospital consists of numerous standard hospital ward rooms, with one room subdivided into four sickbed areas, arranged in a square spiral around the center of the square plan. This technique allows for possible future expansion.

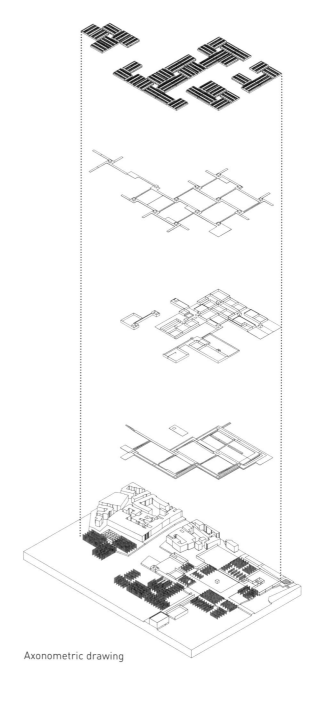

Axonometric drawing

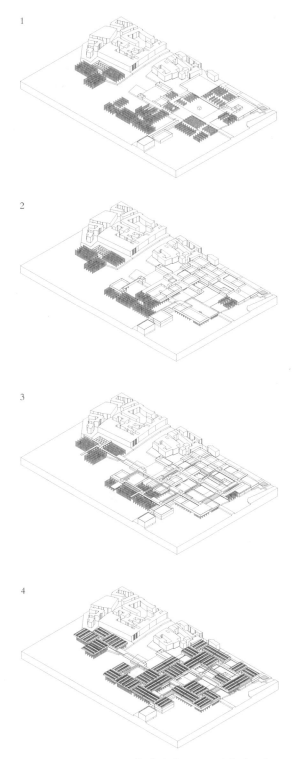

Exploded axonometric drawing

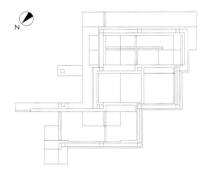

Mezzanine floor plan

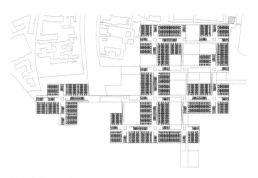

Third-floor plan

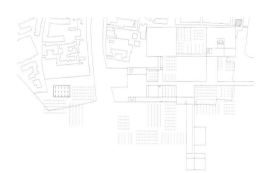

First-floor plan

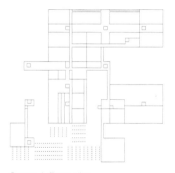

Second-floor plan

Hospital 463

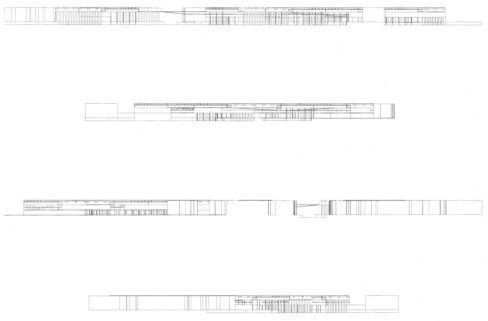

Elevations

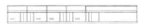

Sections

REFERENCES

Boesiger, Willy, ed. *Le Corbusier Complete Works, Volume 1*. Translated by Y. F. Niu and C. Cheng. Beijing: China Architecture Publishing, 2005.

Boesiger, Willy, ed. *Le Corbusier Complete Works, Volume 2*. Translated by Y. F. Niu and C. Cheng. Beijing: China Architecture Publishing, 2005.

Boesiger, Willy, ed. *Le Corbusier Complete Works, Volume 3*. Translated by Y. F. Niu and C. Cheng. Beijing: China Architecture Publishing, 2005.

Boesiger, Willy, ed. *Le Corbusier Complete Works, Volume 4*. Translated by Y. F. Niu and C. Cheng. Beijing: China Architecture Publishing, 2005.

Boesiger, Willy, ed. *Le Corbusier Complete Works, Volume 5*. Translated by Y. F. Niu and C. Cheng. Beijing: China Architecture Publishing, 2005.

Boesiger, Willy, ed. *Le Corbusier Complete Works, Volume 6*. Translated by Y. F. Niu and C. Cheng. Beijing: China Architecture Publishing, 2005.

Boesiger, Willy, ed. *Le Corbusier Complete Works, Volume 7*. Translated by Y. F. Niu and C. Cheng. Beijing: China Architecture Publishing, 2005.

Boesiger, Willy, ed. *Le Corbusier Complete Works, Volume 8*. Translated by Y. F. Niu and C. Cheng. Beijing: China Architecture Publishing, 2005.

Cohen, Jean-Louis, ed. *Le Corbusier Le Grand*. London, New York: Phaidon Press, 2008.

Frampton, Kenneth. *Modern Architecture: A Critical History*. Translated by X. N. Nan. SDX Joint Publishing Company, 2012.

Le Corbusier. *Accuracy*. Translated by J. Chen. Beijing: China Architecture Publishing, 2009.

Le Corbusier. *A House, A Palace*. Translated by Q. Zhi and L Liu. Beijing: China Architecture Publishing, 2011.

Le Corbusier. *A Journey to the East*. Translated by X. M. Guan. China: Shanghai Renmin Chubanshe, 2007.

Le Corbusier. *Planning of Three Human Settlements*. Translated by J. Y. Liu. Beijing: China Architecture Publishing, 2009.

Le Corbusier. *The City of Tomorrow*. Translated by H. Li. Beijing: China Architecture Publishing, 2009.

Le Corbusier. *Today's Decorative Art*. Translated by L. B. Sun and Y. Zhang. Beijing: China Architecture Publishing, 2009.

Le Corbusier. *Towards A New Architecture*. New York: Dover Publications, 1986.

Le Corbusier. *Towards A New Architecture*. Translated by Z. D. Yang. Phoenix Science Press, 2014.

Le Corbusier. *Yearbook of Modern Architecture*. Translated by Q. Zhi. Beijing: China Architecture Publishing, 2011.

Range, J. *Le Corbusier's Letters*. Translated by Y. F. Niu. Beijing: China Architecture Publishing, 2008.

Sama, S. *Le Corbusier*. Translated by B. Q. Wang. Dalian Technology University Press, 2011.

Samuel, Flora. *Le Corbusier and the Architectural Promenade*. Translated by Q. Ma. Beijing: China Architecture Publishing, 2013.

Samuel, Flora. *Le Corbusier's Detailed Design*. Translated by J. Deng. Beijing: China Architecture Publishing, 2009.

Tafuri, Manfredo and Francesco Dal Co. *Modern Architecture*. Translated by X. J. Liu. Beijing: China Architecture Publishing, 2000.

IMAGE CREDITS

All diagrams are drawn by the author, with the exception of those listed here. All other images in this book are courtesy of China Architecture Publishing, Fondation Le Corbusier, Phaidon France, Phaidon Press, and Flickr IDs: Archigeek, Andrew Stevenson, e.b.archiuav, flickr marago, and Wojtek Gurak.

Figure 1   Phaidon Press; extracted from *Le Corbusier Le Grand*, pg 753: Cohen, Jean-Louis, ed. *Le Corbusier Le Grand*. London, New York: Phaidon Press, 2008.

Figure 5   Fondation Le Corbusier

Figure 6   Fondation Le Corbusier

Figure 8   Fondation Le Corbusier

Figure 17   Fondation Le Corbusier

Figure 19   China Architecture Publishing; extracted from *Corbusier Complete Works Volume 1*, pg 181: Boesiger, Willy, ed. *Corbusier Complete Works Volume 1*. Translated by Y. F. Niu and C. Cheng. Beijing: China Architecture Publishing, 2005.

Figure 27   Fondation Le Corbusier

Figure 29   Fondation Le Corbusier

Figure 41   Fondation Le Corbusier

Figure 43   Fondation Le Corbusier

Figure 46   Fondation Le Corbusier

Figure 48   Phaidon France; extracted from *Le Corbusier Le Grand*, pg 535: Cohen, Jean-Louis, ed. *Le Corbusier Le Grand*. France: Phaidon France, 2014.

Figure 58 (left)   Fondation Le Corbusier

Figure 64   Phaidon Press; extracted from *Le Corbusier Le Grand*, pg 753: Cohen, Jean-Louis, ed. *Le Corbusier Le Grand*. London, New York: Phaidon Press, 2008.

Figure 69 (right)   © flickr marago (Flickr ID)

Figure 71 (right)   © Archigeek (Flickr ID)

Figure 72 (right)   Fondation Le Corbusier

Table 40 (images in the right column)   Andrew Stevenson (Flickr ID)
                                        Fondation Le Corbusier
                                        Fondation Le Corbusier
                                        Wojtek Gurak (Flickr ID)
                                        Fondation Le Corbusier
                                        e.b.archiuav (Flickr ID)

Figure 74   China Architecture Publishing; extracted from *Corbusier Complete Works Volume 1*, pg 86: Boesiger, Willy, ed. *Corbusier Complete Works Volume 1*. Translated by Y. F. Niu and C. Cheng. Beijing: China Architecture Publishing, 2005.

Figure 75 Fondation Le Corbusier

EPILOGUE

This book is a systematic review of the works of the twentieth-century architect Le Corbusier and includes eighty works of public architecture designed by him from 1910 to 1965. The intention is to understand, through the models, as far as possible, the language of his works and the design philosophy behind them. In order to avoid their subjective interpretation, the author has, to his best efforts, been objective and true in the process of analyzing these works; the author also knows that the best interpretation of the works of any great artist lies only in the work itself. (And so began this book.) Through the inspection of the eighty public architecture works, covering the whole process from the functional period of modernist architecture in the early twentieth century, to the period of brutalism in Le Corbusier's later years, it is understood that Le Corbusier created a rich language of architectural expression, which was both a continuation and a new exploration.

Spirals – Starting from the Center, from the Tower of Babel to Musée à Croissance Illimitée

Le Corbusier first adopted the theme of the "spiral" starting with Mundaneum, Musée Mondial in 1929. This theme continued through his career, all the way to the sketching of plans for the twentieth-century museum he designed toward the end of his life—evolving from the rising "Tower of Babel" in the horizontal and vertical dimensions, to the simplified " 卍 " layout. The streamline design and extensibility of the exhibition space in a museum building can pose a central problem to the design. For example, how does one provide a standard scalable pattern that maintains the plane order? Le Corbusier's answer to that was the shell form of the nautilus. The spiral shell of the nautilus—with a curved shell that rotates on a plane and is symmetrical to the left and right—contains the Fibonacci sequence, and the ratio of the previous number to the next number is infinitely close to the golden ratio! The order and function of this natural pattern is undoubtedly in line with the requirements of museum architecture in the context of the industrial age. At both the Musée d'Art Contemporain in Paris and the Musée, Ahmedabad, you can almost hear Le Corbusier describe that visitors who come by will enter the building from the center of the plane and take in the views along the picture rail inside the pavilion, experiencing the museum as well, as they visit the exhibitions.

The Emancipation of the Roof – From Ateliers d'Artistes to École d'Art et d'Architecture

In the design of Ateliers d'Artistes in 1910, Le Corbusier designed a school with a centripetal layout to correspond to the standard theme of industrial technology in the twentieth century. Comparing it with École d'Art et d'Architecture in India, designed in his late career, it can be seen that the two works differ greatly in terms of the number of architectural layers and the composition of forms, but the basic central layout remains the same. Among the elements that enable continuity of the overall composition, a noteworthy evolution lies in the building design of the roof. The "flat-roof garden," one of the "five points of the new building" proposed by Le Corbusier in the 1920s, had not yet been proposed in the first decade of the twentieth century. However, in his early works, as a reaction to traditional nineteenth-century academic architecture, he eulogized the great role of the flat roof in daily use and urban greening. As a result, many of the buildings of that period adopted flat roofs. In his later years—taking as an example, École d'Art et d'Architecture, which are school buildings—it is seen that he turned against the early flat-roofed forms of architecture and replaced them with contrary flexure roofs to provide north-facing lighting for the classrooms in the building. In addition, we can also see that he repeatedly adopted contrary flexure roofs, such as those in the porch of Palais de l'Assemblée and Haute Cour. Le Corbusier's application of the form changes from keeping the complete outline of each block to a trend of fusion. It can be said that the pursuit of the integrity of the geometric form in the early period would have been sure to require that the building's ground, columns, beams, roof, and composition elements maintain a state of indivisible completion. That's where the key elements that led to the gradual melding, and even fusion, of the outlines of the architectural form combination in the late period came in—the roof was liberated!

Transplant and Diversion – From Château d'Eau to Couvent Sainte-Marie de la Tourette

In the little-known work of the public building (water conservancy) architecture, Château d'Eau, Le Corbusier used a spiral staircase attached closely to the outer wall of the circular water tower to reach the top platform. The spiral staircase serves as a bridge between the basic (cylindrical) architectural form and the functional requirements of the water-tower building, for example an observation deck. The essence of the spiral staircase is that its plane is also circular, and thus in Château d'Eau, it was necessary to solve the traffic organization problem under the harsh plane condition, which led to Le Corbusier's re-understanding of this water tower. The architectural form with the circular staircase plane, plus the cylinder, was so fitted that the plane and form achieved a unity. We can see the appearance of the cylindrical traffic entity in the atrium of the Couvent Sainte-Marie de la Tourette and in the outer cylindrical revolving staircase of Église Saint Pierre. The key to the transformation, from water tower to cylindrical revolving staircase, is based on the idea of "transplant." It can be said that Le Corbusier was good at taking the form from one context and transferring it to another very different one, using the same form, but with different functions—just as he once did by re-purposing the prototype of the industrial tower for the assembly hall of Palais de l'Assemblée.

Of course, a piece of architectural work contains a lot of visible and invisible details and the interpretation of these details, unless the architect explains them, retains a certain amount of subjectivity. There is no doubt that it is an important learning experience for students of architecture to research architects, following clues in the process of exploring their ideas and the deep-seated thoughts behind them, whether with a focus on details, or on a macroscopic scale, to learn certain rules.

For Le Corbusier : © F.L.C. / ADAGP, Paris – SACK, Seoul, 2021
For Collaboration work : © FLC / ADAGP, Paris – SACK, Seoul, 2021 and © ADAGP, Paris – SACK, Seoul, 2021

Published in Australia in 2021 by
The Images Publishing Group Pty Ltd
ABN 89 059 734 431

Offices

Melbourne
6 Bastow Place
Mulgrave, Victoria 3170
Australia
Tel: +61 3 9561 5544

New York
6 West 18th Street 4B
New York, NY 10011
United States
Tel: +1 212 645 1111

Shanghai
6F, Building C, 838 Guangji Road
Hongkou District, Shanghai 200434
China
Tel: +86 021 31260822

books@imagespublishing.com
www.imagespublishing.com

Copyright © The Images Publishing Group Pty Ltd 2021
The Images Publishing Group Reference Number: 1590

All rights reserved. Apart from any fair dealing for the purposes of private study, research, criticism or review as permitted under the Copyright Act, no part of this publication may be reproduced, stored in a retrieval system or transmitted in any form by any means, electronic, mechanical, photocopying, recording or otherwise, without the written permission of the publisher.

A catalogue record for this book is available from the National Library of Australia

Title: Le Corbusier Public Buildings: Great Architects Redrawn
Author: Yu Fei
ISBN: 9781864708974

Printed by Everbest Printing Investment Limited, in Hong Kong/China

IMAGES has included on its website a page for special notices in relation to this and its other publications. Please visit www.imagespublishing.com

Every effort has been made to trace the original source of copyright material contained in this book. The publishers would be pleased to hear from copyright holders to rectify any errors or omissions.
The information and illustrations in this publication have been prepared and supplied by Yu Fei. While all reasonable efforts have been made to ensure accuracy, the publishers do not, under any circumstances, accept responsibility for errors, omissions and representations, express or implied.